THE AMERICAN
JUDICIAL PROCESS:
Models and Approaches

DAVID FELLMAN
Vilas Professor of Political Science
University of Wisconsin–Madison
Advisory Editor to Dodd, Mead & Company

THE AMERICAN JUDICIAL PROCESS:

Models and Approaches

CHARLES H. SHELDON
WASHINGTON STATE UNIVERSITY

DODD, MEAD & COMPANY
New York / 1974

To my parents

Preface

The methods and purpose of this book are neither remote nor profound. I have simply described and analyzed the several frames of reference or models by which scholars view the judicial process. In order to give life to the various models, I have reviewed selected studies which illustrate the working of the models. Since I have been selective in my review of the scholarship, the studies included for discussion should be regarded as representative examples only of the large number of meaningful works available. Nonetheless, much remains to be understood in the study of the judicial process, and the questions generated by on-going research often exceed the answers supplied. Today's college students have amply demonstrated to me that they need not wait until the Ph.D. dissertation level to conduct new and revealing research into these questions. All that is necessary is curiosity mixed with a respect for the scholarship in the field. If this book helps to develop such a respect it has served its purpose.

Many people have assisted me in this writing project. Professor Donald G. Baker's suggestions and criticisms of the manuscript, as always, have been invaluable. Professor Walfred Peterson read parts of the book and Professor Taketsugu Tsurutani reviewed the entire manuscript. Both provided me with much needed suggestions. Diana Doerksen's typing, proofreading, and format supervision made my task much simpler. Obviously, I am indebted to those many traditional, conventional, and behavioral scholars who have contributed to the rich materials available on the judicial process. The mistakes and questionable interpretations which remain in the book are, of course, my responsibility.

Finally, the patience and support from my own "micro-group" made the writing of the book possible. Lee Ann, Chris, Ross, and Tom were patient enough to postpone group interaction until the book was completed. Pat provided that touch of intuition and encouragement which made this academic pursuit almost a pleasure.

CHARLES H. SHELDON

Contents

List of Figures

List of Tables

THE AMERICAN JUDICIAL PROCESS:
Models and Approaches

Introduction

THE JUDICIAL PROCESS

The study of politics is the "study of the authoritative allocation of values for a society." [1] The role of the law and the courts is central to this allocation although, obviously, they are not exclusively responsible for it. Although it is not true, as traditionally thought, that courts and judges are above politics and that the judicial process is somehow not part of the large political process, the courts, nonetheless, play a unique role in the allocation of values which distinguishes them from their more political counterparts in the American governmental system. It is not the distinctiveness of the policies emanating from the courts that sets them apart, but the characteristic manner in which these policies are arrived at and the unique nature of the authority accompanying the decisions. Courts, or rather judges, do allocate values among the members of society. But they allocate them through a unique decision-making process and the authority attached to their decisions is characteristic to the bench.

The Nature of Politics

Obviously politics—"the authoritative allocation of values"—does not constitute all that transpires within a society. Even a totalitarian system must, over time, allow some voluntary aspects of social life to exist. Some things are political and some things are not. The keystone to an understanding of what is political is found in the concept of *authority*.

Authoritative decisions are those decisions that affect *all* of society or a major part thereof. Clearly some authoritative decisions are directed to only one or a few members of society. But, given certain

[1] David Easton, *The Political System* (New York: Alfred A. Knopf, 1953), p. 129.

1

conditions, they could apply to many or all. Thus, in Easton's words, to know about politics we must "understand the way in which values are authoritatively allocated, not for a group within society, but for the *whole society*." [2] When leaders of a church decree policies for their membership regarding doctrine, they are not authoritative for society as a whole, only for believers. They lack the breadth of authority needed for our definition.

In addition, the allocation of values is authoritative "when the people to whom it is intended to apply or who are affected by it consider that they must or ought to obey it." [3] But why must these societal decisions be obeyed? Fear, habit, apathy, awe, reason, or agreement may all account for obedience. However, within stable societies it is a rare occasion when people comply mostly from fear that those who possess the power will use it. On the other hand, although the vast majority of governmental decisions are obeyed for reasons other than fear, the perception that coercion may ultimately be brought into play checks those thoughts of disobedience for a few. But authority is not raw power or its threat; authority is *institutionalized power*.[4] Those making the particular allocations of values are perceived to have the "right" to exercise power in order to force compliance if need be.

Obviously, some difficulties are presented when one distinguishes authority ("institutionalized power") from power by merely adding the term "institutionalized." First, we must know what power is. Since Plato, students of politics have been struggling with the concept of *power*. We shall struggle again. Political power involves: (1) a relationship between two or more people, (2) a conflict between these people over the allocation of values in society, and (3) the threat or use of sanctions in order to change or maintain a particular form of allocation. A condition lacking any one of these three elements is not a condition of power. Political power becomes

[2] *Ibid.*, p. 134 (italics added).

[3] *Ibid.*, p. 132.

[4] Robert Bierstedt, "An Analysis of Social Power," *American Sociological Review*, XV (December, 1950). See also the readings in R. Bell, D.V. Edwards, and R.H. Wagner, eds., *Political Power: A Reader in Theory and Research* (New York: The Free Press, 1969); Marvin Olsen, ed., *Power in Society* (New York: Macmillan, 1970); Gerhard Lenski, *Power and Privilege: A Theory of Social Stratification* (New York: McGraw-Hill, 1966); John Champlin, ed., *Power* (New York: Atherton Press, 1971); and Harold Lasswell and Abraham Kaplan, *Power and Society* (New Haven: Yale University Press, 1950).

authority when—through procedures, customs, laws, or practices—those able to threaten or use sanctions appear to most of society to have the right to maintain or make changes in the allocations of values for society. Power is then institutionalized into authority. Power is perceived to be legitimate. In the United States, the authorities are synonymous with government simply because the government is perceived to possess the right to coerce if necessary; the government is legitimate.

THE NATURE OF THE JUDICIARY

Authority (or institutionalized power), which affects society as a whole, is possessed by a variety of governmental institutions. The judicial institutions are clearly one of the several categories of institutions that authoritatively allocate values among members of society. But are the allocations of the judicial institutions unique? Wealth, as a value, is allocated by Congress when laws are passed regarding tax programs. But when a state court awards $100,000 in a damage suit, wealth is also being allocated. Congress authorized the President to disperse funds to state educational systems to improve vocational training—skill as a value is being allocated in society. The Supreme Court declares segregated schools to be inherently unequal and thus in violation of the Constitution—the Court is reallocating the values of skill and enlightenment in society. These obvious examples illustrate sufficiently the point that policies or allocations emanating from courts are not unique when compared with other institutions. If the courts and the judicial process are to be distinguished from other political processes, the separating out apparently cannot be accomplished by concentrating on the substance of the decisions flowing from the bench.

As Theodore Becker so ably points out, "*everything* the court finally does" becomes a "proper study for political scientists" if Easton's definition of politics is to be accepted.[5] Courts, then, appear to be political institutions similar if not identical to legislatures and administrative agencies. But are there not some unique features of the courts as political institutions? What might they be?

In answer to this question some would argue that courts are pri-

---

[5] Theodore L. Becker, *Comparative Judicial Politics* (Chicago: Rand McNally, 1970), p. 18.

marily concerned with legal solutions. For such a solution to take place, Harold J. Berman observes: ". . . *time* must be taken for deliberate action, for *articulate* definition of the issues, for a decision which is subject to public scrutiny and which is *objective* in the sense that it reflects an explicit community judgment and not merely an explicitly personal judgment. These qualities of legal activity may be summed up in the word *formality*." [6] But, as Berman further observes, administrative agencies, legislatures, and executives, as well as courts, are involved in providing legal solutions to issues. The legislative process also involves stages, procedures, and customs which provide time, deliberation, a definition of the issues, along with objectivity and public observation. Perhaps the judicial process, in terms of formality, consists simply of *more* formality.

If there appears to be only a distinction of degree between what courts do and what other political agencies do, why is special training (law school and bar exams) regarded as necessary for the major participants in the judicial process—the judges and lawyers? To answer this question is to provide one dimension of the uniqueness of the judicial process.

In contrast with legislative and administrative processes (recognizing that legislatures and bureaucrats sometimes perform judicial functions, such as legislative investigations or administrative hearings), the judicial process involves a triangle of forces. At the courtroom stage, two antithetical forces—the advocates—appeal for their clients to an objective third party—the judge (and jury)—which must remain aloof from the biases of advocacy. The role of the lawyers is well described by one of the profession's most successful practitioners:

> The litigating lawyer is a mercenary, one of the few remaining examples of the hired combatant. His premise is hostility. . . .
> The need for combativeness arises from the fact that our legal system is an adversary system, the hypothesis being that contention forces out the truth. This presupposes partisanship and bias: since the partisans are opposed, the thrashing and wrangling send the facts to the surface. The judge and the jury will have everything before them—or if not everything, then much more than there would be without the competition. The judge must be relatively passive; the highly partial lawyers

[6] Harold J. Berman, *The Nature and Functions of Law* (Brooklyn: The Foundation Press, 1958), p. 30.

have the responsibility of giving the court the evidence, the authorities and the reasoning.[7]

The judge is to be impartial, aloof, and detached from the combatants before him. Of course, the behavior of judges indicates that there exist varying degrees of impartiality. The authority of the court suffers according to the degree to which the judge joins one of the combatants before him. The judge and his court are cloaked in symbols of objectivity. Robes, high benches, "Your Honor," "would it please the Court," and the demands of courtroom decorum are all examples of a symbolism which protects and reinforces objectivity.[8]

Even though different roles are performed by the lawyers and the judges, collectively they form a partnership. The judge "is relatively passive, listening, moderating, and passing on what is offered to him." [9] But the lawyers are responsible for informing the judge. Then, and only then, can the judge remain aloof and impartial. According to the American Bar Association: "In order to function properly, our adjudicatory process requires an informed, impartial tribunal capable of administering justice promptly and efficiently according to procedures that command public confidence and respect. Not only must there be competent, adverse presentation of evidence and issues, but a tribunal must be aided by rules appropriate to an effective and dignified process. . . ." [10] The decisional process therefore is not the "sole responsibility of the judge." [11] The lawyers must not neglect their role in the partnership. To repeat, the judicial process involves a triangulation of forces—the adversary process—rarely found in nonjudicial circumstances.[12]

---

[7] Charles Rembar, *The End of Obscenity* (New York: Random House, 1968), pp. 216–17.

[8] Richard Johnson refers to the symbolism of objectivity surrounding the court as "dramaturgy." See his *The Dynamics of Compliance: Supreme Court Decision-Making From a New Perspective* (Evanston: Northwestern University Press, 1967), Chapter III.

[9] Judge Edward D. Re, "The Partnership of the Bench and Bar," *The Judge's Journal,* X (April, 1971), 26.

[10] American Bar Association, "Code of Professional Responsibility," Ethical Consideration 7–20 (1969).

[11] Judge Re, "The Partnership of the Bench and Bar," p. 26.

[12] Implicit in this triangulation of forces is a dialectical process. The advocates provide the thesis and antithesis and the judge the synthesis. The courtroom is the setting for the dynamic resolution of the contending forces.

Of course, advocacy of a sort is expressed in the legislative halls as policies and bills are debated. But where is the objective third party which constitutes a portion of the legislature? Bureaucrats might also ideally act as objective third parties—but where are the advocates who would form a partnership with them? This triangulation of forces is therefore one distinguishing feature of the judicial process.

THE SCOPE OF THE JUDICIAL PROCESS

It must be recognized that most of what the lawyer does as he practices the law takes place outside the courtroom. Trial by verbal battle before an impartial observer is simply not the day-to-day concern of much of the legal profession. Nonetheless, when a lawyer is advising or counseling rather than advocating, the ultimate concern is to keep his client out of the courtroom. The consequences of the trial are uppermost in the lawyer's mind. Thus, the professional practice of the law in virtually all of its dimensions must be regarded as part of the judicial process. The possibility of adversary proceedings before a judge (triangulation), however remote in time and removed in space, is the frame of reference for the lawyer's advice and counsel.

When a lawyer-legislator changes wording in a draft bill to conform with a recent court decision, his behavior can be attributed to what has happened in the adversary process. He, like the lawyer advising his client, the prosecutor asking for an indictment, or the public defender suggesting a bargained plea, is part of the judicial process. If a lawyer, legislator, or prosecutor is primarily motivated by a prediction about the consequences of the adversary process, his behavior is a fit subject for students of the judicial process. The boundaries of the judicial process are drawn, in other words, by what is directly related to the actual and potential consequences of the adversary process.

Courts cannot seek out issues for decision. Judges do not supply themselves the stimulus for their responses. Issues must be brought to them according to long-established rules of jurisdiction and standing. The gatekeeping functions of jurisdiction and standing prevent lawyers from utilizing the forum of the courts for frivolous causes.

One must break the law and be apprehended or gain standing before the court before the boundaries of the judicial system are breached. This passivity of the courts enhances the independent position of the judge in the adversary process. No such formal gate-keeping features protect the legislature or the executive.

If structure is important, if the courts are truly unique in the sense that the judge and the lawyer do things differently than others to reach resolution of an issue, we would expect that some features of the decisions emanating from the courts would also be unique. The point has already been made that courts make policy and the sub-stance of their decisions is not unique.[13] There is something unique, however, about the outcome of the judicial decisional process: in contrast with decisions from executives or even legislatures, the courts cannot *enforce* their own decisions. While legislatures and executives can reward and punish in order to gain compliance, the courts are helpless and totally reliant upon others outside the court system for enforcement. President Jackson was reported to have said in response to an unacceptable decision by the Supreme Court: "Chief Justice Marshall has made his decision, now let him enforce it." The uniqueness of the judicial decision was exposed in this statement.

Judicial Authority

Another notable characteristic of the judicial process is the nature of its authority: the courts make authoritative decisions which are surrounded by a symbolic authority quite unique to courts. Although the authoritative rulings of legislatures, bureaucrats, and executives are transitory—and in a democracy that is as it should be since the passions and prejudices of their respective publics are and must be reflected in the decisions of these authorities—the authority of judi-cial decisions represents a constancy in time and space that is absent

[13] It is largely taken for granted now that the courts are involved directly in making public policy. This has not always been an accepted view of the courts. Actually, one of the first major constitutional law textbooks taking a clearly political approach to public law did not appear until 1960. The title of the text clearly describes the "new" approach. See Glendon A. Schubert, *Constitutional Politics: The Political Behavior of Supreme Court Justices and the Constitutional Policies That They Make* (New York: Holt, Rinehart and Winston, 1960).

from the pronouncements of others. Judges are supposed to blend the past with the present and in the process reflect the customs, attitudes, and values which are the ideological and moral underpinnings of the society as a whole. According to Otto Kahn-Freund, some element of government must rise above expediency and provide authoritative links with the past and, thereby, grant an ideological unity to the law.[14] The American legal system, based on written constitutions and *stare decisis* as interpreted and applied by judges, supplies this aura of constancy most often wanting in the authoritative allocations of other officials. The content of the allocation decisions may remain similar but not so the authority accompanying them. The decisions emanating from the courts possess a unique authority.

THE STUDY OF THE JUDICIAL PROCESS

Why must we be so concerned with distinctions and definitions? Definitions are hypotheses about the essential nature of things. Thus, accepting a particular definition of the judicial process tells us where we are to begin our study. When we are able to distinguish the judicial process from other processes we are in a better position to develop an understanding of the interrelatedness of these several processes. To understand how law relates to economics, society, or history we must first know the boundaries of these various subjects. Further, we must know what it is we are to study before we can speculate about how to study it. Proper methods rely upon definitions. Finally, social science research is a cooperative effort in which one builds upon the work of others. We must be confident that the conclusions reached by an earlier scholar and upon which we wish to build are indeed conclusions about the same phenomenon. Agreement on, or at least a comprehension of, definitions is, thus, absolutely necessary.

The ultimate goal of social science is to construct and confirm theories about the social behavior of man. Implicit in models or approaches to the study of the judicial process, too, are theories

[14] Otto Kahn-Freund, "Introduction" to Karl Renner, *The Institutions of Private Law and Their Social Functions* (London: Routledge and Paul, 1949), p. 8.

about motivations behind judicial behavior. Actually all people form —although they seldom clearly articulate them—theories in their heads about the world around them, including the judicial process. These theories, in turn, shape their perceptions of reality. Theories also dictate the parameters of analysis available to the scholar of politics. His choice of a particular model flows from a theory about the political nature of man. From Plato to Marx and beyond, political theorists have addressed themselves to the question of the nature of man. But a single answer is not forthcoming. Nevertheless, this question of man's nature and of what determines his behavior—in terms of politics or the judicial process—is of paramount importance. For, in part, it determines the structuring, collecting, and analyzing of data about the judicial process. If political man (and judicial man) is motivated by power, decision-making models emphasizing the uses of power and the allocations of both power and privilege would be most appropriate as a method of organizing and analyzing judicial data. If man is competitive and self-seeking, although gregarious (forming temporary or permanent coalitions to achieve his objectives), then viewing the judicial process from a group approach would be most meaningful. Man may seek predictability, consistency, and continuity in his relations with others—a condition which may also characterize judges. An analysis of data through role models then would provide an excellent means to understand the judicial process. The foregoing approaches all reflect certain theories about the basic nature of political man.

Models provide the means for constructing or confirming these theories. We need, consequently, to develop an understanding of the nature and functions of models in social science and to analyze the several models of the judicial process. We must critically look at their assumptions and premises, and then view the results of studies which have been based upon a particular model. Perhaps, by following this procedure, we can with confidence broaden our knowledge about the behavior of man in the political and judicial contexts.

THE USES OF MODELS IN SOCIAL SCIENCE

Actually, the process of attempting to identify the judicial process, define its boundaries, and distinguish its features is a form of model building.[15] The concepts of *triangulation* and *authority* have delineated the broad outline of the judicial process. The task at hand now is to describe, analyze, explain, and possibly predict the behavior of that process. Models and approaches supply the means.

Models are valuable to social research for the same reasons they have been of assistance to the "hard sciences."[16] A model of the SST in a wind tunnel tells scientists and engineers about the behavior of the actual supersonic liner under certain conditions. Such is the case with models of social phenomena. Specifically, models in social research provide for classificatory schemes and data organization. Data must be collected and placed into proper categories; the model itself will help the analyst to generate these categories for collection. Description results from the classificatory schemes and data organization that are characteristic of these models. Such models—which aid, instruct, assist memory, and help simplify—perform a *didactic* function and are implicit or explicit in much of the teaching of political science.[17] The table of contents of most text-

[15] Although distinctions exist between a "model," a "theory," or an "approach," the author uses these terms loosely and interchangeably. A *model* is a research tool by which data can be organized, hypotheses generated and tested, predictions made, and theories tested or constructed. A *theory* explains the reasons for the behavior that models hypothesize, test, and predict. An *approach* is a rather amorphous—and not always clearly articulated—model in which the scholar is usually aware of what he wants to research but is not altogether sure of the many components of the model. An hierarchical structure among these three concepts can be visualized. An approach, for example, can lead to a fairly complete model which, when applied to the "real world," can test certain hypotheses that are shown to be consistent or inconsistent with a theory of human behavior. The hierarchical arrangement in this case is bi-directional. A theory can lead to the construction of a particular model. Or a model can help to formulate a theory. We need not become overly concerned at this point with semantic differences. What is called a "model" in the following chapters might well be called an "approach" or a "theory," by someone else. However, all three concepts have contributed and will continue to contribute to our understanding of the judicial process.

[16] There are many books that discuss the uses of models in the social sciences: Maurice Duverger, *An Introduction to the Social Sciences* (New York: Praeger, 1964); J. Hill and A. Kerber, *Models, Methods and Analytical Procedures in Educational Research* (Detroit: Wayne State University Press, 1967); Robert Dubin, *Theory Building* (New York: The Free Press, 1969); and Abraham Kaplan, *The Conduct of Inquiry* (San Francisco: Chandler, 1964).

[17] An excellent analysis of the functions of models is found in A. James Gregor, "Political Science and the Uses of Functional Analysis," *The American Political Science Review*, LXIII (June, 1968), 425–39.

books in constitutional law or the judicial process, providing as it does a classificatory scheme, is an illustration of a didactic model.

A second essential function of a model follows from the data collection and organization. If we have collected all the pertinent data and organized it into adequate categories (normally, arrived at inductively), according to some classificatory scheme, possible relationships between and among the data often emerge. One of the most difficult tasks in social research is the generating of initial hypotheses—and is not always, as might be suspected, the testing of various hypotheses. This is no less true for research focusing on the legal system than for any other academic inquiry, for hypotheses are generally a derivative of the model. The model itself becomes the source of questions. Such *heuristic* models, moving beyond the rather low-level, descriptive characteristics of didactic schemes, generate analytical and often explanatory statements that can be operationally defined and tested.[18] Hypotheses are generated, for example, concerning the relationships of the various classes found in a didactic model. Subsequent testing and assessment allow us to accept with greater certainty, or reject, at least tentatively, the projected relationships among data; and this process in turn generates subsequent testing, appraisal, and validation.

To take a specific example of this process, the heuristic model of stimulus-organism-response (S-O-R), used so fruitfully in psychology, is assumed to represent or be analogous to the decisional process in courts.[19] In this case the researcher would concentrate on testing the relationships among the entities classified as facts (stimulus), judges (organism), and decisions (response), often without any clear indication that the model is sufficiently similar to the actual courtroom process. Should hypotheses generated by the model repeatedly fail to be verified, the fault would lie with the model itself. Modification or, possibly, even rejection of the model might be necessary. Thus, the heuristic value of such a model is measured by the validity of the hypotheses generated.

A third function of models is the *predictive* function. A model can

---

[18] *Ibid.*
[19] Stuart S. Nagel, "A Conceptual Scheme of the Judicial Process," *The American Behavioral Scientist*, VII (December, 1963), 7–10.

suggest answers about a complicated process which cannot be replicated in a tightly controlled laboratory setting. What the model does is supply predictions about how the real phenomenon will behave. Of course, all the crucial aspects of the real phenomenon must be represented in the model. These predictive models are rare in the social sciences. Predictions are certainly made by political scientists; however, the inability to control all the variables of real-life situations usually results in a low probability score on predictions. The problem is getting the model to "fit" the real-life situation, and speculative inferences are often the result.

However, predictive models are helpful; indeed, they constitute the apex of model building—the ultimate in scientific inquiry. If, in fact, the S-O-R model fits or closely approximates the real-life courtroom, then predictions flowing from that model should hold for the thing being represented. Under these circumstances, it would not be necessary to attempt experiments with that institution (even if that were possible); rather, questions would be answered by experimenting with the S-O-R model. Unfortunately, political science has not yet arrived at that level of scientific development.[20]

Models are simplifications of the phenomena they represent. Consequently, all models (didactic, heuristic, and predictive) provide a shortcut in communication; and both configurational and mathematical models are shorthand devices for what otherwise might necessitate extended verbal elaboration. Moreover, such models limit the possibilities of misunderstanding that derive from the ambiguities of words. Hence, models assist in the communication process.

Model construction or scientific inquiry requires four stages in the research process: description, analysis, explanation, and prediction. In the case of the judicial process, description follows from isolating the real or theoretical characteristics of those individuals and groups involved in the process. Analysis occurs when the associations among the characteristics of these constructs or units are identified. Explanation follows when we are able to determine causal relationships among the characteristics of the units. Finally, prediction is achieved when the results of combinations of these characteristics can be anticipated. Obviously, prediction and explanation go hand in hand.

[20] See Gregor, "Political Science," p. 432.

For example, the prediction might be made that A + B will equal C because of X and Y (explanation). Prediction is a statement of the probability that a future condition will occur. Explanation tells why that condition has occurred and will occur.[21]

In the social sciences, there are many kinds of models that develop description, analysis, explanation, and, hopefully, prediction. All models, however, must imitate or duplicate to some degree. Isomorphism—some significant correspondence between the model and the thing being modeled—is their essential characteristic. Several forms of models can perform the didactic, heuristic, or predictive functions attributed to models. The most common form is a *physical* model. Dolls, model cars, an architect's scale model, or a moot court all are physical models. Comparable to psychodrama, a moot court in a law school constitutes a physical model of actual courtroom trial experience.[22] An architect's model of a new courthouse is, obviously, a physical model. Such a modeled scheme of the interior may be of great assistance in planning for the most efficient as well as impressive surroundings befitting a courtroom.

The *symbolic* model is a representation of reality through the use of symbols.[23] Mathematical models are often of this category, espe-

[21] Dubin distinguishes explanation and prediction as follows: "I mean one of two things by prediction: (1) that we can foretell the value of one or more units making up a system; or (2) that we can anticipate the condition or state of a system as a whole. In both instances the focus of attention is upon an *outcome*.

"As I employ the term *understanding* [explanation], it has the following essential meaning: It is knowledge about the interaction of units in a system. Here attention is focused on processes of *interaction* among variables in a system." Dubin, *Theory Building* (n. 16 above), p. 10.

[22] The classical work on psychodrama is J.L. Moreno, *Psychodrama* (New York: Beacon House, 1946). Persons participating in psychodrama play roles and attempt to act as they understand a person in that role would act. In political science, the term "simulation" is used for political psychodramas and the roles played in a simulated situation are models of what people actually do in a real situation. Computers can also be used to simulate roles; computer war games are an example.

See also C.I. Hoveland, "Computer Simulation of Thinking," in Harold Guetzkow, ed., *Simulation in Social Science: Readings* (Englewood Cliffs, N.J.: Prentice-Hall, 1962), pp. 16–28.

[23] An example of a simple symbolic model used in the study of political behavior can be found in James Davies, *Human Nature in Politics* (New York: John Wiley, 1963), p. 3. For an application of Davies' simple model, see Charles H. Sheldon, "The Uniqueness of State Legal Systems: Nevada, Utah and Vermont," *Judicature*, LIII (March, 1970).

cially when applied to social behavior.[24] Symbolic models have two advantages: (1) they provide a shorthand means of representation and (2) they permit the application of statistics and mathematics that may be highly desirable, depending upon the phenomenon being modeled.

Models can also take the form of *mental images*. Abstractions as a mental exercise result from the use of models of this sort. "Political man" or "economic man," for example, are composite abstractions, mental images, of persons who pursue power or who enhance their capacity for profit.[25] "Legal man," a man who furthers his interests through the use of law, may describe a composite of a large number of lawyers but seldom reflects any single advocate. Nonetheless, the model may be a useful one in generating questions. For example, what causes lawyers to deviate from such an image?

Models may also be of the *ideal type*.[26] Model codes illustrate this use of the term.[27] Such models tend to be prescriptive in the sense that imitation is hoped for. Again, the ideal model may be useful in understanding reality by acting as a standard against which real conduct can be compared.[28]

Thus, models in the social sciences are statements, taxonomies, images, or symbols of an isomorphic nature—sometimes constituting categories, implicit or explicit, which are hypotheses about human behavior. Because of the partial development of the social sciences, our best models are still tentative. To test a model is to test a theory about the behavior of man in social circumstances. Social scientists

[24] See Hayward Alker, Jr., *Mathematics and Politics* (New York: Macmillan, 1965); Fred Kort, "Predicting Supreme Court Decisions Mathematically: A Quantitative Analysis of 'Right to Counsel' Cases," *The American Political Science Review*, LI (March, 1957); Werner F. Grunbaum, "Analytical and Simulation Models for Explaining Judicial Decision-Making," in Joel B. Grossman and Joseph Tanenhaus, eds., *Frontiers of Judicial Research* (New York: John Wiley, 1969), pp. 307–34.

[25] Robert P. Wolff, ed., *Political Man and Social Man* (New York: Random House, 1966).

[26] The German sociologist, Max Weber, began the contemporary concern for pure or ideal types with which reality can be compared. See Max Weber, *Theory of Social and Economic Organization* (New York: Oxford University Press, 1947), and *Methodology of the Social Sciences* (Glencoe, Ill.: The Free Press, 1949).

[27] See, e.g., "Model Code of Criminal Procedure" (1930).

[28] One study has compared the actual behavior of lawyers in New York City with the "model" or ideal as expressed in the Canons of Professional Ethics. Jerome Carlin, *Lawyers' Ethics* (New York: Russell Sage Foundation, 1966).

are in the fortunate, or unfortunate, position of being unable and unwilling to manipulate the social situation in order to test various hypotheses. Simply put, people many times cannot be and ought not to be manipulated for the sake of science. Thus, models for social scientists become even more important than they are in those sciences where laboratory experiments can sometimes substitute for field work. But we are still testing. Our predictions are many times speculations. At best a model of the judicial process, then, is a statement about how men tend to behave in a judicial situation; and empirical research is directed toward testing this statement against reality.

THE CONSTRUCTION OF A MODEL

By describing the construction of a model of the judicial process, it is possible to illustrate the workings—and parameters—of that process.[29] Many of the existing models, as will become evident, describe and explain only parts, or fragments, of the total judicial process. Where they fit in the total process, and their implications for the process, clearly emerge when the major components of the total judicial process are analyzed.

The basic assumption underlying the following description evolves from legal positivism and realism. According to this view, the law is what the courts say it is. Law is the behavior of those people who practice, define, and enforce that body of prescriptions called law. If we want to understand the law (or the judicial process), we must understand the people who work with laws.[30] The issue among the various schools of jurisprudence need not be joined here. The above

[29] For references, see Robert Dubin, "Working Bibliography," in his *Theory Building* (New York: The Free Press, 1969), pp. 250–57. An example of model construction relating to the judicial process is Charles H. Sheldon, "Structuring a Model of the Judicial Process," *Georgetown Law Journal*, LVIII (June, 1970). (This section, "The Construction of a Model," borrows much from this article.) See also Malcolm M. Feeley, "Two Models of the Criminal Justice System: An Organizational Perspective," *Law and Society Review*, VII (Spring, 1973), 407.

[30] In 1897, Oliver Wendell Holmes, Jr., gave expression to this when he said: "The prophecies of what the courts will do in fact, and nothing more pretentious, are what I mean by the law." Holmes, "The Path of the Law," *Harvard Law Review*, X (1897), 460–61. Karl N. Llewellyn added to this definition: "What these officials [judges, sheriffs, clerks, jailers, lawyers, etc.] do about disputes is, to my mind, the law itself." Karl N. Llewellyn, *The Bramble Bush* (New York: Oceana Publications, 1951), p. 12.

expressions do not exclude the ideals or "oughts" of law—the forces of custom, natural law, comity, or precedents. It merely means that an understanding of the law (process) comes from an understanding of those who establish, apply, interpret, and enforce the law. Our goal in social research is to describe, explain, and possibly predict. Only then can we judge the law adequately in terms of right and wrong, good and bad.

The construction of a model is a most crucial task for the social or legal scholar. He invents models and then discovers whether or not they are consistent with reality. The construction of the model is pure research; the process of appraising the utility of the model is applied research. Models in the social sciences must be regarded as representing some aspects of social life. They contain, or are constructed from, defined units possessing attributes or variables.

COMPONENTS OF A MODEL

The immediate participants—and processes—involved in cases brought before judges are rather obvious; but in model building it is necessary to determine if there are not other relevant factors, units, and components that must be included or excluded. On what basis is one unit considered relevant and another rejected? Normally, the dynamism of the judicial process results from the interaction among the accusers, the accused, and the settlor of the dispute—triangulation. If the judge is the center of the judicial process, then all of the actors who assist him in his role must be determined. The "accuser-accused-settlor" scheme is too narrow to comprehend the entire process, however. Excluded, for example, is the important role of "friends of the court," those outsiders whose briefs are filed by neither the accuser nor accused. A more comprehensive view of the whole can be arrived at in another way. Clearly, the function of adjudication involves decisions. The flow of decisions—whether political, administrative, or judicial—follows five stages: (1) recognition of a problem, (2) statement of the issue, (3) deliberation, (4) resolution of the issue, and (5) solution of the problem.[31] The components of the model can be isolated by identify-

[31] Herbert J. Spiro, *Government by Constitution* (New York: Random House, 1959), pp. 23–26. See also Harold Lasswell and Daniel Lerner, eds., *The Policy Sciences* (Stanford: Stanford University Press, 1951).

ing those who are involved in the several stages of this decisional process.

Recognition. The recognition of a problem or the recognition of a violation of the rules of society involves police, pressure groups, and litigants. The police make an arrest. A pressure group watches for a possible test case to further its interests. An individual may, in a civil suit, recognize transgression by another on his rights and call his lawyer.

Statement. The statement of the issues is a phase of the decisional process that formulates alternatives. Different means of dealing with the recognized problem are articulated. Lawyers are primarily involved in defining the alternatives for their clients and before the magistrates. Indictments, prosecutors, and grand juries exemplify this stage.

Deliberation. Deliberation is the process involving the weighing of alternatives in terms of possible consequences. Rationalizations are involved in the deliberations. Obviously, the adversary process exemplifies this stage of the decisional process. Again, lawyers along with pressure groups acting as friends of the court are the units. Witnesses, bailiffs, and "audiences" are all embraced within this stage.

Resolution. Resolution of the issue is by a judge, assisted in some cases by juries, clerks, and other judges. The issue is thereby legally resolved, although the decisional process may at this point revert back to the statement stage for resolution by an appellate court. The judge, however, remains at the center of the resolution stage.

Solution. Finally, the solution embraces (1) the stipulations found in the judicial order and written opinion, and (2) those actors who enforce or administer the decision. Bureaucrats, executives, police, federal marshals, probation officers, and personnel of penal, corrections, or rehabilitation institutions are included. In most cases, litigants accept the decision as binding (or carry the issue to higher courts, when possible), and comply with it because court decisions constitute legitimate decisions. It is at this stage that the judicial process has its greatest impact on the broader cultural context of society. The judicial ruling becomes a standard by which the larger society accepts or examines or reexamines its position.[32]

Thus, the five-stage decisional process provides a method for isolating the components of the model. Figure 1 lists the various components which participate in the several decisional stages in the judicial process.

LITIGANTS
Plaintiff
Defendant
Criminal
Public
Pressure Groups

LAWYERS
Prosecutor
Defender
Grand Jury
Researcher-Investigator
Bar Association
Witnesses

JUDGES
Jury
Clerks
Bailiffs
Other Judges

PENAL PERSONNEL
Parole Boards
Rehabilitation Centers
Reform Institutions
Jails, Prisons

POLICE
Investigators
Arresting Officers
Marshals

FIGURE 1.   Components of the Judicial Process

MODEL VARIABLES

The components possess certain attributes or variables (characteristics) which flesh out the model. For example, a judge is fifty-

[32] Perhaps the classic example of a society reexamining its position in the wake of a judicial decision occurred in the aftermath of *Brown* v. *Board of Education*, 347 U.S. 483 (1954). It has been argued that one of the basic functions of the law and courts is to teach "right" behavior. See Harold J. Berman, *The Nature and Functions of Law* (Brooklyn: Foundation Press, 1958).

eight-years old, a graduate of an Ivy League law school, sitting at the appellate level, in a large metropolitan area. Through the assigning of such attributes, the component (the judge) gains an identity within the model. Although the following categories of variables are somewhat arbitrary and some overlap may appear, the classification provides for a convenient summary.

Demographic. Although often referred to as "sociological," demographic variables are sufficiently important to constitute a separate category. Demographic data are compiled from population features thought to account for some variation in human behavior. For instance, a judge raised in an extremely large family might approach custody cases with a different orientation than does a judge from a small family. First- or second-generation, foreign-born lawyers involve themselves with different practices than white Anglo-Saxon lawyers. Defendants in criminal courts who speak with an accent or perhaps are unable to speak English adequately may fare differently than those more facile with the language. Lawyers practicing in rural settings may develop attitudes which contrast with those of their metropolitan counterparts. Therefore, population data are obviously important in understanding the judicial process.[33] Biological characteristics can also be classified as demographic factors. Age, sex, and race variables need to be explored as determinants of attitudes and behavior.[34]

Sociological. Sociological factors flow from the patterns of social interaction between and among the several components of the judicial model. There are numerous sociological variables—including religion, class, legal office organization, work experience, and educa-

---

[33] Harry Jones, ed., *The Courts, The Public and the Law Explosion* (Englewood Cliffs, N.J.: Prentice-Hall, 1965); William de Rubertis, "How Apportionment with Selected Demographic Variables Relates to Policy Orientation," *Western Political Quarterly,* XXII (December, 1969); Robert H. Birkby, "The Supreme Court and the Bible Belt: Tennessee Reactions to the Schempp Decision," *Midwest Journal of Political Science,* X (August, 1966); and John Schmidhauser, "Judicial Behavior and the Sectional Crisis of 1837–1860," *Journal of Politics,* XIII (November, 1969).

[34] H.A. Bullock, "Significance of Racial Factor in Length of Prison Sentence," *Journal of Criminology, Criminal Law and Police Science,* LII (November–December, 1961); Stuart Nagel, "Ethnic Affiliations and Judicial Propensities," *Journal of Politics,* XXXLV (February, 1962); and Derrick A. Bell, Jr., "Racism in American Courts: Cause for Black Disruption or Despair?" *California Law Review,* LXI (January, 1973).

tional variables—which, as evident from several studies, are related to and do influence the judicial process and judicial behavior.[35]

Economic. Economic variables and attributes have been a traditional concern of political scientists as well as of legal scholars. Litigants with a greater economic base win more cases. The poor have traditionally been "victims" of the legal process. The income of lawyers significantly shapes their perception of and orientation toward the law.[36]

Political. Political variables are related directly to the exercise of authority outside the judicial process but having an impact thereon. For example, party politics directly affects judges. Democrats on the bench tend to favor the underprivileged in their decisions to a greater degree than Republicans.[37] Republicans tend to be pro-business. There are political variables which affect the selection of judges too. The Missouri plan for the selection of judges, for example, removes direct partisan pressures from the final recruitment process but transfers group pressures to the nominating stages.[38] Partisan and nonpartisan elections of judges may lead to the recruitment of judges who hold different legal orientations.[39] The effects on the judicial process of political parties, pressure groups, and of political and governmental figures therefore constitute a major concern for the student of the judiciary.

Institutional. Institutional factors must also be considered in the appraisal of the judicial process. Judges and lawyers, while influenced by sociological and political factors, must nonetheless work

[35] Jack Ladinsky, "The Impact of Social Backgrounds of Lawyers on Law Practice and the Law," *Journal of Legal Education,* XVI (1963); Stuart Nagel, "Judicial Backgrounds and Criminal Cases," *Journal of Criminology, Criminal Law and Police Science,* LIII (September, 1962); and John Schmidhauser, "Stare Decisis, Dissent and the Background of the Justices of the Supreme Court of the United States," *University of Toronto Law Journal,* XIV (1962).

[36] Skelly Wright, "The Courts Have Failed the Poor," *New York Times Magazine,* March 9, 1969; and Jerome E. Carlin, *Lawyers on Their Own* (New Brunswick, N.J.: Rutgers University Press, 1962).

[37] Stuart Nagel, "Political Party Affiliation and Judges' Decisions," *American Political Science Review,* LV (December, 1961); and S. Sidney Ulmer, "The Political Party Variables in the Michigan Supreme Court," *Journal of Public Law,* XI (1962).

[38] Richard A. Watson and Rondal G. Downing, *The Politics of the Bench and Bar* (New York, John Wiley, 1969).

[39] Bradley C. Canon, "The Impact of Formal Selection Processes on the Characteristics of Judges—Reconsidered," *Law and Society Review,* VI (May, 1972).

within the constraints of the legal-institutional systems. Thus, constitutions, statutes, and precedents in part shape and determine the alternatives available to judges and lawyers. An activist or restraintist judge must still deal with precedent; a liberal or conservative judge must face similar constraints. Hence, the institutional factors raise new questions, new issues to be explored, including, among others: the impact of federalism on judicial behavior; and possible procedural differences in state systems which have either one or two appellate levels. Institutional factors are important. Although these are institutional, not individual, variables, they must be taken into consideration in the judicial model.

The institutional factors are different from the other factors herein reviewed because they are not attributes or variables of the units or persons participating in the judicial process. More correctly, the institutional factors constitute the legal and customary practices or circumstances within which the units interact. They form the situational context for the components. For example, a lawyer "possesses" age, income, status, and training. He does not, however, possess a precedent or a solo practice. Rather, these variables and attributes

---

DEMOGRAPHIC
Family
Immigration
Sex
Age
Race
Urban-Rural

POLITICAL
Party Affiliation
Family Politics
Political Attitudes
Ideology
Activism
Public Opinion
Group Membership

SOCIOLOGICAL
Class-Status
Education
Work Experience
Religion
Peer Group

ECONOMIC
Income

INSTITUTIONAL
Statutes
Constitutions
Precedents
Custom-Rules
Structure
Facts of Case
Jurisdiction

FIGURE 2.   Attributes and Variables of Components

constitute an arena within which the other factors operate. These arenas may impose limits on the lawyer's behavior.[40]

The factors discussed above, then, can be set out as noted in Figure 2.

THE WORKING OF THE MODEL

One major task remains in the construction and use of models. After the components of a model have been isolated and the characteristics of these components defined, the model must be so constructed as to establish the linkage or interaction among the characteristics of the components. The variables of a component must be related to variables of the same component and to variables of other components. Thus, a model, to "work," must generate hypotheses and operational statements that can be tested. For example, it is possible to determine the degree to which Ivy League graduates differ from non-Ivy League lawyers in annual earnings; legal office organization; attitudes; and, for judges, sentencing behavior, pro-labor decisions, and political activities.

The judicial process is not a static thing; the process is continuous. Thus, a model that simulates real properties and actions must take the time/change factor into consideration. Linkages and relationships must be identified and then importance determined through time. The model must be in motion. To portray such motion through time and space, models may assume numerous forms, dependent upon the creator of the model: revolving wheels, flow arrows, dimensional spaces, mathematical formulas, or some other combination of symbols are common.

Models currently in vogue usually concentrate on a part of the broad outline of the total process described above.[41] For instance, decision-making, role, group, and traditional models tend to be con-

---

[40] See Jerome Carlin, *Lawyers on Their Own;* Herbert Jacob, "The Effect of Institutional Differences in the Recruitment Process: The Case of State Judges," *Journal of Public Law,* XLLL (1964); Jack Ladinsky, "Careers of Lawyers, Law Practice and Legal Institutions," *American Sociological Review,* XXVIII (February, 1963); and Walter F. Murphy, "Lower Court Checks on Supreme Court Power," *The American Political Science Review,* LIII (December, 1959).

[41] Sheldon Goldman and Thomas P. Jahnige point out that several models are currently utilized to explain the conversion stage of the judicial process. See their *The Federal Courts as a Political System* (New York: Harper and Row, 1971), pp. 149–200.

cerned more with the center of the process—the judges. Systems and impact models attempt to focus on the total process involving the broader schema set out previously. What is especially significant is that a particular scholar's choice of a model is, in part, determined by the questions he asks. Because of the symbiotic association between theory and models (and the development of the former by means of the latter is much of what social science is all about), it behooves the student of the judicial process to view critically the several models in vogue in terms of their assumptions, logic, and scope and then to become familiar with the empirical studies which have evolved from those models.

The focal point of the following chapters is a discussion of these two facets (assumptions and studies) of the major models and approaches to the study of the judicial process. Some overlap in the types of appropriate data for each model will become evident. For example, a study of the background characteristics of judges would be important for decision-making, role, and small-group models. The differences lie in how the student articulates background with other components of the model and how much weight is given each component. The chapters are organized so that the reader is able to move from the narrower to the more comprehensive models—resulting, hopefully, in an appreciation of the total judicial process. The book concludes with an appeal for an eclectic approach to the study of the judicial process. Each model has its unique but important contribution to make.

CHAPTER ONE

Decision-Making Models

DESCRIPTION AND ANALYSIS OF JUDICIAL DECISION MAKING

Benjamin N. Cardozo, eleven years before he assumed his seat on the United States Supreme Court, observed in 1921 that: "The work of deciding cases goes on every day in hundreds of courts throughout the land. Any judge, one might suppose, would find it easy to describe the process which he followed a thousand times or more. Nothing could be further from the truth."[1] It is exactly this process of deciding that the decision-making models attempt to describe, analyze, and explain. What puzzled Cardozo in 1921 has intrigued observers of the judicial process to this day. To know how and why judges decide as they do is to know the very essence of the judicial process. Many scholars believe that decision-making models provide the means to achieve such knowledge.

Although scholars have recognized that courts make political or policy decisions, until recently very few considered these political factors in their analyses. Traditional models relied too heavily upon *stare decisis* as the explanatory variable. If a court or a justice disregarded precedent, he was criticized for deviating from the law, thereby preventing satisfactory explanations for the court's decision. Decisional models were designed to go beyond these narrow, "legal" explanations for decisions of judges.

C. Herman Pritchett's *The Roosevelt Court: A Study in Judicial Politics and Values, 1937–1947* (1948) reshaped the study of constitutional law. As a consequence, studies of decision making specifically and public law generally took on a new life.[2] Pritchett

[1] Benjamin N. Cardozo, *The Nature of the Judicial Process* (New Haven: Yale University Press, 1960), p. 9.

[2] C. Herman Pritchett, *The Roosevelt Court: A Study in Judicial Politics and Values, 1937–1947* (New York: Macmillan, 1948).

concentrated on the many nonunanimous decisions of the Supreme Court and, through bloc analysis and scaling of the votes, illustrated how the justices revealed "information about their attitudes and their values. . . ." [3] Pritchett noted that court decisions clearly demonstrated that even judges begin with "different assumptions, that their [often] inarticulate major premises are dissimilar, [and] that their values systems are differently constructed and weighted." Consequently, "their political, economic and social views contrast" and influence their decisions.[4] Judicial votes are decisions. But what underlies those votes—the justices' attitudes and values—constitutes the explanatory and predictive elements of the decisional approach.

Even though Pritchett's work was recognized as a breakthrough in public law research, few scholars followed his lead until the late fifties and early sixties. Decision-making studies had in the meantime developed outside the legal area—namely in the areas of public policy, public administration, and foreign policy—quite separate from Pritchett's work.[5]

The decision-making framework assumes the presence of two or more alternative actions, one of which may be no action. In the selection of these alternatives, the actor follows a "sequence of activities involving stages of problem recognition, search for information, definition of alternatives, and the selection of one . . . [alternative] consistent with the ranked preferences identified in the first three stages that will maximize . . . the actor's goal." [6] Because of varying evaluations, people perceive problems differently, search for different sources of information, and accept only some alternatives. The reasons for these different evaluations or "preferences" account for the actor's decision. The search for judicial preferences, and reasons for and effects of these preferences, constitute the core of decision-making models. Attitudes, ideologies, or values of judges become most important as explanations for votes and decisions. It is

---

[3] *Ibid.*, p. xii.

[4] *Ibid.*

[5] For example, Herbert A. Simon, *Administrative Behavior* (New York: Macmillan, 1949); R.C. Snyder, H.W. Bruck, and B. Sapin, *Decision-Making as an Approach to the Study of International Politics* (Princeton, N.J.: Monograph No. 3, Foreign Policy Analysis Project Series, 1954); and Julius Turner, *Party and Constituency: Pressures on Congress* (Baltimore: The Johns Hopkins University Press, 1951).

[6] Stephen L. Wasby, *Political Science—The Discipline and Its Dimensions* (New York: Charles Scribner's Sons, 1970), p. 131.

this emphasis that distinguishes decision-making models from the other approaches discussed in this book.

Most decision-making models are forms of the stimulus-organism-response (S-O-R) model common to psychology.[7] Under the classification scheme of this model, legal policies (decisions) are regarded as responses. Constitutions, statutes, case law, and court rules along with informal norms such as customs, legal treatises, and concepts of justice, are regarded as one kind of stimuli.[8] Evidence, circumstances of the cases, the nature of the parties to the dispute, constitute the "facts" of the case and are regarded as another kind of stimuli. The individual characteristics (attributes and attitudes) of the judges and their position *vis-à-vis* other judges and participants in the courtroom are the relevant dimensions of the organism. The model is mechanistic and unilinear in the sense that nothing happens unless a stimulus is present and the sequence is from S through O to R. Thus, the model (see Figure 3) is not complete in itself and is dynamic only when an appropriate stimulus is present. It is neither self-starting nor sustaining.

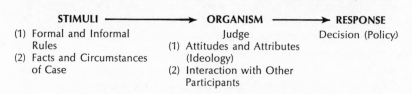

FIGURE 3.   Simple Decision-Making Model

Decision-making models of varying complexity have been constructed and applied to the judicial process. Most, but not all, studies have focused on the decision-making process at the U.S. Supreme Court level. Following Pritchett's pioneering study, other political

[7] See, for example, Stuart Nagel, "A Conceptual Scheme of the Judicial Process," *The American Behavioral Scientist,* VII (December, 1963), 7.

[8] For example, the impact of procedural rules (*en banc* proceedings vs. rotating panels) on decision making is analyzed in Burton M. Atkins, "Decision-making Rules and Judicial Strategy on the United States Courts of Appeal," *The Western Political Quarterly,* XXV (December, 1972), 626.

scientists have promoted the renaissance in the study of public law using decisional schemes.[9] Although emphasis is still directed toward the "S" and "R" of the model, increasingly the "O" has received attention. For it is the "organism," the judge—and his attitudes, ideologies, values, and attributes—who shapes the outcome of judicial decisions.

Three categories of attributes and variables contribute to the development of the attitudes, values, and ideologies which may become part of a judge's decisions. In this development certain hereditary factors interact with social background and experience, which are in turn shaped by a professional socialization process. The result is a set of attitudes and values which may or may not fit into a fairly coherent ideology. A particular set of facts (case, issue, defendant) triggers certain attitudes resulting in a characteristic decision, as illustrated in Figure 4.

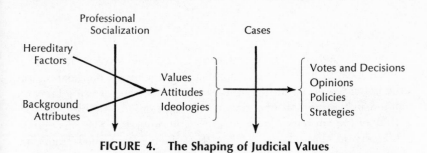

FIGURE 4.   The Shaping of Judicial Values

Game theory is a mathematical expression of a decision-making model.[10] "Gaming" is an attempt to explain and predict *rational*

[9] Perhaps most instrumental in the later developments of the study of judicial behavior and decision making was Glendon A. Schubert. See his *Quantitative Analysis of Judicial Behavior* (Glencoe, Ill.: The Free Press, 1959); *Judicial Behavior* (Chicago: Rand McNally, 1964); *Judicial Decision-Making* (Glencoe, Ill.: The Free Press, 1963); and *The Judicial Mind* (Evanston: Northwestern University Press, 1965).

[10] William A. Gamson, "A Theory of Coalition Formation," *American Sociological Review*, XXVI (June, 1961); Glendon A. Schubert, "Policy Without Law: An Extension of the Certiorari Game," *Stanford Law Review*, XIV (March, 1962), 284; and Schubert, "The Study of Judicial Decision-Making as an Aspect of Political Behavior," *The American Political Science Review*, LII (December, 1958), 1007.

decisional behavior in a conflict situation in which all factors cannot be controlled because other people are involved in the game. Given a certain goal, the model assigns relative weights to several decisional alternatives available to two or more players or decision makers. Players adopt strategies (plans) in order to increase their payoff (winnings or losses) within given "rules" when coalitions are available. Thus, game theory ". . . consists first of all in analyzing simplified prototypes of games such as chess, poker, and others; then in calculating as accurately as possible the winning chances for each player and each hand; and in determining the conditions under which advantageous coalitions can be made or alternative strategies can be evaluated for their chances of success." [11]

By utilizing a game model it is possible to reconstruct the voting behavior of justices, assuming that they are motivated by several clear-cut factors. When "reality" approximates the hypothesized game, we can suggest that, in fact, what the game postulates is "true."

CRITIQUE

Several methodological criticisms have been leveled at studies which have utilized the decision-making models in the analysis of the judicial process. Earlier studies were criticized for using facts as stated in the opinion of judges as an appropriate stimulus for the study of the Supreme Court. As one critic suggests: "The conceptual difficulty in this scheme is that these facts, as gleaned from the opinion verbiage, are not stimulus at all. Are the facts as stated in the judicial opinion the same facts presented to the court for decision? No, they are not. The case opinion itself was not that which confronted the perceiving organisms (the judges) at the argument." [12]

According to this criticism, decision-making analysis must include facts which were rejected as well as those which were accepted—and by which judges individually—rather than simply including those facts stated in the majority opinion. Another point made is that facts as stimuli are seldom perceived uniformly, so that a knowledge

---

[11] K.W. Deutsch, "Game Theory and Politics: Some Problems of Application," *The Canadian Journal of Economics and Political Science*, XX (February, 1954), 76.

[12] Theodore Becker, *Political Behavioralism and Modern Jurisprudence* (Chicago: Rand McNally, 1964), p. 14.

of pertinent facts found in the written opinion tells us little about perceptions of those facts by each individual judge.

Except as applied to those limited studies relying on *stare decisis* to explain and predict voting behavior in terms of past voting behavior of justices, the above criticism is unwarranted. First, what are called in this line of criticism the "facts" of a case or cases are clearly more complex than those stated in a justice's opinion. In the decision-making model, the *cases* are the stimuli which force judges to respond to policy issues. By the time cases have gone through lower courts and are placed on an appellate docket for oral argument and decision, the issues are largely well defined and will demand answers to substantive policy questions. Otherwise, the cases would not warrant review.[13] Issues presented to the higher court normally generate what might be called "ideological" responses on the part of the justices. The attitudes, values, and beliefs of justices (i.e., "ideologies," particularly concerned with such issues as economic and political conservatism or liberalism, dogmatism or pragmatism, libertarian or statist, activist or restraintist views) determine their responses. Because judges' ideologies and perceptions of the issues vary, the decision-making model becomes multidimensional, that is, the judges' ideologies cut across each other.[14] Thus, by exploring the "O" aspect of the model, scholars can more readily explain the responses than when only the "facts" of cases are the central concern.

To determine the ideology of a judge, however, it is necessary to probe more deeply than into the cases in which the justice participated, voted on, and wrote opinions about. Off-bench speeches, writings, memoirs, biographies, interviews, and other data must also be studied to establish sets of beliefs.[15] Consequently, criticism of decision making that faults the model because it appears as if it utilizes "the response itself as a stimulus" is unwarranted.[16] Decisional scholars can go beyond mere facts and votes.

[13] A substantial number of cases turn on minor legal issues which simply do not generate any important ideological responses but must be resolved by courts of last resort. Thus, decisional studies utilize cases which have broad policy implications and are most likely to lead to division on the high courts.

[14] See, for example, Schubert, *The Judicial Mind* (n. 9 above).

[15] David J. Danelski goes beyond cases to establish judicial values in "Values as Variables in Judicial Decision-Making: Notes Toward a Theory," *Vanderbilt Law Review*, XIX (June, 1966), 721–40.

[16] Becker, *Political Behavioralism*, p. 14.

A more valid criticism which can be leveled at decision-making studies is not aimed at the model but at its limited application. Studies have focused almost exclusively on the Supreme Court. Although the Court is at the apex of the judiciary, the dynamics of the judicial process are also displayed in lower federal and state courts. Indeed, these courts more often than not can set the limits within which the Supreme Court must act. Moreover, the vast majority of cases are decided by lower courts—the courts' greatest impact on individuals being felt at the trial level. Consequently, a neglect of the lower courts in decision-making studies means a large void exists in our knowledge of the judicial process. However, it is questionable whether or not the decisional models used so successfully with the Supreme Court level can be applied to trial courts.[17] The problem is that the cases presented before the trial judge seldom are adequate stimuli to elicit the broad sets of values held by the judge. Policy issues are not the kinds of questions commonly posed to trial judges. The lower courts are to a great degree locked into procedures and practices which limit discretion. Perhaps to understand trial courts, the decision-making model will have to focus on the "S" aspect of the model rather than the "O." [18]

Some critics have said that the decisional model oversimplifies the decision process.[19] But simplification, at least to some extent, is what models are about. Schubert quite clearly indicates the functions of a model:

> The test of the value of a scientific model, concept or theory is not *whether* it oversimplifies empirical reality; but rather, what effect it has upon our understanding of that reality. The lawyer's model of judicial decision-making, which is based upon traditional logic and depends upon the *stare decisis* norm for its *deus ex machina*, is also a vast over-simplification of empirical reality. . . . [O]ur criterion should be: Which helps us the better to acquire valid and reliable understanding about how and why judges make their decisions? [20]

---

[17] *Ibid.*

[18] Kenneth M. Dolbeare, *Trial Courts in Urban Politics* (New York: John Wiley, 1967).

[19] Notably, Becker, *Political Behavioralism* (n. 12 above); and *Comparative Judicial Politics* (Chicago: Rand McNally, 1970).

[20] Schubert, *The Judicial Mind* (n. 9 above), p. 286.

With the newer emphasis on judicial values and attitudes in decision making, there is a danger that the scholar may neglect gradual changes which can, over a time period, creep into the attitudinal makeup of the judge. Thus, a constant rechecking of the value assumption of the judge is essential, and possible changes in a judge's perceptions of the issues presented in cases can be accounted for. The late Justice Hugo Black may be, considering the shift in his voting in the later few years of his tenure, a case in point.

The decision-making model assumes patterned behavior on the part of those making decisions. That is to say, under given circumstances a judge will accept a certain alternative fairly consistently. The judge attempts consistently to enhance his "preferences" and to urge his choice upon other members of a court. It is important to note that random or unique behavior cannot be explained adequately by decisional models, except through probability models.[21] Certainly of all the forms of decisional processes, the situation, procedures, and standards of the courtroom are designed to lead to consistent decisional behavior on the part of judges. But if such a design is unsuccessful, "an empirical decision theory is impossible."[22] However, because of the distinctive nature of the judicial process and legal reasoning, the lack of patterned decisional behavior on the part of judges is not as great as with other types of decisions, even though we might see obvious examples of random—at least in our view—judicial decisions.

Another problem with decision-making models generally, and as they apply to courts specifically, is the problem of locating the decision makers, that is, of determining who actually makes or influences decisions.[23] Obviously, the judge makes the decision. But what needs to be determined also is the impact of clerks, bailiffs, court administrators, witnesses, and lawyers on the judicial decision. To ignore the role of other decision makers in the judicial process, focusing only on the decisions of the judges, severely circumscribes the value of the model. For in following such a procedure major components

[21] Joanne Poparad Paine, "Some Frames of Reference," in Wasby, *Political Science*, p. 132.
[22] *Ibid.*
[23] *Ibid.*, p. 135.

of the judicial process are ignored. Including other individuals as "fact" stimuli could resolve this problem.

Voting on judges on collegial courts has been most commonly utilized as an indicator of a judge's response to certain case stimuli. As Murphy and Tanenhaus point out, though, such a limited view of responses may distort the image of judicial decision making. Often a judge's response is recorded merely as a "for," "against," or "abstain" on, say, a civil liberties case. But voting seldom constitutes the total response of a judge. He may vote "for" after having argued in vain "against" in conference. He may have voted contrary to his values in order to be able to write the opinion of the court. He may have cast his vote "for" the defendant in a case of lesser importance while hoping to vote "against" in a more important case, hoping also to win the support of other judges who needed his vote in the first case. Moreover, a judge's "pro" vote does not indicate the intensity with which he holds his views. Consequently, analyses of decision-making responses must consider more than the judge's voting behavior.[24]

Some decision-making models neglect the direct and indirect impact of written briefs, oral arguments, juries, conferences, opinion-writing, and a myriad of other cultural and psychological factors that influence judicial attitudes. Even though it is recognized that these many other factors may be embodied in attitudes or values *vis-à-vis* issues presented by the cases, we must know more about their impact to understand adequately judicial decision making. The shift from the broader dimensions of the stimuli toward a more narrow concern for the organism has led to an imbalance. Neither "S" nor "O" must be neglected. Some return to a more thorough traditional analysis of cases and of the rules and regulations circumscribing decisions may be called for.[25]

Actually, the application of decision-making models is not new in legal scholarship. Only the techniques and methods of testing hypotheses are different today. Traditionalists attributed to judges a unique form of reasoning which accounted for their decisions: reasoning by logic or through syllogisms, the judges would arrive at an

[24] Walter F. Murphy and Joseph Tanenhaus, *The Study of Public Law* (New York: Random House, 1971), p. 110.

[25] H. Frank Way, Jr., "The Study of Judicial Attitudes: The Case of Mr. Justice Douglas," *Western Political Quarterly*, XXIV (March, 1971), p. 12.

answer after establishing a major premise, a minor premise, and then deducing therefrom the rule to be applied. According to this view, a form of decision making—reason by analogy—could be seen in operation as judges performed the mechanical function of discovering an already existing law. However, the legal realists and the sociological school of jurisprudence challenged the traditionalists and crusaded for a broader scope to the study of the judicial process. Oliver Wendell Holmes, Jr. expressed the "new" approach in the oft quoted statement: "The life of the law has not been logic; it has been experience." [26]

Game theory also presents some difficulties when applied to court decision making. It assumes rational decisions (i.e., that the judge will act to increase his power or to achieve his goals). But we cannot be certain that judges decide "rationally," in this sense. To be of use, games must always have payoffs (i.e., some judges win something and others lose the same thing). Power is the payoff in political games. If a judge is motivated by "justice," "being right," and adhering to court norms or an individual ideology rather than being powerful, he is deciding "irrationally." But the value of game theory is to test the rationality and power aspects of judicial decision making. It is of importance that we know those judges who are and who are *not* motivated as game theory postulates.[27]

Game analysis of judicial decision making has been static; we are unable to view the decisional process as a dynamic or transitional process in which one decision or action is related to another in time. In other words, gaming can only tell us about possible decisional alternatives in a game situation. Also, even if the actual behavior of a player fits the postulated behavior of the game, we are still at a loss to explain the "whys" of his actions in terms of background, attitudes, and political or social forces outside the courtroom.

Our basic goal is to uncover the broadest possible explanations for judicial behavior. Consequently, the limited scope of the decisional model is the most telling criticism. However, as one student of decision making correctly concludes, perhaps at this particular stage of development of the study of the courts, adequate and valid re-

[26] Oliver Wendell Holmes, Jr., *The Common Law* (Boston: Little, Brown, 1881), p. 1.
[27] For an explanation of game theory, including its difficulties, see Glendon A. Schubert, *Quantitative Analysis,* Chapter 4.

search means limited research.[28] Nevertheless, we must be willing to broaden the scope of our studies in order to discover broader explanations of judicial phenomena.

DECISION-MAKING STUDIES

Decision-making studies have contributed to our understanding of two dimensions of the decisional process. First, the impact of backgrounds, hereditary attributes, and professional experience on attitudes or values has been one major area of concern of students applying decisional models. Second, the effects of attitudes and values on voting and other decisional outputs has interested the decisional scholar. These two emphases provide us with convenient categories for our review of decisional scholarship.

JUDICIAL BACKGROUNDS AND ATTITUDES

In 1959, John Schmidhauser compiled background data for all ninety-two Supreme Court justices who had served up to that time on the high bench. As expected, the justices were an unrepresentative lot. Warning against relying too heavily on backgrounds as predictive instruments, Schmidhauser, nonetheless, concluded that if the Supreme Court is the "keeper of the American conscience, it is essentially the conscience of the American upper middle-class sharpened by the imperative of individual social responsibility and political activism," conditioned by conservative legal training and professional socialization.[29] Schmidhauser also observed that prior judicial experience seemed not to lead to more objective and better qualified justices. In a subsequent study, he pursued this topic in more detail and found no positive correlation between prior experience and a restraintist approach to Supreme Court cases. Also, his data showed that the dissenters on the high bench tended not to be the "great innovators" willing to disregard precedent for some social

[28] Schubert, *The Judicial Mind*, p. 287.
[29] John Schmidhauser, "The Justices of the Supreme Court: A Collective Portrait," *Midwest Journal of Political Science*, III (February, 1959), 49; and *The Supreme Court: Its Politics, Personalities, and Procedures* (New York: Holt, Rinehart and Winston, 1961).

cause. Quite the contrary, the dissenters were more often supporters of precedent which they felt was being abandoned by the majority.[30]

Although judicial biographers have concerned themselves with the background-and-values relationship, only a few legal scholars and political scientists had attempted systematically to study this aspect of decision making until Schmidhauser's work.[31] In the sixties, such concerns became common among those scholars attempting to understand the judicial decision-making process.

Kenneth Vines investigated the possibility that Southern Federal District judges were influenced more by their backgrounds than by their legal training. Using race relations cases between 1954 and 1962 as his source, he identified "integrationists" (voted pro-black), "moderates" (split vote regarding blacks), and "segregationists" (anti-black). The mere fact that Vines found extremes within the South on race cases indicated that environment or background was more important than legal training, which presumably would have led to a more homogeneous voting record. More segregationists were Democrats than Republicans; but birthplace, law school, and practice location were not significantly different for the three types of judges. The segregationists tended to have held a state position prior to selection to the bench while integrationists had federal experience. The segregationists tended to be Protestant while the integrationists were often Catholics or indicated no religious preferences. Thus, the more a judge was tied to the South by his background (Protestant, state office, and Democrat), the more likely he would be anti-black in his voting behavior.[32]

Stuart Nagel's study of nearly 300 state and federal Supreme Court judges also showed that religion as well as ancestral nationality were correlated with liberal-conservative attitudes and decisions. The Anglo-Saxon Protestants in his survey tended to be more conservative

[30] John Schmidhauser, "Stare Decisis, Dissent and the Background of the Justices of the Supreme Court of the United States," *University of Toronto Law Journal*, XIV (1962), 194.

[31] Examples of early background studies are C.A.M. Ewing, *The Judges of the Supreme Court, 1789–1937* (Minneapolis: University of Minnesota Press, 1938); and R. Mott *et al.*, "Judicial Personnel," *Annals*, CLXVII (May, 1933), 143.

[32] Kenneth Vines, "Federal District Judges and Race Relation Cases in the South," *Journal of Public Law*, XXVI (1964), 338.

than non-Anglo-Saxon Catholics. Although his data were not conclusive and the correlations not particularly strong, Nagel concluded
that "so long as court cases frequently involve value-oriented controversies . . . and so long as different ethnic group affiliations tend
to correspond to different value orientations, there will probably
always be some correlation between ethnic affiliations of judges and
their decisional tendencies." [33] In another study, Nagel found significant correlations between a conservative approach to criminal defendants and membership in the American Bar Association, public
prosecuting experience, and Protestant religion.[34] As reported in
Chapter 4, in certain categories of cases political party affiliation also
is associated with liberal or conservative attitudes.

An analysis of the backgrounds of Eisenhower and Kennedy lower
federal court appointees indicated that, unlike the Supreme Court
justices, the backgrounds of these appointees were middle class. Law
school education apparently provided them with the credentials to
move up and into the judiciary. Partisan activism appeared to be an
important variable that led to their appointments in both administrations, but whatever the background variance between Eisenhower
and Kennedy appointees it could be attributed to the nature of
the national parties themselves. For example, Republican appointees
tended to be of a higher socioeconomic status than Democrats. The
study showed no evidence to demonstrate that judges at the lower
federal level were members of the "power elite" on their way to the
top echelons of power.[35]

Kenneth Dolbeare's work on 124 federal district court judges
showed that little association existed between backgrounds and
voting on urban public policy. Age, residency, law school, appointing
president, career, and political party were not significantly related to
their decisions, however prior judicial experience was. Judges with
prior experience on the bench tended to void police practices in the

[33] Stuart Nagel, "Ethnic Affiliations and Judicial Propensities," *Journal of
Politics*, XXIV (February, 1962), 110.
[34] Stuart Nagel, "Judicial Backgrounds and Criminal Cases," *Journal of Criminal Law, Criminology, and Police Science*, LIII (September, 1962), 333; and
"Testing Relations Between Judicial Characteristics and Judicial Decision-
Making," *Western Political Quarterly*, XV (September, 1962), 425.
[35] Sheldon Goldman, "Characteristics of Eisenhower and Kennedy Appointees
to the Lower Federal Courts," *Western Political Quarterly*, XVIII (December,
1965), 755.

civil rights areas more than judges who lacked such a background. Beyond this statistically significant relationship, Dolbeare found little to cause much optimism regarding the value of compiling and analyzing the backgrounds of judges.[36]

Several explanations for the dearth of explanatory materials in background studies are possible. Much of the statistical work uses the nonunanimous decisions of appellate courts to identify judicial decisional differences. As Joel Grossman has pointed out, this ignores the vast majority of cases which are decided without dissent at all levels of the court system and may be associated with backgrounds.

> Contrasting background experiences are pictured as the major cause of dissensus, while unanimity or consensus are considered evidence of the "non-operation" of background factors. By treating consensus in this limited way, the potential impact of background factors is severely circumscribed, if not distorted; no provision is made for cases where background experience could lead to consensus, and no attention is given to the possibility that dissensus could result from non-background factors.[37]

In addition, we are not altogether sure what backgrounds lead to what attitudes or sets of values. Actual individual experiences may well cut across background characteristics, resulting in the former blotting out the latter. Finally, as Grossman warns, background studies assume that the judge makes a "rational" decision in which the alternatives are clear and the choice through which his values can be furthered apparent—an assumption which may fail to hold true.

It may well be that when a student views the life and times of one particular judge, the discovery of several meaningful background variables is possible. Danelski's biography of Justice Pierce Butler, for example, related his past railroad experience to bench decisions quite adequately.[38] Materials from other biographies seem also to lead to success in associating bench behavior with the past. But

---

[36] Kenneth M. Dolbeare, "The Federal District Courts and Urban Public Policy," in Joel B. Grossman and Joseph Tanenhaus, eds., *Frontiers of Judicial Research* (New York: John Wiley, 1969), p. 373.

[37] Joel B. Grossman, "Social Backgrounds and Judicial Decisions: Notes for a Theory," *Journal of Politics,* XXIX (May, 1967), 336.

[38] David J. Danelski, *A Supreme Court Justice Is Appointed* (New York: Random House, 1964).

when many judges are considered in aggregate, background characteristics become so varied and numerous that explanation is lost.
Furthermore, when several presumably important background variables are considered for a great number of judges, the results are
not impressive. Don Bowen found that, at best, 10 percent of decisional variance could be explained by one background characteristic
of the judges and when six leading variables were considered together, only 30 percent of the variance was accounted for.[39] The
alternative is not to abandon consideration of backgrounds but to
pay closer attention to the relationship of background to other intervening variables (e.g., institutional rules and procedures, roles, consideration of power, individual experiences) before the dependent
variables of votes or decisions are considered.

S. Sidney Ulmer suggests that the problem with socialization
studies may not be with the indirect and intangible influence of
backgrounds on attitudes and responses, but with the statistical
methods used to measure significance. Using Supreme Court justices
as his source, Ulmer discovered that being Catholic, being born in
a rural area, and being a nonpolitician lawyer prior to selection to
the bench were related to a justice's tendency to dissent. For Ulmer,
predicting a justice's predisposition to dissent on the basis of these
three variables, separately and in combination, holds some promise.[40]

Attitudes, Values, and Decision Making

The scholars who have contributed to our knowledge of the relationship between attitudes and decision making take background as
a given factor. If important, it will be reflected in the attitudes and
values held by the judges. The initial task must be to isolate judicial
attitudes and then to determine the decisional impact of these attitudes. The questions become, "What values do judges hold?" and
"How are these values reflected in their decisions?" When these are
answered, the research can expand to encompass backgrounds.

C. Herman Pritchett, whose book *The Roosevelt Court: A Study
in Judicial Politics and Values, 1937–1947* had such a great effect
on the study of constitutional law, is generally recognized as the

[39] Don R. Bowen, "The Explanation of Judicial Voting Behavior from Sociological Characteristics of Judges" (unpublished Ph.D. dissertation, Yale, 1965).
[40] S. Sidney Ulmer, "Dissenting Behavior and the Social Backgrounds of
Supreme Court Justices," *Journal of Politics*, XXXII (August, 1970), 580.

"founder" of contemporary empirical decisional research. As Pritchett states in the Preface to that seminal work, he was struck by the degree and various combinations of dissent on the highest bench: "I began to wonder what it was in that case and in the autobiographies of those justices that led them to disagree with the majority of the Court on the issue there raised. I decided that it might be profitable to examine into the actual patterns of disagreement among the justices, and so went back to preceding terms of the Court for additional data." [41]

The voting record and the written opinions of the justices during ten years of the Roosevelt Court provided Pritchett with instances of consistent liberal and conservative dissenting blocs on the Court. Issues of civil liberties, rights of the accused, state economic regulation and taxation, federal economic regulation, and labor split the members of the Court quite distinctly. The split was, to Pritchett, along attitudinal or values lines. Justices Murphy, Douglas, Black, and Rutledge were civil libertarians and economic liberals, as evidenced by their voting and opinion records. Justices Reed, Frankfurter, Jackson, Stone, Burton, Vinson, and Roberts composed the conservative bloc. Several sets of values coalesced to compel the justices to vote either liberal or conservative in the broadest sense. The liberal-conservative dimension was slightly fragmented by differences of attitude with respect to individual freedoms where matters of economic liberalism and political liberalism were concerned. For example, Justice Murphy voted for individual liberties in 94 percent of the cases, but only in 82 percent for liberal approaches to economic issues. Judicial pragmatism was also seen as a set of values motivating the votes of some justices. Finally, the justices' attitudes toward restraint and activism influenced their votes in many of the cases studied by Pritchett. These several sets of values held by the justices "explain" their votes in nonunanimous cases.

Pritchett also demonstrated the existence of "libertarian activists" on the Vinson Court between 1943 and 1950. Justices Murphy, Rutledge, Douglas, and Black consistently supported libertarian claims and favored a broad application of judicial power to protect those claims. Pritchett felt that to further individual freedom, a justice had to adopt an activist stance. Frankfurter, for example, was liber-

[41] Pritchett, *The Roosevelt Court,* p. xi.

tarian, but his restraintist approach to decision making prevented him from consistently joining the liberal bloc.[42]

Subsequent decision-making studies of judicial attitudes benefited substantially from the quantitative methods developed in sociology, psychology, and political behavior. Cases were determined statistically to present to the justices the same basic policy issues which would generate varying voting responses. The response variance, then, could be attributed to the different attitudes, values, or ideologies of the justices. The consistency and strength of the justices' responses were also more reliably measured and response prediction was implied if not specifically attempted in much of the attitudinal scholarship.[43]

S. Sidney Ulmer has confidence in his ability to predict the degree of support by Supreme Court justices for civil liberties cases on the basis of his ranking of justices on a libertarian scale over a six-year period.[44] Stuart Nagel, Reed Lawlor, Werner Grunbaum, Albert Newhouse, and Glendon Schubert are also impressed with the predictive power of attitudinal studies. Through the use of sophisticated statistical methods and computers, their decisional models appear to hold promise for further scientific development.[45]

Harold Spaeth found that the attitudes of some Supreme Court justices led them to support labor in labor cases and to withhold support for business cases where government regulation of business

[42] C. Herman Pritchett, *Civil Liberties and the Vinson Court* (Chicago: University of Chicago Press, 1954), p. 192.

[43] For a discussion of the statistical methods applied to courts, consult Glendon A. Schubert, *Quantitative Analysis of Judicial Behavior* (Glencoe, Ill.: The Free Press, 1959); and Walter F. Murphy and Joseph Tanenhaus, *The Study of Public Law* (New York: Random House, 1972).

[44] S. Sidney Ulmer, "A Note on Attitudinal Consistency in the United States Supreme Court," *Indian Journal of Political Science*, XXII (1961), 204.

[45] Stuart Nagel, "Predicting Court Cases Quantitatively," *Michigan Law Review*, LXIII (June, 1965), 1411; "Testing the Effects of Excluding Illegally Seized Evidence," *Wisconsin Law Review* (Spring, 1965), 283; and "Applying Correlative Analysis to Case Prediction," *Texas Law Review*, XLII (October, 1964), 1006; Reed Lawlor, "What Computers Can Do: Analysis and Prediction of Judicial Decisions," *American Bar Association Journal*, XLIX (April, 1963), 337; Werner Grunbaum and Albert Newhouse, "Quantitative Analysis of Judicial Decisions: Some Problems in Prediction," *Houston Law Review*, III (Fall, 1965), 201; and Glendon A. Schubert, "Judicial Attitudes and Voting Behavior: The 1961 Term of the United States Supreme Court," *Law and Contemporary Problems*, XXVIII (Winter, 1963), 100; and "Behavioral Jurisprudence," *Law and Society Review* II (May, 1968), 407.

was involved.[46] Illustrating the inferential jump characteristic of attitudinal studies, Schubert, reviewing Spaeth's study, observed that his pro-labor and antibusiness relationship ". . . suggests, of course, that attitudes toward labor and attitudes toward business . . . were both subcomponents of a more basic attitudinal variable." [47]

Joseph Tanenhaus selected a great number of Supreme Court cases that were appealed from the rulings of federal administrative agencies during the 1947–56 terms of the Court in order to test the statistical significance of judicial voting behavior. Only Justices Black and Douglas consistently voted in a specific direction in several categories of cases, with Justices Vinson, Minton, Frankfurter, Reed, and Jackson occasionally displaying consistency. At least Black and Douglas had definite attitudes toward the particular issues presented by the cases. For example, they voted pro-labor, pro-business competition, and for freedom of the person in draft and immigration issues. However, Tanenhaus was careful to point out that his study was designed only to determine whether certain voting patterns are statistically significant. Why they are significant must be left to further study.[48]

But Justices Black and Douglas did not always agree. Harold Spaeth discovered that Black was more pro-states rights, restraintist, and pro-business than Douglas. Although Spaeth's article displayed a fine combination of statistical applications with a traditional reading of the dissenting opinions of the two justices, Spaeth did not attempt to classify the justices into the opposing ideological categories which might be indicated by their divergent attitudes.[49] Spaeth also discovered that Justice Frankfurter's restraintist approach to the law, at least in business and labor cases, was a myth.

[46] Harold Spaeth, "Analysis of Judicial Attitudes in Labor Relations Decisions of the Warren Court" (paper delivered to the Midwest Conference of Political Scientists, April, 1962); and "Warren Court Attitudes Toward Business: The 'B' Scale," in Glendon A. Schubert, ed., *Judicial Decision-Making*, Chapter 4.
[47] Glendon A. Schubert, "Biographical Essay: Behavioral Research in Public Law," *The American Political Science Review*, LVIII (June, 1963), 443.
[48] Joseph Tanenhaus, "Supreme Court Attitudes Toward Federal Administrative Agencies, 1947–1956—an Application of Social Science Methods to the Study of the Judicial Process," *Vanderbilt Law Review*, XIV (March, 1961), 473.
[49] Harold Spaeth, "An Approach to the Study of Attitudinal Differences as an Aspect of Judicial Behavior," *Midwest Journal of Political Science*, V (May, 1961), 165.

Instead of voting for federalism and granting deference to federal regulatory commissions (a restraintist reaction), Frankfurter more consistently voted against labor and for business when the restraintist and labor-business issues overlapped. Frankfurter's restraint arguments appeared, to Spaeth, to be but a rationalization to clothe his more basic economic conservatism.[50]

But restraint vs. activism is still an important distinction to apply to members of the high bench—including Frankfurter. In those issues which present to the Court a question of judicial power, the justices split into a bloc that votes to protect or expand their power and a bloc that does not wish to assume any further power. Justices Douglas, Reed, Minton, Warren, Black, and Clark were "activists," in this sense, and Justices Whittaker, Stewart, Burton, Harlan, Frankfurter, and Jackson were "restraintists." Thus, the commitment to restraint or activism is present for all justices but may be sublimated for values of a higher order when the issue before them is perceived to involve a more basic question.[51]

Glendon Schubert is the political scientist who has perhaps had the greatest impact on the development of attitudinal decision-making studies. In a series of articles and books, he has reported new methodological applications of decision-making models leading to highly suggestive conclusions. Beginning where Pritchett ended his study of the Vinson Court, Schubert demonstrated the continued existence of a left bloc in civil liberties cases. The attitudes of Justices Warren, Black, Douglas, and Brennan toward individual freedom consistently led them to vote for civil liberties, which was not the case with Justices Whittaker, Burton, Harlan, and Frankfurter. Justice Clark often felt compelled to align with the left until Brennan joined the Court in 1956. As Schubert pointed out: "Faced with pressures from both the augmented libertarian bloc and the right bloc of four justices, Clark began to move to the right, and to establish closer ties with the second John Marshall Harlan and with Burton." Attitudes toward civil liberties apparently were not strong in Clark's case.[52]

[50] Harold Spaeth, "The Judicial Restraint of Mr. Justice Frankfurter: Myth or Reality," *Midwest Journal of Political Science*, VIII (February, 1962), 22.

[51] Harold Spaeth, "Judicial Power as a Variable Motivating Supreme Court Behavior," *Midwest Journal of Political Science*, VI (February, 1962), 54.

[52] Glendon A. Schubert, *Constitutional Politics* (New York: Holt, Rinehart and Winston, 1960), p. 158.

Through scalogram analysis, Schubert has also shown that Supreme Court justices have persistent attitudes toward claims of injured workmen in Federal Employers' Liability Act cases, toward the claims of aliens, and toward the claims of the individual in right to counsel and search-and-seizure cases. The apparent attitudes motivating some justices in these cases is a sympathy toward the underprivileged in the American system.[53] Although the justices' attitudes led them to join liberal or conservative blocs, there was evidence of Justice Black moving to the right in the later years of the Warren Court, as Clark did during the early period. But Black's change, according to Schubert, was an attribute of age more than a change in his attitudes.[54]

Schubert's most complete work, *The Judicial Mind*, pulls together and develops his attitudinal approach to judicial decision making. As with all of his other works, Schubert assumes that justices of the Supreme Court are political types (i.e., they are participants in power struggles and they are motivated by private interests in their pursuit of power). Of course, private interests does not mean to imply selfish pecuniary motives but rather a "process analogous to the implementation of the attitudes of the justices toward issues of public policy through the act of voting on decisions on cases."[55] Schubert further assumes that justices make rational decisions. The training and experience of judges and the norms of the Court all contribute to the exercise of rationality. Finally, Schubert assumes that the public views of the justices (i.e., written opinions, speeches, writings, and decisional votes) approximate the private beliefs held by members of the Supreme Court. It is exactly this relationship between beliefs and political action (votes of judges) that he investigates. His goal is to give content to the beliefs. Cases provide the stimulus for certain attitudes and ideologies, and the votes are the response.

Each case asks the justices to respond to the question: is your attitude toward value X sufficiently favorable that you believe that a claim of degree Y should be upheld? (For example: Is your attitude

[53] Schubert, *Quantitative Analysis* (n. 43 above), Chapter 5.
[54] Glendon A. Schubert, *The Constitutional Polity* (Boston: Boston University Press, 1970), p. 129.
[55] Schubert, *The Judicial Mind* (n. 9 above), p. 13.

toward political freedom sufficiently favorable that you believe that a
witness before a congressional investigating committee cannot "consti-
tutionally" be compelled to reveal his past associations, if any, with the
Communist Party . . . ?) [56]

From 1946 through 1963, 1,657 cases involved disagreement among
members of the high court and 1,099 of these evoked liberal-conservative responses from the justices. The cases were almost evenly
divided between economic and civil liberties issues. From these two
sets of cases, Schubert constructed "C" (political liberalism) and
"E" (economic liberalism) scales. The "C" scale had five subcomponents: political equality, political freedom, religious freedom, fair
procedure, and individual privacy. The "E" scale encompassed fiscal
claims, governmental regulation of business, union-management disputes, freedom of competition, and the constitutionality of state
taxing. Justices Murphy, Rutledge, Douglas, Black, Warren, and
Brennan occupied the six top ranks of the "C" scale (i.e., they voted
most often in favor of the extension of civil liberties). Justices Reed,
Minton, Vinson, Clark, Burton, and Whittaker ranked lowest on the
"C" scale. Liberal attitudes toward the "E" scale measured by votes
on economic issues were most strongly held by Justices Murphy,
Black, Douglas, Rutledge, Warren, and Brennan (i.e., they voted
most often for the economically underprivileged), and Justices Whittaker, Jackson, Harlan, Frankfurter, Burton, and Stewart gave least
support to the underprivileged. The remaining justices fell between
these two extremes.

Scales other than "C" or "E" could be constructed to measure other
attitudinal dimensions, such as attitudes toward governmental taxing
authority, federalism, judicial activism, and judicial centralization.
The data collected by Schubert allowed him only to measure the
significance of the taxing authority and federalism dimensions in
those few terms where the issues were numerous. However, he believed that these other attitudes should be considered as important
attitudinal dimensions.

High correlation existed between "C" and "E" attitudes. That is, as
the rankings noted above indicate, most of the justices who rated

high on political liberalism also rated high on economic liberalism. However, significant differences exist among the subcomponents of the scales which led Schubert to ask meaningful questions about liberalism-conservatism as the *single* major dimension of judicial attitudes. Votes on fiscal claims and anti- or pro-business cases correlated highly with one another and with the general "E" scale. In other words, these votes (attitudes) were all of the same genus. Political freedom and fair-procedure attitudes were highly correlated with the general "C" scale attitudes. Again, these three apparently represented the same thing. But attitudes toward political equality and right of privacy correlated more closely with "E" than with "C" attitudes! Attitudes toward government taxing authority had little to do with "C" and a pro-union attitude, as expected, correlated with "E." Religious freedom appeared not to be highly correlated with either "C" or "E." Schubert was willing to accept liberalism-conservatism as the overriding attitudinal dimension of both political and economic issues ("C" and "E" are highly correlated), but he also believed that some of the discrepancies in the subcomponents of the two major scales indicate that attitudes of some of the justices are on a different plane, perhaps between economic and political dimensions although intersected at some point with them. In other words, the judicial mind is more subtle than commonly described and is likely multidimensional.

Nonetheless, political-equality attitudes correlated the highest of all the subcomponents with both the general "C" and "E" scales and, therefore, was the "core value" of general liberalism. Also, the strengths of other "E" and "C" attitudes led Schubert to suggest that they were expressions of more general ideologies. When justices vote, they are expressing attitudes which flow from three ideological dimensions of general liberalism: equalitarianism, libertarianism, and individualism, or their antitheses.

The scale of equalitarianism-traditionalism indicates the "extent to which justices believe in the desirability of changing the status quo in order to bring about a society in which there is greater equality of opportunity for all persons"; libertarianism-authoritarianism refers to the "extent to which justices believe in the importance of extending the scope of freedom as opposed to authority"; and individualism-collectivism measures the "extent of the belief that the most important ultimate interest is that of the individual human being, as distinguished from the interests of societies composed of interacting individuals." [57]

According to this analysis, the Court was dominated by a conflict between equalitarianism and traditionalism during the 1946–48 and 1955–62 periods, with traditionalism dominating in the earlier period and equalitarianism winning the majority in the later era. 1949 and 1954 were periods on the Court when collectivism won most of the votes. From 1950 through 1953, authoritarianism dominated "E" and "C" issues presented to the Court. The changes in dominant ideology were primarily due to the changes in Court personnel rather than to any fluctuation in individual justices' attitudes.

But what was striking about the individual attitudes of justices was that political and economic conservatives *outnumbered* the liberals on the bench during the time covered and yet the Court's output, especially in the latter years (1955–62), was clearly *liberal*. Schubert believed this was due to an ideological plane of pragmatism-dogmatism, which intersects liberalism-conservatism and divides the conservatives but not the liberals on the bench.

Liberal and conservative ideologies are reference points for justices to evaluate external social, political, and economic issues. Pragmatism and dogmatism are reference ideologies which deal "with fundamental personality attributes." The pragmatist believes in individual freedom and the dogmatist believes in social restrictions upon the exercise of individual freedom. Schubert believed the pragmatism and dogmatism ideologies overlapped and replaced (at least for the conservatives on the bench) the individualism and libertarianism ideologies and became a "super-ideological dimension." Schubert states: "Both Individualism and Libertarianism are ideologies which strongly emphasize freedom of the individual . . . while the counter-ideologies of Collectivism and Authoritarianism strongly emphasize the socialization of compulsion. . . ." [58] This conflict over the degree of individual freedom is what pragmatism-dogmatism is about. So, by adding this new ideological level, we can now graphically portray Schubert's "judicial mind."

[57] *Ibid.*, p. 202.
[58] *Ibid.*, p. 259.

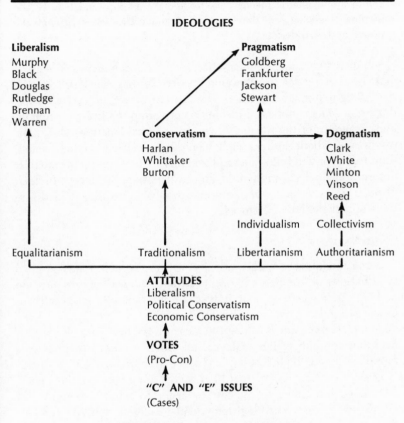

FIGURE 5. The Judicial Mind

Thus, Schubert was able to explain the shift in Court output on the basis of these ideological divisions on the high court:

> . . . during all except the most recent of the seventeen terms studied, the attitudinal differences of Supreme Court justices toward political and economic issues have reflected the para-ideological division of conservatives; and since conservatives, but not liberals, were further divided ideologically between pragmatists and dogmatists, the more

cohesive and intense ideology of the liberal minority tended to be the dominant ideology of the Court throughout the latter half of the period of this study.[59]

Schubert's continued contribution to the development of decision making as a model for studying the courts has been substantial. According to him, and to others, if we can ascertain judicial attitudes, these will reflect an overall ideology motivating the judges. From an understanding of the ideology, we can gain explanations and make predictions about judicial behavior. The decision-making model, thus, fulfills or will fulfill the requirements we have set up for models: description, analysis, prediction, and explanation. Schubert's *Judicial Mind* is a fine example of the application of a decisional model to the study of the judicial process.

GAME ANALYSIS

Game models are mathematical constructs which, when applied to situations of conflict, suggest possible explanations for decision making. If we assume that judges are participants in politics or power struggles, then the prerequisites for a conflict situation have been met. Game models attempt to measure the best possible *rational* decisions through which a player can either maximize winnings or minimize losses. If, for example, Justice Roberts and Chief Justice Hughes, in 1937, wished to (1) develop unanimity on the bench, (2) move the Court to the left in order to blunt the anti-Court attacks of the New Deal legislators and President, and (3) enhance their own power, several strategies were available. First, they should both remain the "swing men" between the three-man left coalition (Brandeis, Cardozo, and Stone) and the four-man right (Van Devanter, Sutherland, Butler, and McReynolds) and thereby enhance their power on the bench. This required voting with the right when the situation was such that their two votes could not possibly win the decision for the left because of nonparticipation or defections. Second, when the bench was not divided among the coalitions, their goal was a unanimous or near unanimous decision. Third, in order to move the Court to the left, obviously, Hughes and Roberts had to vote with the liberals when that coalition, with their votes, could

[59] *Ibid.*, p. 272.

win. Schubert showed that the voting behavior of Roberts and Hughes approximated these postulated strategies of the game and thereby demonstrated that the two justices were likely motivated as the game suggests.[60]

A side payoff in the above game would be "winning" the assignment of an opinion in the 1937 conflict. In fact, the assignment of opinions by Hughes corresponded with the power ranking of the justices.[61]

Game models applied to the Insular Cases of 1901 suggested that Justice Brown also played the "swing" role between two coalitions and increased his power as well as receiving most of the opinion assignments as a side payoff. Power and game strategies could have also been involved in Federal Employers' Liability Act cases between 1938 and 1957. A coalition of four justices was able to force the Court to grant review in those favorable cases in which a decision on merits went for the plaintiffs (the workers).[62]

Decisional models utilizing game theory have not been numerous and not all scholars are overjoyed with the heuristic and predictive power of game analysis. Nonetheless, the few examples have the value of testing some commonsense hypotheses as well as generating further hypotheses which could be investigated by other models or approaches. For example, if unanimity, power, and liberal motivations were involved in the 1937 decisions, traditional research into the personal papers, opinions, and biographies of the justices might well support or refute what the game suggests.[63]

Decision-making models—whether they concentrate on backgrounds, attitudes, or game strategies—are directed toward an understanding of the heart of the judicial process: how and why judges decide as they do. Obviously, the student of the judicial process, whatever his or her interest may be, must have a working knowledge of judicial decision making before wider interests can be pursued.

[60] Schubert, *Constitutional Politics* (n. 52 above), p. 161.
[61] *Ibid.*, p. 164.
[62] Schubert, *Quantitative Analysis* (n. 43 above), Chapter 4.
[63] E.g., Felix Frankfurter, "Mr. Justice Roberts," *University of Pennsylvania Law Review*, CIV (December, 1955), 313; Alpheus T. Mason, *Harlan Fiske Stone, Pillar of the Law* (New York: Viking, 1956); M.J. Pusey, *Charles Evans Hughes* (New York: Macmillan, 1951); and Robert H. Jackson, *The Struggle for Judicial Supremacy* (New York: Alfred A. Knopf, 1941).

CHAPTER TWO

Micro-Group Models

DESCRIPTION AND ANALYSIS OF SMALL-GROUP MODELS

Small-group analysis (micro-group model) has been extremely popular in sociology and social psychology but has only recently gained adherents in political science.[1] "Small groups," "face-to-face groups," or "primary groups" are terms which can be interchanged with "micro-groups" without loss of meaning. The prerequisites of a small

[1] See, for example, Sidney Verba, *Small Groups and Political Behavior* (Princeton: Princeton University Press, 1961). Verba writes of "a new and exciting field of research," p. 3. Examples of micro-group applications to courts are S. Sidney Ulmer, "Leadership in the Michigan Supreme Court," in Glendon A. Schubert, ed., *Judicial Decision-Making* (New York: The Free Press of Glencoe, 1963), p. 13; Walter F. Murphy, "Leadership, Bargaining, and the Judicial Process," in Glendon A. Schubert, ed., *Judicial Behavior: A Reader in Theory and Research* (Chicago: Rand McNally, 1964), p. 395; Richard J. Richardson and Kenneth Vines, "Interpersonal Relationships on Three United States Courts of Appeals," in Thomas P. Jahnige and Sheldon Goldman, eds., *The Federal Judicial System: Readings in Process and Behavior* (New York: Holt, Rinehart and Winston, 1968), p. 145; David J. Danelski, "The Influence of the Chief Justice in the Decisional Process of the Supreme Court," in Walter F. Murphy and C. Herman Pritchett, eds., *Courts, Judges, and Politics* (New York: Random House, 1961), p. 497; Walter F. Murphy, "Courts as Small Groups," *Harvard Law Review*, LXXIX (June, 1966), 1565; S. Sidney Ulmer, "Homeostatic Tendencies in the United States Supreme Court," in Ulmer, ed., *Introductory Readings in Political Behavior* (Chicago: Rand McNally, 1961), p. 167; Eloise Snyder, "The Supreme Court as a Small Group," *Social Forces*, XXXVI (March, 1958), 232; S. Sidney Ulmer, "The Analysis of Behavior Patterns in the United States Supreme Court," *Journal of Politics*, XXII (November, 1960), 629; S. Sidney Ulmer, *Courts as Small and Not So Small Groups* (New York: General Learning Press, 1971); Gordon Bermand and Rob Coppock, "Outcomes of Six- and Twelve-Member Jury Trials: An Analysis of 128 Civil Cases in the State of Washington," *Washington Law Review*, XLVIII (May, 1973), 593; and Note, "Applicability of Three-Judge Courts in Contemporary Law: A Viable Legal Procedure or a Legal Horsecart in a Jet Age?," *American University Law Review*, XXI (April, 1972), 417.

group, whether a collegial court or a peer group, are face-to-face contact, awareness of members as individuals in the group, and common goals.[2] Hence, the emphasis on face-to-face communications and reciprocal awareness distinguish a micro-group from a macro-group. Goal orientation is present in both, if not in all, human endeavor.[3]

The popularity of micro-group models has developed largely because of the lack of explanatory power of other models. First, small-group theory is designed to explain behavior which seems inconsistent with the psychological makeup of the individual and which appears explainable in terms of that individual's membership in a large group, society, or a nation.[4] Obviously, the basic assumption underlying micro-group models is that when men (judges) get together into some structured situation (collegial court), their behavior is altered. What they would decide individually is changed when they decide collectively. Implicit in this assumption is that the collective will is not just the sum total of individual wills but more a "general will," qualitatively different from individual wills. Being in a group makes a difference.[5]

Micro-group models are also popular because small groups can be directly observed, experimented with, and simulated. This makes such studies apparently more scientific. R.T. Golembiewski reports: "Size is, of course, the key to the usefulness of the small groups. Small size permits the intensive study of meaningful social units." [6] By analogy, the discoveries of simulated or laboratory group experiences can be projected to the "real" world of the courts and hypotheses, explanations, and predictions generated. If, for example, seating arrangements alter communications among members of a small group in the laboratory, the seating arrangements of judges in conference would display distinct patterns of communication.[7]

[2] Verba, *Small Groups*, pp. 11–12.
[3] *Ibid.*, p. 13.
[4] R.T. Golembiewski, *The Small Group* (Chicago: University of Chicago Press, 1962), p. 17.
[5] Some psychologists have challenged the "general will" aspects of micro-group models. See George C. Homans, "The Study of Groups," in David L. Sills, ed., *International Encyclopedia of the Social Sciences* (New York: Macmillan, 1968), VI, 263.
[6] Golembiewski, *The Small Group*, p. 19.
[7] S. Sidney Ulmer, *Courts as Small and Not So Small Groups* (New York: General Learning Press, 1971), pp. 10–12.

Micro-group approaches are designed to examine the internal makeup and characteristics of the group. Macro-group models (Chapter Four), although paying attention to the internal structure of groups, are more directly concerned with intergroup relations and access to governmental units. Macro-group models look outward for their content and micro-group models look inward. The student of micro-groups is concerned with the interactions among the members of the group rather than with the activities of the group collectively. The student of macro-groups, on the other hand, although clearly interested in how the members of the group interact, usually is concerned with the group's behavior as expressed through a spokesman or leader and with the interaction among groups. The ACLU's court participation is the macro-group student's concern, while the interaction between members of the Smallvilles' ACLU committee, meeting in a member's home, interests the micro-group scholar.

A multimember court clearly fulfills the requirements of a small group. The small group is a miniature society with its own boundaries, patterns of relations, and norms. The research goal may be to understand larger societies by studying the more manageable smaller group or to limit one's conclusions to that small group without projecting them as hypotheses about all societies.[8] This latter goal is most prevalent in the micro-group studies involving courts.

Although social psychologists have amassed an impressive amount of empirical and theoretical data regarding a wide variety of subjects encompassed by the term "small group," political scientists studying courts have thus far remained rather conservative in their search for relevant data. Basically, three questions have been asked by those using small-group analysis applied to the courts: (1) What is the influence of "structure" on the behavior of judges and others involved in the courtroom? (2) What are the patterns of interaction among the members of the court? and (3) Have the members of the court achieved their goals? Of course, questions concerning the how, why, to what degree, etc., follow from the major queries. The micro-group model configuration can be portrayed as follows:

[8] *Ibid.*, pp. 90–109.

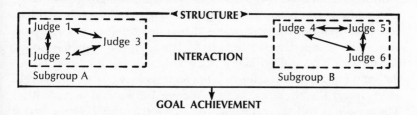

FIGURE 6. Micro-Group Model

The fundamental concern of the micro-group studies is to discover what part of a person's behavior can be attributed to his/her membership in the group. Different groups mean different behaviors. Thus, the various dimensions of the difference constitute the variables to be considered by the student of small groups. In a loose sense, the structural aspects of the model are composed of independent variables; the interaction process involves intervening variables; and the goal achievement characteristics are the dependent variables.[9]

Structural Variables	*Interaction Variables*	*Goal Variables*
Group Size	Member Characteristics	Cohesiveness
Norms	Communication	Effectiveness
Rules	Leadership	Equilibrium
Organization	Subgroup Formation	
Statutes	Expertise	
	Roles	

We would want to know, for example, what impact a nine-man court (size) has on the degree of productivity (effectiveness) when two subgroups form under two different sorts of leaders, as compared with a seven-man court without distinctive subgroups and only one leader.

[9] These variables follow generally those suggested by Morton Deutsch, "Group Behavior," in David L. Sills, ed., *International Encyclopedia* (n. 5 above), pp. 265–75.

Structural variables are those aspects of the small group that tend to regulate group behavior through standing rules, laws, or written and unwritten prescriptions which define the group as an organization. (E.g., a law degree is required of judges; the Supreme Court has nine members; the Chief Justice assigns opinion-writing tasks; the supreme court of Washington State meets in departments as well as *en banc;* the court meets in conference after oral arguments.) Those elements of the courtroom or jury room which can be identified without knowing anything about the people interacting within the organization would fall into the structural variables category.

The interaction variables center on the people in the group. As members of a small group interact in their effort to achieve goals, leadership roles tend to form; expertise is recognized or developed; subgroups may form; and the individual attributes and social, economic, and status variables may dictate the direction, intensity, and frequency of the interaction among members. (E.g., a businessman with high status is designated leader of a jury; a former tax lawyer is assigned opinion-writing tasks in a complicated tax case; Democrats on the bench form a liberal voting bloc.) "Who interacts with whom concerning what?" is the question that delineates the broad dimensions of the interaction process.

The degree to which goals are achieved may determine the cohesiveness, the effectiveness, and the equilibrium of the group. These three goal variables can overlap or be mutually exclusive. As the group performs its tasks with dispatch and thoroughness, the members tend to have a greater commitment to each other as a group. They are satisfied. On the other hand, a haphazard approach to tasks may result in a crowded docket, but members still get along well. The pressures of inefficiency may actually force the group to coalesce even more. The persistence of the group (equilibrium) may not be threatened although it is not achieving its goals. Many groups have existed long after their function has been assumed by others. But equilibrium means more than persistence. Conflicts on the bench, consistent subgroup formation, and maverick roles may threaten the equilibrium of the group but not necessarily its existence.

Although the direction of the data accumulation is determined by the questions the researcher wishes to ask of the courts and judges, generally speaking, small-group studies of courts center upon leadership. Who influences whom and how? Who leads the court in various cases through his personality, prestige, and expertise (interaction variables)? Procedures in most courts favor the chief justice or the presiding judge (structural variable). He could assume task leadership and, possibly, social leadership (interaction variable) and thereby develop cohesion and productivity in the court (goal variable).[10]

Interviews, questionnaires, courtroom observations, and participants' memoirs and biographies constitute the sources for small-group data. Simulated experiments where "players" attempt to act out the "reality" of the courtroom could also suggest some characteristics to be investigated by the micro-group scholar.

CRITIQUE

Micro-group models of courts have been highly suggestive but as yet have limited application. Because of the special nature of the judicial process, observations of a court as a small society would be of little value in explaining the nature of the larger society. Also, the manner in which judges interact makes observations extremely difficult, if not impossible. Scholars cannot directly experiment with nor actually view much of what constitutes the day-to-day interaction among judges as they discuss, debate, and decide cases in conference and circulate memoranda and written opinions regarding cases before them. Consequently, the "whys" of interpersonal relations remain speculative. What goes on inside a jury room? The "purple curtain" still shields the inner workings of courts from the prying eyes of the scholar. Some would argue that the curtain should remain closed.

Micro-group laboratory studies have only a limited value for an understanding of courts simply because of the professional and specialized nature of judicial interaction. Much of what social psychologists have done in the labs can only be suggestive regarding courts.

Small-group studies of influence or leadership postulate that power is the overriding, if not sole, motivational factor in the inter-

[10] For an excellent application of task and social leadership in the U.S. Supreme Court, see David J. Danelski, "The Influence of the Chief Justice in the Decisional Process," in Walter F. Murphy and C. Herman Pritchett, eds., *Courts, Judges and Politics* (New York: Random House, 1961), p. 497.

action among judges. Cooperation, cohesion, and agreement factors remain unaccounted for but nevertheless may be crucial. Disagreement exists as to the definition of leadership, making it difficult for a researcher to check his results and for comparative studies to be made.[11] There is also the possibility that some courts at various times perform their tasks without leadership.

Multimember courts are certainly small groups. But most courts in the American system, state and federal, are presided over by one judge. Models which concentrate on the interaction of several judges would need revision to represent adequately and accurately the trial court levels. Also, not all court cases involve juries. Knowledge of the group dimensions of the jury would still leave much to be explained about the judicial process.

In a collegial court setting, deciding involves both individual and group interaction. Federal and state appellate court procedures allow, if not dictate, that a judge review individually much of the preliminary materials demanding decision (e.g., petitions for review, issuances of certain writs, study of briefs, etc.). Although judges decide collectively in preliminary conferences, they draft opinions individually. The final vote is a group function, but concurring and dissenting opportunities interpose into the collective action. Varying combinations of collective and individual decision making exist among courts. Efforts must be made to separate the influence of these two settings if small-group studies are to be more meaningful. Micro-group models transferred unchanged from social psychology to the judicial process may provide inadequate description, explanation, or prediction.

To be effective, micro-group studies must be comparative. To know the impact of the size of a court or jury on individual behavior, for example, comparisons must be made between groups of different sizes. Most of the contemporary studies make comparisons also in time. When new members are appointed to the Supreme Court, a "new" group is formed which is compared and contrasted with the previous group; however, the variable of size remains constant. It should be noted that more studies of state courts are needed. Wide variations in structure exist at that level, allowing for meaningful comparisons.

[11] Danelski, "The Influence of the Chief Justice," p. 498.

A word should be mentioned about the tendency for micro-group models to be closed models, not accounting for environmental or cultural input and impact. Indirectly, the background characteristics of the group participants and the types of cases heard by the judges and jurors do reflect environment. However, the factor of environment is not easily operationalized into categories lending themselves to easy measurement, quite apart from the problem of analyzing how it finds its way into the small-group model. Thus a reluctance to open the small-group model is understandable.[12]

Finally, there has been a tendency among micro-group students of the judicial process to rely heavily upon votes to verify the existence of subgroups or blocs on the courts. Walter F. Murphy has offered this criticism: "The fact that two or more Justices vote together is rather weak evidence that their votes are the result of interaction; standing alone, voting records tell very little about the force or direction of any interpersonal influence that may exist. Small group analysis requires other kind of data and a more general understanding of the impact of a group decisional situation on individual behavior." [13]

Micro-group models, like most of the frameworks discussed in this book, do not provide the means for an explanation of all that happens within the judicial process. They were not designed to be all-encompassing. Nonetheless, despite the limited scope and particular problems of micro-group models as applied to courts, micro-group scholars have broadened our knowledge of the judicial process, as exemplified in the numerous studies described below.

MICRO-GROUP STUDIES

The impact of structure on judicial and juror behavior has been a traditional concern of legal scholars and political scientists. The interaction among jury and court members interested sociologists first and only recently has begun to concern political scientists. Goal achievement, finally has perhaps the richest tradition in political science; for, after all, Aristotle and Plato were concerned with "justice." Thus, the studies which have utilized micro-group models represent an ecumenical collection.

[12] Deutsch, "Group Behavior," p. 271.
[13] Murphy, "Courts as Small Groups" (n. 1 above), p. 1567.

STRUCTURE

Few would question the importance of federalism, separation of powers, or the political party system as crucial structural variables pressing on judges and other participants in the judicial process.[14] Less obvious, but important, structural variables are the varied and often invisible rules of procedure which may have been forced on the courts by legislatures, adopted by the judges under their rule-making powers, or accepted as custom simply because through time the courts have deemed such procedures to be of value in performing their tasks.[15]

State and federal collegial courts vary in size from three to nine members. If psychologists are correct, size of the court has some meaningful effects upon the interaction of members of the bench and upon achievement of goals.

> The larger the . . . group . . . , then the greater the demands upon the leader and the more he is differentiated from the membership at large; the greater the group's tolerance of direction by the leader and the more centralized the proceedings; the more the active members dominate the interaction within the group; the more the ordinary members inhibit their participation and hence, the less exploratory and adventurous the group's discussion; the less intimate the group atmosphere, the more anonymous the actions, and generally the less satisfied the members as a whole; the longer it takes to get nonverifiable (judgmental) decisions; the more acceptable the unresolved differences; the more subgroups formed within the membership; and the more formalized the rules and procedures of the group.[16]

Each one of these statements cries for verification within the context of the collegial court. S. Sidney Ulmer has suggested some implications for size of group; but his observations, like those above, come from group studies other than courts and are based upon prob-

[14] For a discussion of the impact of general structural variables on the judicial process, see Stuart S. Nagel, *The Legal Process from a Behavioral Perspective* (Homewood, Ill.: Dorsey Press, 1969), Chapter 4.

[15] *Ibid.*, Chapter 5. The importance of deciding cases in panels and in *en banc* situations where the entire court membership sits is discussed by Burton M. Atkins, "Decision-making Rules and Judicial Strategy on the United States Courts of Appeals," *The Western Political Quarterly*, XXV (December, 1972), 626.

[16] Bernard Berelson and Gary A. Steiner, *Human Behavior: An Inventory of Scientific Findings* (New York: Harcourt, Brace, and World, 1964), p. 358.

ability theory. The larger the group, the greater the probability that members will, through interaction, recall information and reach a more accurate decision. Also, the larger the membership, the more members will tend to look to "experts" within their group for explanations and interpretations, thereby increasing the influence of the experts.[17]

Section 2281 of the U.S. Code requires that a special three-judge court be established to hear cases involving the question of the constitutionality of state statutes. Appeal is directly to the U.S. Supreme Court. Between 1958 and 1962, .48 percent of all petitions to the high bench for review involved decisions from these special courts. Of all the plenary decisions of the Court, 3.5 percent dealt with the three-man court cases.[18] "Thus, despite some freedom to avoid decision, the court seems to feel obliged to give plenary treatment to a substantially higher proportion of three-judge appeals than to other forms of petition to review." [19] Structure has an effect, however slight, in altering the behavior and goals of the Supreme Court. Because of the pressures of time, this may lead gradually to a "decrease in the Court's ability to grant writs of *certiorari* [in other cases] and, hence, in its freedom to choose the cases to be heard before it." [20]

The major Congressional motivation behind the enactment of Section 2281 was to impress the federal judiciary with the importance of the special cases assigned to it and to gain a greater respect for and compliance with their decisions.[21] There was hope that through their collective knowledge, the judges would in effect, do a more judicious job. It appears that, as the Yale study suggests, the three-judge court has given more careful consideration to cases, resulting in greater compliance and legitimation.[22] Size alone does not explain the impact of the three-judge court, but it is an important factor.

[17] S. Sidney Ulmer, *Courts as Small and Not So Small Groups,* p. 5; and "Toward a Theory of Sub-Group Formation in the United States Supreme Court," *Journal of Politics,* XXVII (February, 1965), 133. For further comments on the impact of size, see William H. Riker, *The Theory of Political Coalitions* (New Haven: Yale University Press, 1962), Chapters 2, 3, and 4.

[18] Comment, "The Three-Judge Court Reassessed: Changing Roles in Federal-State Relations," *Yale Law Journal,* LXXII (Summer, 1963), 1655.

[19] *Ibid.*

[20] *Ibid.*

[21] *Ibid.,* pp. 1646–1647.

[22] *Ibid.,* p. 1654.

Bradley C. Canon and Dean Jaros have isolated structural factors which have an impact on judicial behavior.[23] Using dissensus on state supreme courts as the basis for their study, they discovered that the presence or absence of an intermediate appellate court influenced the rate of dissent at the highest court level. The dissent rate is higher for those supreme courts which are protected from trivial cases by an intermediate appellate court.[24] This higher dissent rate may, in turn, be explained by the fact that states with second-level appellate courts tend to be industrialized, urbanized, and heterogeneous.[25] In addition, as expected, the case load is lower for those Supreme Courts which are assisted by other appellate structures.[26]

Methods of selection and tenure on the bench (both of which can be classified as structural variables) are related moderately to the rate of dissent on the high bench. Appointive courts dissent less than elective judges.[27] Also, the longer the tenure of the judge, the greater the tendency to dissent.[28] If we are to view dissent on a collegial court as an interaction variable (related to formation of subgroups, lack of strong leadership, etc.), the structural variables of tenure, selection, and court organization can be seen to have some impact on this interaction variable. At the same time, case load decreases with the presence of an intermediate appellate court having, possibly, an influence upon a court's goal variable of effectiveness.

Several state appellate courts and the federal circuit courts make decisions primarily in departments or panels rather than en banc with the entire membership sitting.[29] Richardson and Vines suggest several interaction implications flowing from such a structural arrangement. First, the composition of the various panels or committees can vary according to the assignments made by the presiding

[23] Bradley C. Canon and Dean Jaros, "External Variables, Institutional Structure and Dissent on State Supreme Courts," Polity, III (Winter, 1970), 175.

[24] Ibid., p. 192.

[25] Dean Jaros and Bradley Canon, "Dissent on State Supreme Courts: The Differential Significance of Characteristics of Judges," Midwest Journal of Political Science, XXXV (May, 1971), 324.

[26] Canon and Jaros, "External Variables," p. 193.

[27] Ibid., p. 190.

[28] Ibid., p. 192.

[29] Richard J. Richardson and Kenneth N. Vines, The Politics of Federal Courts (Boston: Little, Brown, 1970), p. 122. See also Delmar Karlen, Appellate Courts in the United States and England (New York: New York University Press, 1963).

judge.[30] Each "new" assignment should change the nature of the panel. Moreover, a decision coming from a panel as opposed to a full *en banc* decision would be scrutinized more closely by a higher court.[31] Dissent rates would decrease as the size of the panel decreases. The probability of disagreement among three is clearly less than among the entire court members of perhaps seven or nine. One study indicates that panel arrangements lend themselves to negotiations leading to consensus.[32]

The chief judge or chief justice is placed in an excellent leadership position. He selects the membership of the panels, presides over both panels, and often assigns cases to the panels. Also, the presiding judge often appoints retired or *pro tem* judges to relieve congested dockets and to fill vacancies. By his control over appointments, case assignments, and through presiding prerogatives, the chief judge can influence the interactions among sitting judges.[33] The panel situation also enables a judge who had been in the minority in an *en banc* ruling, to ignore or change the meaning of the decision of the larger body in subsequent panel cases.[34]

En banc proceedings, on the other hand, display structure-interaction relationships which are the opposite of panel behavior or are unique to the larger body. When the whole court sits together, there appears to be a tendency toward the institutionalization of conflict. Eighty percent of the *en banc* cases in federal circuits involve dissents and in a large number of cases the vote is close.[35] Despite the increased chances of disagreement, *en banc* proceedings tend to gain greater acceptance from other courts and from the litigants and their publics.[36]

Some other organizational factors have been isolated as having a strong behavioral influence. In an attempt to explain why the political party influences were significant in the Michigan Supreme Court

[30] Richardson and Vines, *The Politics of Federal Courts,* p. 122.

[31] *Ibid.,* p. 123.

[32] Sheldon Goldman and Thomas P. Jahnige, *The Federal Courts as a Political System* (New York: Harper and Row, 1971), p. 178.

[33] Richardson and Vines, *The Politics of Federal Courts,* pp. 123–24.

[34] *Ibid.,* p. 125. See also Burton M. Atkins, "Decision-making Rules" (n. 15 above).

[35] *Ibid.,* and A. Lamar Alexander, Jr., "En Banc Hearings in the Federal Courts of Appeals: Accommodating Institutional Responsibilities," *New York University Law Review,* XL (May, 1965), 583.

[36] Richardson and Vines, *The Politics of Federal Courts,* pp. 125–26.

but not on the Wisconsin high bench, David Adamany suggested that the contrasting structural arrangement between the states may account for some of the behavioral difference.[37] The Wisconsin Supreme Court, in contrast with that in Michigan, is a resident court. All the justices live in the capital and have adjacent offices, providing ample opportunity for informal consultation before final decision. Time limitations in Wisconsin act against the filing of dissenting opinions also. Thus, structure discourages dissent and encourages accommodation in Wisconsin, but a different structural arrangement has the opposite effect in Michigan.

The opportunity for the study of the influence of organizational variables is overwhelming and demands the return of many behavioral scholars to the traditional concerns of political scientists and legal scholars. Daryl R. Fair, in a fine summary of the variations in state intermediate appellate courts, has provided some descriptions which cry for comparative research.

> In Georgia, all three judges in a panel must agree in order to reach a decision; when there is a dissent in a panel the court meets *en banc* to decide the case. . . . For all practical purposes, all three judges must agree in New Jersey also; if there is a dissent an appeal is taken to the Supreme Court. In Ohio, two votes of three are usually required to decide cases, but a unanimous vote is necessary to reverse a lower court on the weight of the evidence. The vote on the disposition of cases takes place in eleven states at a conference held prior to the writing of opinions. In five states this process is handled differently. Texas uses a system by which a tentative opinion is prepared prior to conference by the judge who draws the case. California relies strictly upon signatures on written opinions which are circulated. In Indiana, both the conference technique and the system of circulating written opinions are used; . . . .[38]

---

[37] David Adamany, "The Party Variable in Judges' Voting: Conceptual Notes and a Case Study," *The American Political Science Review*, LXIII (March, 1966), 57. See also S. Sidney Ulmer, "Leadership in the Michigan Supreme Court," in Glendon A. Schubert, ed., *Judicial Decision-Making* (n. 1 above), pp. 16–17; and Edward N. Beiser and Jonathan Silberman, "The Political Party Variable: Workmen's Compensation Cases in the New York Court of Appeals," *Polity*, III (Summer, 1971), 521.

[38] Daryl R. Fair, "State Intermediate Appellate Courts: An Introduction," *Western Political Quarterly*, XXIV (September, 1971), 423. See also Herbert Jacob, *Justice in America* (Boston: Little, Brown, 1972), pp. 194–95.

Procedures vary greatly among state supreme courts as well. If Adamany is correct in his appraisal of the Wisconsin Supreme Court, we can assume that structure looms large in other states as an influence on behavioral variations. Certainly, students of the judicial process do not have a paucity of research (and researchable) questions available in this area.

INTERACTION

Rules of procedure have an impact on the dimensions of interaction in the U.S. Supreme Court. The Chief Justice is *primus inter pares* as a result of rules, norms, and customs which have developed in the Supreme Court. Procedure dictates that he preside over open court and conference. He presents his views first after oral argument and he votes last. He assigns opinion-writing tasks when with the majority and he initiates considerations of petitions for writs of *certiorari*. He controls the time to be spent on many matters. The opportunities for leadership are therefore available although not all chief justices will seize them.

Through a study of the private papers of Supreme Court members sitting from 1921–46, David Danelski was able to identify two leadership roles—task and social—which were partially a result of procedural opportunities available to the Chief Justice.[39] Chief Justice Taft was a social leader on the bench during his tenure, but Associate Justice Van Devanter pushed the Court toward completion of its assigned tasks. Chief Justice Hughes performed both leadership roles. Chief Justice Stone failed to lead the Court in either "getting its business completed" or in keeping personal conflicts at a minimum.[40]

Subgroup formation, an interaction characteristic, is common with small groups; and collegial courts are no exception. In order to enhance his position in a court, a judge may join with other judges to win the vote and also to control the tone of the written opinion or to add weight to the court's decision. Structural characteristics can en-

[39] Danelski, "The Influence of the Chief Justice" (n. 10 above), pp. 497–508.
[40] See also Walter F. Murphy, "Marshalling the Court: Leadership, Bargaining, and the Judicial Process," *University of Chicago Law Review*, XXIX (Summer, 1962), 640.

courage coalition formation. However, the formation of subgroups is primarily a function of the interaction process itself.

C. Herman Pritchett, who was so instrumental in revitalizing the study of the judiciary by political scientists, assumed that much of what judges decide can be related to their particular ideology or attitudes rather than merely to their perceptions of the facts and relevant law in each case. Nonunanimous opinions provided the basis for Pritchett's analysis and have continued to be the source from which the students interested in subgroup formation draw their conclusions. In recording their dissenting votes and writing their reasons for not accepting the majority's opinions, the justices are "informing the public of their divisions and their reasons." But to Pritchett, the justices are also "supplying information about their attitudes and their values which is available in no other way." According to Pritchett: "For the very fact of disagreement demonstrates that members of the Court are operating on different assumptions, that their inarticulate major premises are dissimilar, that their value systems are differently constructed and weighted, that their political, economic, and social views contrast in important respects." [41] Subgroups are formed around the "preferences and prejudices of the justices." [42]

Through bloc analysis, Pritchett isolated the degree to which justices agreed and disagreed with one another. The justices did indeed form voting alignments which lasted through time although their interagreement waned in the latter part of the time period covered by his study. Legal scholars and political scientists had already known of liberal and conservative wings on the Court, but Pritchett gave statistical support for their earlier impressions. The formation of such coalitions was attributed to the values and attitudes held by the justices toward social, economic, and political issues.

[41] C. Herman Pritchett, *The Roosevelt Court: A Study in Judicial Politics and Values, 1937–1947* (New York: Macmillan, 1948), p. xii. See also his *Civil Liberties and the Vinson Court* (Chicago: University of Chicago Press, 1954); "Divisions of Opinion Among Justices of the U.S. Supreme Court, 1939–1941," *The American Political Science Review*, XXXV (October, 1941), 890; "Dissent on the Supreme Court, 1943–1944," *The American Political Science Review*, XXXIX (February, 1945), 42; and "The Roosevelt Court: Votes and Values," *The American Political Science Review*, XLII (February, 1948), 53.

[42] C. Herman Pritchett, "Divisions of Opinion Among Justices," p. 890.

Today's student of the judicial process must be familiar with bloc analysis and scalograms in order even to read much of what is published in scholarly journals dealing with courts. Certainly to do research into the judiciary, knowledge of these methods is required. Subgroups on collegial courts, identified by these techniques, appear to be common with almost all multimember courts. Ulmer and Schubert, for example, have updated Pritchett's work by identifying blocs on the Warren Court.[43] State courts are also characterized by subgroups. Studies have reported that the Michigan Supreme Court contains two blocs which parallel the party affiliations of the judges.[44] The supreme courts of Illinois, Iowa, Washington, Wisconsin, and New York display similar bloc formation although party background may not be associated with the membership of a justice in a particular subgroup.[45]

Eloise Snyder identified three subgroups in the U.S. Supreme Court: liberal, conservative, and pivotal.[46] New justices tended to

[43] Ulmer, "The Analysis of Behavior Patterns," p. 633; and Glendon A. Schubert, Quantitative Analysis of Judicial Behavior (Glencoe, Ill.: The Free Press, 1959), Chapter 3.

[44] Glendon A. Schubert, "The Study of Judicial Decision-Making as an Aspect of Political Behavior," The American Political Science Review, LII (December, 1958), 1014; S. Sidney Ulmer, "The Political Party Variable in the Michigan Supreme Court," Journal of Public Law, XI (1962), 352; and Malcolm M. Feeley, "Another Look at the 'Party Variable' in Judicial Decision-Making: An Analysis of the Michigan Supreme Court," Polity, IV (Fall, 1971), 91.

[45] E. Ferguson, "Some Comments on the Applicability of Bloc Analysis to State Appellate Courts" (paper delivered to the Midwest Conference of Political Scientists, May, 1971); Jerry K. Beatty, "An Institutional and Behavioral Analysis of the Iowa Supreme Court—1965–1969" (unpublished Ph.D. dissertation, University of Iowa, 1970); David Flint, "The Supreme Court of Washington: A Quantitative Analysis of Judicial Behavior" (unpublished Master's thesis, Washington State University, 1964); David W. Adamany, "The Party Variable in Judges' Voting: Conceptual Notes and a Case Study," The American Political Science Review, LXIII (March, 1969), 57; Edward N. Beiser and J. Silberman, "The Political Party Variable: Workmen's Compensation Cases in the New York Court of Appeals," Polity, III (Summer, 1971), 521.

[46] Eloise Snyder, "The Supreme Court as a Small Group," p. 232. A study by S. Sidney Ulmer has verified some of Snyder's propositions. Groups did form, but not necessarily only three in number. The movement among groups was from the polar groups to the pivotal and not directly from polar to polar. New justices did not consistently join the pivotal group before moving to the polar groups. S. Sidney Ulmer, "Toward a Theory of Sub-Group Formation in the United States Supreme Court," Journal of Politics, XXVII (February, 1965), 133. Kennedy appointees to the high court displayed bloc behavior described by Snyder. See Dennis L. Thompson, "The Kennedy Court: Left and Right of Center," The Western Political Quarterly, XXVI (June, 1973), 263.

join the pivotal group before aligning themselves with the left or right subgroups. During the thirty-three years covered by Snyder's study, no long-term liberal subgroup member had associated himself with the conservative group and no conservative had joined the liberals without passing through the pivotal subgroup.

A brief survey of the relevant works clearly indicates subgroup formation as a characteristic of the interaction process among judges sitting on collegial courts. What remains to be adequately explained is the reason for the formation of these subgroups. Power and influence seem the most obvious explanation. However, we are not altogether sure that, because judges vote alike, part of their strategy is to join with others and to persuade others to join with them. We may know something about the intensity of the strengths of the subgroup by measuring the degree and consistency of voting agreement through time. But it may well be that Judge A votes consistently with Judge B simply because they perceive facts, law, and issues similarly without consultation, discussion, or debate. In other words, interaction may well be at a minimum between the two judges, but their voting records indicate the contrary. The problem here is not with the concept of interaction and subgroup formation but, rather, with the present methods used to measure the interaction. Also, concentration on nonunanimous cases and dissenting voting ignores the vast number of cases on which judges agree. That agreement might well be a product of certain forms of interaction as yet unidentified through empirical research.

S. Sidney Ulmer has concluded that power or influence is not necessarily the major reason for the formation of subgroups. Rather than using the terms "coalitions" or "power blocs" for subgroups on the Court, he prefers the term "clique," which implies that members may actually sacrifice power to vote consistently with their ideology or values.[47] Samuel Krislov has also been disturbed by the assumption that power motivates judges' subgroup behavior: "It would be foolish, of course, to assume that in a real sense 'power' . . . represents the totality of any sane judge's motives. General views of justice and the judicial role, the relation of the court's position to other agencies in the governmental structure, to say nothing of the facts

[47] Ulmer, "Toward a Theory," p. 133.

of the case, all play a fundamental role in determining actual votes and outcomes." [48]

David Rohde has added another dimension to the explanation of coalition formation among appellate court judges. The size of a particular winning coalition on civil liberties cases during the Warren era was a function of perceived threat situations. If a threat to the Court's power exists (e.g., the Jenner-Butler Bill of 1958 or the draft Omnibus Crime Bill of 1968), the size of a winning coalition will increase. In a nonthreat circumstance, the winning coalition tends to be a bare majority. In addition, the nonthreat coalition is composed of justices who consistently agree on civil liberties issues, whereas the threat coalition includes justices with divergent views. Clearly, then, the political environment has an impact on the size and nature of coalitions on at least the Supreme Court.[49] For whatever reason—power, values, attitudes, coincidence, friendship, or threat— it cannot be denied that the formation of subgroups within collegial courts is a common form of interaction.

The leader-follower relationships on a collegial court have been investigated by several students of the judicial process, but as with most of the small-group studies of the court, the "purple curtain" prevents direct observation. Two major sources have been consulted to part the curtain: voting records and memoirs. By manipulating voting records in terms of agreement and disagreement among the court members, suggestions are generated about who leads whom. In addition, the personal papers of justices supply insights into the personal interactions behind the voting records. Any substantial appraisal of leadership should include both sources. Unfortunately, memoirs are not normally available until long after a justice leaves the bench and some caution must be exercised in their use because of biases and misperceptions often built into any personal account of political events.

Traditionally, personal characteristics have been viewed as guides to leadership. Certain people possessing specific traits were always placed into formal influence positions. But leadership has been found

---

[48] Samuel Krislov, "Theoretical Attempts at Predicting Small Group Behavior," *Harvard Law Review*, LXXIX (June, 1966), 1580.

[49] David Rohde, "Policy Goals and Opinion Coalitions in the Supreme Court," *Midwest Journal of Political Science*, XXXVI (May, 1972), 197.

to be more difficult to identify. Who occupies a formal leadership position (e.g., Chief Justice or presiding judge) is an obvious beginning point for analysis of leadership. But the position approach is not altogether satisfying simply because of the not uncommon existence of "the power behind the throne," or of individuals who manipulate the formal leaders. Also, leadership has been shown to be related to situation, and different situations may consequently lead to different leaders. In courts, the difficulty of position analysis is increased because of the many individual aspects of judicial decision making. The Chief Justice has the opportunity to be first among equals but may not seize the opportunity. Thus, small-group studies of leadership assume, at the beginning, that all judges on the bench have an equal chance to be leaders.

Ulmer has defined leadership on the bench as "a process of exerting influence on that behavior, in an organized group, which leads to the establishment and achievement of goals." [50] He has clearly delineated the relationship of an interaction variable (leadership) with goal variables consistent with the micro-group model. Votes on collegial courts are a reflection of power, but the image may be distorted. Judges may vote with one another but for different reasons. Blended with the voting statistics must be the degree of concurrences in reasons or opinions associated with the votes.

Through a study of voting in all nonunanimous civil liberties cases in the 1958 term, Ulmer identified a Frankfurter, Harlan, Whittaker, Stewart, and Clark voting bloc and a Warren, Douglas, Brennan, and Black bloc. Justices Frankfurter and Warren attracted the highest voting agreement rate among the members of their respective blocs and thus appeared to be the leaders. But by determining the degree to which the bloc members concurred in the opinions of others (e.g., how many times Warren concurred with Brennan as compared with how many times Brennan concurred with Warren), it was discovered that "Brennan received almost twice the ratio of supportive acts from Warren than Warren received from Brennan." [51] Brennan, not Warren, appeared to be the leader of the 1958 civil liberties bloc. Frankfurter gained slightly more support from Harlan, making him the leader of the other bloc. Ulmer also noted that when power is defined in terms of who has the crucial swing vote between the two

---

[50] Ulmer, "Leadership on the Michigan Supreme Court" (n. 37 above) p. 15.
[51] Ulmer, "The Analysis of Behavior Patterns" (n. 43 above), p. 252.

blocs, Whittaker rated highest, leading him to conclude that "it would seem that firm conclusions about leadership . . . must await more conclusive evidence, although Warren, Brennan, Frankfurter, and Harlan seem more likely candidates for this mantle than other members of the court." [52]

Ulmer also found degrees of leadership in his work on the Michigan Supreme Court. By using three indicators of leadership: (1) degree of interagreement between two pairs of justices; (2) degree of interagreement among three or more justices; and (3) the number of majority opinions each justice wrote, Ulmer established a rank order of leadership on the Michigan high bench.[53] He found that the Chief Justice ranked only third, suggesting that formal position at the state level is not a clear indication of leadership.[54] However, leadership may be manifested in forms other than power. Between 1880 and 1958, the relative power positions of justices on the U.S. Supreme Court remained stable and tended to correlate highly with the stability of the power position of the Chief Justice. If the power ranking of the Chief Justice fluctuated through time, so also did the rankings of the other justices. Although the Chief Justice may not be number one on several indices of power, the stability of his position says much about the stability of power relations on the Court generally. Thus, Ulmer concluded that "the role of the Chief Justice is perhaps more significant than is generally conceded." [55] But it is the person that makes the office; the office only allows for the opportunity for leadership.

David Danelski and Walter Murphy have contributed substantially to our understanding of the position of Chief Justice in the U.S. Supreme Court.[56] Their data indicate that indeed the Chief Justice of the U.S. Supreme Court is in a unique position to provide subtle forms of leadership. Their approach has been to use private papers, memoirs, and biographies, rather than votes, in order to

[52] *Ibid.*, p. 254.
[53] Ulmer, "Leadership in the Michigan Supreme Court," p. 25.
[54] *Ibid.*, p. 27.
[55] Ulmer, "Homeostatic Tendencies" (n. 1 above), p. 176. Ulmer suggests that age and geographical origins of the Chief Justice have an impact on his and the Court's stability.
[56] Danelski, "The Influence of the Chief Justice" (n. 10 above), p. 497; and Walter F. Murphy, *Elements of Judicial Strategy* (Chicago: University of Chicago Press, 1964).

analyze the leadership interaction process within the Court. We have already seen that procedures favor the Chief Justice. But these procedures only grant the Chief Justice the opportunity to lead. In addition, the Chief Justice must be persuasive, esteemed, able, and well liked.[57] Through preparation, personality, and prestige, Danelski has shown that some chief justices have clearly assumed task and social leadership, whereas others have relinquished the leadership role to associate justices. Because Chief Justice Hughes established an unanimous consent procedure to handle the great number of petitions for *certiorari* and was apparently well prepared to justify denials and grants during conference, he was, thereby, able to lead the Court at the early stages of the decisional process. During conference, Hughes, as presiding officer, expedited matters and kept personal animosities to a minimum. His personality fit well with the other members of the bench and he was clearly respected by his colleagues. Chief Justice Hughes combined the qualities of personality, esteem, and preparation to fulfill the requirements of leadership on the high bench. Chief Justices Taft and Stone, on the other hand, lacked these qualities and failed to lead their respective Courts as effectively as Hughes.[58] Persuasion on the merits of the case, sociability, bargaining, threatening, and exercising influence on selection of colleagues are tactics available to most chief justices.

In our pursuit of explanations of judicial behavior, we must not forget that judges are lawyers trained to be convinced by meaningful legal and policy arguments. As Walter Murphy points out: ". . . judges can be persuaded to change their minds about specific cases as well as about broad public policies, and intellectual persuasion can play an important role in such shifts."[59] We should also note that justices who are held in high regard in terms of their ability to get along socially with their colleagues can often add to their leadership. Again, according to Murphy: "Observance of the simple rules of human courtesy and thoughtfulness . . . can do much to keep interpersonal relations on a plane where a meaningful exchange of

[57] Danelski, "The Influence of the Chief Justice," p. 497.

[58] The leadership alternatives and strategies available to all justices on the high bench are ably reviewed by Walter F. Murphy's fine study, *Elements of Judicial Strategy*. See also his "Marshalling the Court: Leadership, Bargaining, and the Judicial Process," *University of Chicago Law Review*, XXIX (Summer, 1962), 640.

[59] Murphy, *Elements of Judicial Strategy*, p. 44.

ideas is possible." [60] Simply being nice may make others susceptible to one's arguments. Should persuasion or sociability fail, a judge can sanction or threaten his colleagues by withholding his vote or writing an opinion which may attack the viewpoint of his colleagues. Bargaining over votes and viewpoints in written opinions is a common tactic among members of a collegial court during the stage when opinions are drafted and circulated among the judges. Compromising on part of a written argument from a draft opinion may allow the judge to retain or gain another argument or a vote on the final disposition of a case.

The assignment of opinion-writing tasks provides the Chief Justice or senior justice with a strategy opportunity to reward, punish, and to develop unity on the bench. Chief Justices Vinson and Warren and Associate Justices Frankfurter and Black, motivated by ideological considerations, used much of their opinion-assignment responsibilities to reduce tension on the bench during their tenures. The ideological commitments created the tension and the opinion assignments were designed to reduce that tension. [61]

Under favorable circumstances, judges can exert some influence on the selection of "friendly" colleagues to their bench. Murphy has shown many examples of the efforts, some successful, to influence the president or senators to promote a friend to the Supreme Court. [62] Co-option, persuasion, sociability, bargaining, and sanctioning—in combinations or separately—are all tactics available to members of a multimember court and can be utilized effectively to enhance the power and leadership influence of a judge. Micro-group models can tell us much about the interaction among members of a collegial court, and leadership is clearly an important relationship needing further analysis.

Micro-group analysis appears to be applicable only to a collegial court situation, leaving an understanding of the trial judge to different approaches. But such a conclusion ignores the role played by juries in the trial court system of America. The jury, which certainly is involved in decision making at the trial level, is a small group.

[60] *Ibid.*, p. 49.

[61] William P. McLauchlan, "Research Note: Ideology and Conflict in Supreme Court Opinion Assignment, 1946–1962," *Western Political Quarterly*, XXV (March, 1972), 16.

[62] Murphy, *Elements of Judicial Strategy*, pp. 73–78.

Structural, interaction, and goal variables are clearly applicable to this institution also. For example, answers to questions of size, leadership, and effectiveness are most crucial for an understanding of the jury. Of course, we must recognize that only a very small percentage (perhaps two percent) of cases are even tried by jury. But small-group analysis can help us to understand this two percent and, in our quest for knowledge, we must not ignore even this small part of the larger phenomenon we are attempting to understand. An appraisal of the extensive micro-group literature on juries would be quite beyond the scope of this review of small-group studies on the judicial process. We should be aware, however, of the role of juries and of their amenability to micro-group models.[63]

---

[63] The best general works on juries from a small-group approach in which simulation as well as field interviews were used came out of the extensive University of Chicago Jury Project initiated in 1953. See Harry Kalvin, Jr., and Hans Zeisel, *The American Jury* (Boston: Little, Brown, 1966); and Rita James Simon, *The Jury and the Defense of Insanity* (Boston: Little, Brown, 1967). See also American Judicature Society, *The Jury Process, A Bibliography*, Report No. 1 (January, 1968); and H.S. Erlanger, "Jury Research in America: Its Past and Future," *Law and Society Review*, IV (February, 1970), 345.

CHAPTER THREE

Role Models

DESCRIPTION AND ANALYSIS OF ROLE MODELS

Role theory has a respected history in sociology, anthropology, and psychology but only recently has the concept had any great impact on legal research. Role theory is based upon a rather simple assumption about human behavior: man seeks predictability in his relations with others. Psychological drives, resulting from something innate or learned or both, account for the need for predictability. Whatever the cause, man expects certain behavior from others; and largely his expectations are confirmed. Because of the continued confirmation of expectations, "positions" or "statuses" are defined; and we begin to identify a person by the position he holds. The actions or behavior associated with the position constitute a role.[1]

Although man's psyche demands predictability in his social transactions, the development of a position encompasses more than the coming together of random psychological expectations. Positions are also products of social needs. Judges are expected to perform a social function; namely, to allocate justice within a set of fairly well-defined rules of procedure. The continued existence of a social system requires that someone perform this function.[2] Thus, positions are institutional products of the psychological need for predictability in our

[1] For a general introduction to role theory, see B.J. Biddle and E.J. Thomas, eds., *Role Theory: Concepts and Research* (New York: John Wiley, 1966); S.F. Nadel, *The Theory of Social Structure* (New York: The Free Press of Glencoe, 1957); Neal Gross *et al.*, *Exploration in Role Analysis* (New York: John Wiley, 1958); John C. Wahlke *et al.*, *The Legislative System* (New York: John Wiley, 1962); and Theodore Sarbin and Vernon Allen, "Role Theory," in Gardner Lindzey and Elliot Aronson, eds., *The Handbook of Social Psychology* (Reading, Mass.: Addison-Wesley, 1968), Vol. 1.

[2] Gabriel Almond and James S. Coleman, eds., *The Politics of the Developing Areas* (Princeton: Princeton University Press, 1960); and Gabriel Almond and G. Bingham Powell, Jr., *Comparative Politics: A Developmental Approach* (Boston: Little, Brown, 1966).

relations with one another and of the need for the performance of certain social functions. Roles are the behavioral dimensions of these positions. No matter who is found in any particular position, he will be expected to act in a way we consider characteristic of the position or status. Professor Smith, for instance, is both an individual and a professor. He is expected to act a certain way simply because experience has shown that professors act that way. Moreover, he normally does act in the expected way and that confirms our expectations. This does not discount the contribution, however unique, that Smith brings to his professorship. It is merely to recognize that his position as professor to some degree adds to or subtracts from the actions of Smith the individual. To understand the "additions" and "subtractions" is to understand Smith's role.

Judges also are expected to behave in a characteristic manner, which is to say they occupy a definite position. Judges perform roles as a result of their having donned the robes of judicial office. Perhaps even more than professors, judges have constraints upon their behavior which result from confirmed expectations about the judicial office. Recently, attention has been directed to these judicial roles, and emerging studies of them should lead to a substantial growth in our knowledge of the judicial process.[3]

A role involves the actions of two or more people who are inter-

[3] Theodore Becker, *Political Behavioralism and Modern Jurisprudence* (Chicago: Rand McNally, 1964); Becker, "A Survey Study of Hawaiian Judges: The Effects of Judicial Role Variations," *The American Political Science Review*, LX (September, 1966), 677; Joel B. Grossman, "Role Playing and the Analysis of Judicial Behavior," *Journal of Public Law*, XI (1962), 285; Charles H. Sheldon, "Perceptions of the Judicial Roles in Nevada," *Utah Law Review*, MCMLXVIII (September, 1968), 355; Kenneth Vines, "The Judicial Role in American States: An Exploration," in Joel B. Grossman and Joseph Tanenhaus, eds., *Frontiers in Judicial Research* (New York: John Wiley, 1969); Grossman, "Dissenting Blocs on the Warren Court: A Study in Judicial Role Behavior," *Journal of Politics*, XXX (November, 1968), 1068; S. Sidney Ulmer, *Courts as Small and Not So Small Groups* (New York: General Learning Press, 1971); Dean Jaros and Robert Mendelsohn, "The Judicial Role and Sentencing Behavior," *Midwest Journal of Political Science*, XI (November, 1967), 471; Henry Glick, *Supreme Courts in State Politics* (New York: Basic Books, 1970); Henry Glick and Kenneth Vines, *State Court Systems* (Englewood Cliffs, N.J.: Prentice Hall, 1972); Theodore Becker, *Comparative Judicial Politics* (Chicago: Rand McNally, 1970); and Beverly Blair Cook, "Perceptions of the Independent Trial Judge Role in the Seventh Circuit," *Law and Society Review*, VI (May, 1972), 615.

acting or communicating with one another.[4] The nature of the interaction is controlled by the respective positions in which these people
place themselves; their perceptions of the norms surrounding each
position; and, consequently, the behavioral expectations each holds
for the other.

Judges occupy distinct positions on the bench. A lawyer in the
courtroom arguing a case holds the position of an advocate. Each
has learned the norms (or most of them) surrounding his respective
position; each expects certain behavior from his role partners; and
each acts accordingly—that is, each plays a role. These reciprocal
expectations, it should be noted, will be regulated by the situation
in which the position incumbents find themselves. At a bar association meeting, the lawyers and the judge behave in one manner and
in the courtroom, in another. Each situation manifests different sorts
of customs or norms which have developed through time to give
predictability to the situation. Thus, three major sources account for
role performance (behavior): (1) the position incumbent has expectations about how he should act; (2) the person in a position
with whom the incumbent is interacting has expectations about the
incumbent's behavior (and, of course, his own); and (3) these
expectations are developed through a learning of norms or standards
which are part of a distinct situation.

The sets of norms to be "called into being" to regulate the situation depend upon who is interacting with whom and the type of
situation. A judge will act a certain way with a fellow judge and
another way when he is interacting with a lawyer in the courtroom.
Outside the courtroom situation, his role behavior with the same
positions may vary. Given the varying perceptions, situations, and
role partners, many role possibilities are evident even within the
relatively stable and "simple" judicial process. Despite his background, the individual who becomes a judge must act out a certain
role demanded by that position. His learning of the judge's role,
however, comes at the end of a long process of legal socialization.
Upon graduation from law school and successful completion of the

---

[4] The communication need not be a face-to-face or verbal form of interaction.
Legal briefs, lower-court records, probation officers' reports, or recollections of
past experiences in anticipation of a new encounter with a person would be
forms of communication other than face-to-face interaction.

bar exam, the student becomes a lawyer and begins to be socialized in his role or roles, although the process will not be near completion until after years of practice. When he is selected to the bench further socialization is necessary.[5] He now comes into relations with other judges, lawyers, and courtroom participants; and new demands are made on him to conform to the normative imperatives of his position.

Symbolically, the role model could be portrayed as $R = f [S + (P \times P) + N]$. Role is a function of Situation plus Position interaction plus Norms. The symbols are given the following content.

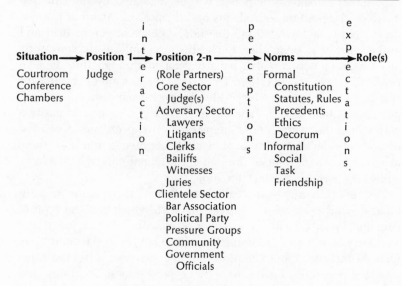

Situation →	Position 1 → interaction	Position 2-n → perception	Norms →	expectations Role(s)
Courtroom	Judge	(Role Partners)	Formal	
Conference		Core Sector	Constitution	
Chambers		Judge(s)	Statutes, Rules	
		Adversary Sector	Precedents	
		Lawyers	Ethics	
		Litigants	Decorum	
		Clerks	Informal	
		Bailiffs	Social	
		Witnesses	Task	
		Juries	Friendship	
		Clientele Sector		
		Bar Association		
		Political Party		
		Pressure Groups		
		Community		
		Government		
		Officials		

FIGURE 7.   Judicial Role Model

SOURCE: This scheme is a revision of the one suggested by Kenneth N. Vines, in "The Judicial Role in the American States: An Exploration," in Joel B. Grossman and Joseph Tanenhaus, eds., *Frontiers of Judicial Research* (New York: John Wiley, 1969), p. 461.

[5] Robert Carp and Russell Wheeler, "Sink or Swim: The Socialization of a Federal District Judge," *Journal of Public Law*, XXI (1972); and Beverly Blair Cook, "The Socialization of New Federal Judges: Impact on District Court Business," *Washington University Law Quarterly*, MCMLXXI (Spring, 1971).

Obviously, many types of roles can result as judges interact with many different role partners under varied situations. In Figure 7 the term "sector" has been utilized to delineate the categories of roles associated with the various situations and partners. The *core sector* involves the immediate relations judges have with colleagues on the bench at the appellate level. These relationships are at the center of the judicial function. The *adversary sector* involves communication between judges and lawyers, witnesses, litigants, juries, and bailiffs, and is most characteristic of the trial level. The *clientele sector* includes the relations judges have with those who make direct or indirect demands on their behavior (thus, clients); but the interaction most often is in situations other than the courtroom and its immediate environs. Encounters with political party, pressure group, bar association, community, and governmental positions constitute the interaction of the clientele sector. Thus, over time, a judge may perform a variety of roles. The composite of these roles would, according to role theory, tell us much of what we want to know about the judicial system.

Why must a judge perform these roles? The role partners expect certain behavior simply because, through time, norms have developed around the position of a judge in order to allow the judge to perform his crucial functions of "judging." Moreover, sanctions are available to those with whom the judge interacts. If he fails to live up to expectations, he may not be reelected or promoted; he may be overruled by a higher court; he may be in disgrace with his profession; and he may simply not be invited to social gatherings. In turn, when the lawyer, for example, fails to perform his role as viewed by the judge, contempt citations, loss of his case, or verbal chatisement may be in order.[6] Thus, the norms are not accepted merely because they have been in existence time out of mind. They can be enforced. Rarely is there a need for enforcement, however, simply because actors tend to meet the demands of their role adequately. Predictability in behavior is a requirement of social life. In a sense, the role model can be regarded as an ideal type. Actual behavior is measured in terms of how close it approximates the ideal. Role theorists assume that judges are aware of how they ought to behave

[6] Part of a judge's view of the lawyer's role may involve expectations regarding proper strategy, use of precedent, and procedure. When the lawyer fails to live up to these expectations, his case may be lost.

under certain conditions as they interact with certain role partners. They further assume that judges will consciously or unconsciously attempt to emulate the behavior demanded of them. While exact coincidence between the role demands and the judge's behavior is not necessary, the judge must recognize the role constraints and adjust his behavior to some degree.

Role models attempt to go beyond description. Explanation accrues when the researcher seeks to analyze the association between background and training, socialization, selection processes, and special skills—and the role or roles he has described. The selection process (formal or informal) recruits characteristic lawyers to the bench. If the selection process means anything, it means that some lawyers will be elected or appointed to the bench and others, because they lack certain prerequisites, will fail. Graphically, the relationship of other factors to roles can be portrayed thusly:

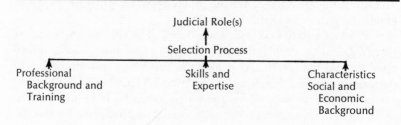

FIGURE 8.   Role Potential and Recruitment

By an analysis of those characteristics which are most closely associated with a judicial role (role potential) and which are characteristic of a certain selection process, the student of the judicial process develops explanation. The whys of the roles are generated if not answered. The precedent-oriented judge, for example, performing a law-interpreter decisional role, is discovered to have been trained at a local law school; he has practiced primarily in civil and criminal defense areas under solo conditions, possesses a conservative ideology, and was selected to the bench by partisan elections.

Role models are often associated with small-group approaches but are both more limited or wider in scope than small- or micro-group models. Again, the scope is determined largely by the questions the researcher wishes to pose. If the major concern is the interaction among the members of an appellate court, from three to nine judges constitute the research boundaries. If all the major role partners with whom the judge must interact are to be analyzed, then the role approach involves more than the interactions of the immediate members of a collegial court. Clerks, witnesses, lawyers, jurymen, party members, constituents, other judges, and a myriad of direct and indirect role partners would need to be understood.[7]

Although the scope of the study may vary, the role approach is qualitatively different from small-group analysis. Small-group models do not concern themselves necessarily with the "oughts" of interaction among group members. Because the role model is an ideal type, behavior is measured in terms of the degree to which a judge adheres to the norms of his position. Small-group models eschew these normative standards for measuring behavior.

Role theory also overcomes one major difficulty with most forms of small-group analysis. Often small-group models are characterized by impenetrable boundaries. Nine members of a collegial court are viewed as members of a closed group. Through small-group analysis we can gain a greater understanding of the inner workings of the court, but important factors which lie outside the group are hidden from our view; we learn about individuals in the group, but seldom can we suggest the nature of the contribution those individuals make to the larger system. Role models, in contrast, are open constructs allowing for the inflow and outflow of social forces. Henry Glick has described this function of roles: "Role . . . performs a more general integrating function when individual roles are viewed as units contributing to larger systems. In this way systems are seen as complex organizations of interacting roles, not as relationships among individuals."[8]

Also, role models do not assume the presence of conflict, leadership, or competition as is common with group approaches, although certainly such political behavior is not discounted. Cooperation, friendship, kinship, persuasion, and social behavior are all common

[7] For a fine account of the scope of role interactions, consult the appropriate sections of William Chambliss and Robert Seidman, *Law, Order and Power* (Reading, Mass.: Addison-Wesley, 1970).

[8] Glick, *Supreme Courts* (n. 3 above), p. 12.

forms of role behavior and may be important to an understanding of the judicial process.

CRITIQUE

The methods associated with the role model (biographies, questionnaires, and interviews) have a distinct value in that the student of the judicial process is going directly to the source of his study. He is asking the judge himself about his view of what he does and why.[9] Nonetheless, therein lies one of the difficulties of the role model. The judge may not be willing to express his real perceptions of what norms regulate his behavior. Possibly the judge may not be conscious of the specific norms which he embodies in his behavior. This criticism is leveled at survey methods rather than the role model, however. It is true that methodological techniques must be refined to deal with the subtle dimensions of roles. What is further needed is an extensive study of policy outcomes—decisions and votes through time—to determine if the judge's role, as constructed from reactions to questions, is consistent with his actual behavior. Various roles must be more closely related to actual decisional outcomes.

Role conflict is another problem to be resolved. Two roles displayed by a judge may present a contradiction to him. An appellate judge may view one of his roles as restraintist: laws passed by the legislature ought to be given overriding weight. However, these laws and the public opinion that led to them may transgress upon the rights of the individuals. Should the judge then perform his restraintist role or his libertarian role regarding individual rights? In a civil liberties case, instead of voting with the majority as his restraintist role dictates, and instead of dissenting as his libertarian role dictates, the judge may only concur, without writing an opinion. The concurrence appears to be inconsistent behavior. In fact, given the role conflict, it is clearly consistent. The role data which fail to account for conflicting norms may therefore confuse rather than clarify.

Role perceptions may also create a difficulty with the role model. A judge may not perceive the norms defining his role, or he may not accept these norms. Such a judge can be categorized as a maverick,

[9] Theodore Becker, "Surveys and Judiciaries, or Who's Afraid of the Purple Curtain," *Law and Society Review,* I (November, 1966).

but this hardly contributes to meaningful explanation and certainly not to prediction.[10] Time is also necessary for a judge to learn his role. Until the norms are learned, a judge's behavior cannot be explained by the role model.[11]

Another difficulty with role models is how to define the limits of the scope of the study to be conducted. If the judge behaves according to his perception of the expectations of others, the question of "Who are the others?" must, of course, be answered.[12] Thus far, the research in judicial role performance has been largely limited to interaction with other judges but, as we have suggested, to take full advantage of role models, other role sectors must be investigated. How broad should those sectors be? A point of diminishing returns may be reached but we as yet do not know where. S. Sidney Ulmer reports: "Obviously, . . . the number of persons, groups, and institutions holding expectations for the behavior of judges far outnumber the elements effectively exerting influence on the choice of the judicial role." [13]

Not only can the scope of concern overwhelm the student, but an understanding of the relationship between expectations and actual influence is necessary. For instance, the ACLU expects judges to play a libertarian role. The judge, in turn expects the ACLU to push for libertarian decisions. When the judge decides in favor of a defendant in a libertarian issue, was it due, in part, to the ACLU influence? If the lawyer arguing the case is not an ACLU cooperating attorney and an *amicus* brief was not filed, can we identify an actual line of influence from the ACLU? Actually, this criticism should be regarded as a note of caution rather than as a question regarding role models. Also, before we take advantage of the potential of role models by widening the scope of our study, we must know more about the core role sector of the judicial process—especially at the

[10] Legislative studies have isolated a maverick or "outsider" role which may have its counterpart in the judiciary. See Ralph K. Huitt, "The Outsider in the Senate—An Alternative Role," *The American Political Science Review,* LV, (September, 1961), 566. See also Malcolm E. Jewell and Samuel C. Patterson, *The Legislative Process in the United States* (New York: Random House, 1973), Chapters 15 and 16.

[11] For a fine discussion of the time lag in learning, see Beverly B. Cook, "Role Lag in Urban Trial Courts," *Western Political Quarterly,* XXV (June, 1972), 234.

[12] Ulmer, *Courts as Small and Not So Small Groups* (n. 3 above), p. 19.

[13] *Ibid.*

trial level, where most of what goes on in the judicial process happens.

The applications of role theory to political and judicial phenomena is fairly recent. Borrowing a research model like the role model from sociology and social psychology results in some ambiguities. As yet, political scientists have not agreed upon boundaries, terminology, nor methods for role studies. Thus, some difficulty exists in building a more complete and consistent body of data in the area of roles. Gaps remain which, through a more general acceptance of terminology, etc., could be filled in. Time, however, should solve this problem.

Current studies of judicial role, however suggestive and thorough, have displayed several limitations which may well be attributed to the relative newness of the application of role theory to the judicial process. First, they have been limited to collegial courts (i.e., to the appellate level); the single judge at the trial level has been ignored. Second—and this characteristic is related to the collegial focus— the current studies have dealt only with judges' expectations of their role partners' behavior; role partners other than fellow judges have not been surveyed as to their perceptions of the judges.[14] Third, comparative state studies have assumed that similar roles are performed by judges in different states; federalism as an independent variable has not been adequately researched, with the exception of the question of the influence of the selection process.[15] Finally, the current studies have relied on interviews as the main source of data collection. The costs both in terms of time and money are therefore high. Mail questionnaires should be further utilized. By such a method a wider universe could be surveyed at minimal cost. Further, questionnaires which guarantee anonymity may elicit more "realis-

[14] Recent exceptions are Michael W. Giles, "Lawyers and the Supreme Court: A Comparative Look at Some Attitudinal Linkages," *Journal of Politics*, XXXV (May, 1973), 480; and Jonathan D. Casper, *Lawyers Before the Warren Court: Civil Liberties and Civil Rights, 1957–1966* (Urbana: University of Illinois Press, 1972). Although Casper failed to utilize a role model for his study, his book presents many insights into the lawyer's perception of his function, goals, and clients. Giles's short work deals with lawyers' perceptions of the Supreme Court. See also Edward N. Beiser, "Lawyers Judge the Warren Court," *Law and Society Review*, VII (Fall, 1972), 139.

[15] Glick, *Supreme Courts* (n. 3 above), p. 24. For a discussion of the impact of federalism, see Charles H. Sheldon, "The Uniqueness of State Legal Systems," *Judicature*, LIII (March, 1970), 333.

tic" answers on norms and constraints than an interview in which the mere presence of the interviewer has an influence on responses. Questionnaires may assist in closing the gap between biased data and real data.

ROLE STUDIES

Role studies of courts contain a unique and certainly not undesirable combination of scholarship. Historians, traditional political scientists, and legal scholars have all contributed greatly to our knowledge about roles.[16] They have also told us much about the role backgrounds and behavior of individual justices, usually at the U.S. Supreme Court level. The biographer is also a role theorist although he or we may not have known this. How did Harlan Fiske Stone view his role and did he behave accordingly? [17] What was John Marshall's view of the role of Chief Justice of the high court? [18] What constraints did Frank Murphy feel on his position as justice? [19] It is largely from these traditional biographical "beginnings" that the more rigorous role theorists have drawn their criteria for measurement and their hypotheses for testing.

SITUATIONAL VARIABLES

Role models have been "formulized" into $R = f[S + (P \times P) + N]$. In this formula, Role is a function of Situation plus Position interaction plus Norms. Situations in which judges find themselves, on and off bench, are characterized by unique norms. For instance, a judge ought to do certain things in the courtroom but in conference or in chambers he ought to behave differently. Unfortunately, few

[16] Ungs and Baas recognize the great value of traditional legal scholarship for establishing criteria for empirical research. See Thomas D. Ungs and Larry R. Baas, "Judicial Role Perceptions: A Q-Technique Study of Ohio Judges," *Law and Society Review*, VI (February, 1972), 343. For a discussion of the problems of using traditional sources, see S. Sidney Ulmer, "Bricolage and Assorted Thoughts on Working in the Papers of Supreme Court Justices," *Journal of Politics*, XXXV (May, 1973), 286.

[17] Alpheus T. Mason, *Harlan Fiske Stone: Pillar of the Law* (New York: Viking Press, 1956).

[18] Albert J. Beveridge, *The Life of John Marshall* (Boston: Houghton Mifflin, 1919).

[19] J. Woodford Howard, *Mr. Justice Murphy: A Political Biography* (Princeton: Princeton University Press, 1968).

studies have investigated the varied situational norms ordering the behavior of judges. We know something about the lawyer in non-judicial situations.[20] We must know more about the judge's off-bench perceptions of role.

Beiser, Goodman, and Cornwell surveyed judges in a nonjudicial setting and discovered that the situation did make a difference regarding their role behavior.[21] Their study dealt with judges who were among the delegates to recent New York and Maryland constitutional conventions. Prior to the convention the judges maintained a predominantly "idealistic" attitude regarding politics and constitutional making. The judges felt that the activities at the constitutional convention ought to be above politics. In contrast, lawyers and other delegates were more political in their approach to the convention. However, the judges were taking their judicial role norms with them into a new situation.[22] The New York convention polarized around political party interests, whereas the Maryland situation remained nonpartisan. The impact of the New York partisan situation on judicial norms was significant. According to Beiser et al.: ". . . having undergone an intensely partisan experience, the New York judges abandoned their idealistic conception of what a constitutional convention is all about. The judges in Maryland, whose convention experience was non-partisan, continued to espouse the idealist position." [23] New York judges, in a different situation, found their judicial norms wanting. It would be interesting to see if such an experience had an impact on their subsequent judicial norms in the courtroom.

[20] E.g., John Sprague and Heinz Eulau, *Lawyers in Politics: A Study in Professional Convergence* (Indianapolis: Bobbs-Merrill, 1964). Despite their special legal training and experience, lawyers tend to assimilate legislative roles quite similarly to legislators without legal background. Sprague and Eulau's analysis of these lawyers in legislative roles indicates the strengths of the legislative norms at least in the legislative situation.

[21] Edward Beiser, J.S. Goodman, and E.E. Cornwell, Jr., "Judicial Role in a Nonjudicial Setting," *Law and Society Review*, V (May, 1971), 571.

[22] An earlier report on the New York convention clearly indicated that there was a distinctive role associated with the judges. See John Sprague, E.E. Cornwell, Jr., and J.S. Goodman, "Judicial Role in a Nonjudicial Setting: Some Survey Evidence," *Law and Society Review*, IV (February, 1970), 371.

[23] Beiser et al., "Judicial Role in a Nonjudicial Setting," p. 574. The convention situation also changed role attitudes for participants other than judges. See W.R. Swanson, S. Kelleher, and A. English, "Constitution-Makers: Political Experiences, Role Conflicts, and Attitude Change," *Journal of Politics*, XXXIV (February, 1972), 183.

Trial and appellate situations traditionally have been regarded as special circumstances requiring different sorts of tasks, behavior, and decisions. The trial judge is the trier of fact and the appellate jurist reviews the trial results in terms of law and procedure. The trial judge sits alone, occasionally aided by a jury; the appellate judge decides in a collegial situation. They interact with different positions under different rules of procedure. These two contrasting situations can lead to characteristic role perceptions.

According to Ungs and Baas, the trial judge is more concerned than his colleague at the higher level with following precedent, clearing the docket, ascertaining truth, and seeking justice in the immediate case.[24] As trier of fact, the trial judge would have to be oriented toward seeking justice in a single case. Under constant pressure to keep up with the docket, his administrative concern would be great. The trial judge is also responsible for applying the decisions of higher courts, requiring him to be overly concerned with precedent. Although the demands of these norms would certainly be present at the appellate level, the trial judge feels them more acutely.

Adjudicator and law-making roles are rejected by trial judges.[25] As an adjudicator, a judge attempts to mediate and accommodate the interests represented by the conflicting parties before him. The trial judge in such a situation chooses to apply law and precedent, resulting in little accommodation between the conflicting interests. Law-making or policy decisions are alien to his perception of his role.[26] Trial judges are much more integrated with the local political system than appellate jurists. They are not as ideologically oriented as their colleagues on the higher benches and are less innovative. They tend to be more concerned with property issues than with larger social and policy issues. Change through case law will come from above, not from the trial judge who eschews the law-making role.[27]

Why is the trial situation different from the appellate one? One survey indicates that several factors make their contribution and that situation as a factor cannot be wholly discounted. Judges were asked to respond to a list of reasons for the uniqueness of the appellate

---

[24] Ungs and Baas (n. 16 above), p. 358.
[25] *Ibid.*
[26] Glick, *Supreme Courts* (n. 3 above), p. 38.
[27] Kenneth M. Dolbeare, *Trial Courts in Urban Politics* (New York: John Wiley, 1967), pp. 122–27.

level; as noted in Table 1. If we can associate unique procedures and structural arrangements with the factor of situation, these data suggest the importance of this role variable.[28]

TABLE 1.   Reasons for the Uniqueness of the Appellate Judge

Appellate Characteristics	Percentage
*Appellate procedures allow more opportunity for contemplation and creativity	50.7 (n = 130)
Decisions have a greater impact on the state	47.6
Deals more in the area of abstract justice	35.3
*Group atmosphere of a multimember court contributes to creativity	31.5
Appellate judge has more experience than a trial judge	20.7
Less practice of judicial self-restraint necessary at the appellate level	10.7
Handles more important cases	10.0
Appellate judges are generally more competent	8.4
Appellate judges play a more political role than trial judges	3.0
Other reasons	2.3
(Percentages total more than 100 because of opportunity for more than one choice)	

* Situational factors

Jaros and Mendelsohn have documented the importance of role to the trial judge in their study of sentencing behavior of judges and attributed its importance to the situation of the trial court. Because of the "structured and routinized circumstances" of the trial court, the judges "are more influenced by role considerations than by personal factors."[29] Jaros and Mendelsohn have suggested an explanation for trial and appellate situational differences which is reflected in the above list of reasons. Creativity, contemplation, and justice—appellate-level characteristics—are not easily manifested in the highly

[28] Charles H. Sheldon, "State Judicial Roles: Trial vs. Appellate" (unpublished research report, Washington State University, 1972), p. 20.

[29] Jaros and Mendelsohn (n. 3 above), p. 471.

structured and routinized trial situation. Thus, situation obviously generates characteristic norms that grant freedoms to and put constraints on the judges. Situation cannot be investigated adequately, however, unless other units of the role formula are considered.

Position interaction, usually comprised of judges interacting with other judges on a collegial bench, has been given content by culling statements of *norms* from traditional materials, classifying them, and then searching for those judges who appear to fit into the various categories. The emphasis in this kind of study is upon the norms surrounding the position rather than the interaction process itself although certainly assumptions about the interaction can be made from position norms.

JUDICIAL NORMS

Because of his efforts in judicial biography, Carl Brent Swisher has been called "one of the first . . . 'judicial behavioralists.' " [30] Indeed, it is interesting to note many of the traditional political and legal scholars concerned with the life and times of individual judges were implicitly viewing their subjects from a role perspective. What motivated a particular justice on the Supreme Court bench? How did the judge view his function on the bench? What judicial constraints on his philosophy and politics did he feel? How did he treat his colleagues? These are questions of particular interest to students of role.

J. Woodford Howard, Jr., one of the better biographers, has compiled a catalogue of behavioral concepts selected from leading judicial biographies, illustrating the contemporary uses of traditional materials. For example, he found that the use of conversion propositions ("attitudes or values affecting judicial behavior, including 'role of the court' attitudes") to be widespread in fifteen biographies he surveyed.[31] It is from materials such as these that the role theorists obtain their list of possible norms which guide the behavior of the judges.

A fine blend of the old and new was exemplified by Dorothy B. James's work on the role perceptions and behavior of Justices

[30] C. Herman Pritchett, "In Memoriam: Carl Brent Swisher," *Villanova Law Review*, XIII (Summer, 1968), 708.

[31] J. Woodford Howard, Jr., "Judicial Biography and the Behavioral Persuasion," *The American Political Science Review*, LXV (September, 1971), 710.

Douglas and Jackson.[32] The design of her work was to isolate role demands from the values of the two justices. To discover the values held by the two justices, she consulted memoirs, speeches, biographies, Court opinions, and Justice Douglas himself, through an interview. Her goal was to determine when the justices followed their philosophy and when they adhered to the norms of the Court. History tells us that norms for any Supreme Court justice are likely to be (1) maintaining an orderly judicial process, (2) acting as an umpire of the federal system, (3) maintaining judicial independence, (4) exercising self-restraint, and (5) avoiding extrajudicial political activity.

Although regarded as being motivated by conflicting judicial philosophies, Justices Douglas and Jackson both accepted as binding on their behavior the requirement of maintaining an orderly judicial process. Adherence to precedent was not regarded as a strong norm, however. Both justices felt that supervision of the federal system was an important function of the Supreme Court, but they disagreed on the relevant criteria for judging the balance to be maintained between federal and state concerns. Thus, the importance of this norm appeared marginal. Judicial independence was a strong norm for both justices. We can assume, since these two jurists represented the extremes in philosophy on the bench, that independence was a strong Supreme Court role demand. Judicial self-restraint, the subject of many role studies, was also discovered to be important for Douglas and Jackson; but avoidance of political activity was at best a weak norm, if not irrelevant to the judicial role. Given the various strengths of norms described by James, might not we be able to make some predictions about the role behavior of other justices on the high bench?

Justice Frankfurter, for example, has been regarded by some as a civil libertarian. It was his restraintist role that intervened, requiring him to decide against the defendant in civil liberty cases. But when the *Ashwander* rules of self-restraint were not applicable, he voted for the defendant.[33] Joel Grossman, using scalogram analysis in which

<hr>

[32] Dorothy B. James, "Role Theory and the Supreme Court," *Journal of Politics*, XXX (February, 1968), 160.

[33] Mr. Justice Brandeis, concurring in *Ashwander* v. *T.V.A.*, 297 U.S. 288 (1936), listed the various circumstances under which the Supreme Court would exercise restraint as it exercised judicial review.

civil liberties cases were classified in terms of whether they presented an activism-restraint (A-R) problem or not, discovered that indeed in all A-R cases in 1958–59, Frankfurter voted for exercising restraint. But in non-A-R cases, he still cast a libertarian vote only occasionally.[34] To conclude that the reason he voted against civil liberties was because of his concept of role is therefore an inadequate explanation. The self-restraintist norm was important for Frankfurter, as it was for Douglas and Jackson, but it fails to explain enough of his anti-civil liberties voting behavior. Perhaps either personal philosophy or another norm influenced his vote.

Norms which order the judicial role and, in most cases, judicial behavior, change with role partners and with situations. Role studies of state court systems have separated role norms into those that flow from the perception held by the judge regarding the purposes or the goals of courts (purposive norms) and the perceptions of how a judge goes about making a decision (decisional norms). Not all students agree upon the criteria to measure the two forms of norms nor do they all agree on the classification labels. A composite of *purposive* and *decisional* roles identified by Ungs and Baas, Vines, and Glick [35] illustrate the level of agreement among these role scholars, as seen in Table 2.

Under the category of purposive roles, the norms of the law interpreter emphasizes *stare decisis*, restraint, and the preservation of existing law. However, Glick notes that the law interpreter is no more conservative in his decisions than is the law maker.[36] The law or policy maker views the function of a judge as one of establishing public policy through the courts. According to this view the judge makes law as do legislators, only the procedure is different. Personal philosophy and values enter into the judicial decisions of the law maker. This role orientation seems more natural with appellate courts than with trial judges. For example, a study of the Nevada court system indicates that trial judges rely heavily on precedent whereas appellate judges, at least in Nevada, turn to some general concept of "justice" for guidance. Also, trial judges attempt "to apply the law"

[34] Grossman, "Role-Playing and the Analysis of Judicial Behavior" (n. 3 above), p. 287.

[35] Ungs and Baas (n. 16 above), p. 343; Vines, "The Judicial Role" (n. 3 above), p. 461; and Glick, *Supreme Courts* (n. 3 above), p. 50.

[36] Glick, *Supreme Courts* (n. 3 above), p. 50.

TABLE 2.   State Judicial Roles

Purposive Roles* (The Goals of Judges)		Decisional Roles* (How a Judge Decides)	
Law Interpreter	(U, G)	Trial Judge	(U)
Law Maker	(G)	Mechanist	(G)
Adjudicator	(U, G, V)	Formalist	(G)
Administrator	(U, G, V)	Realist	(G)
Peacekeeper	(U)	Law Interpreter	(V)
Task Performer	(G)	Law Maker	(V)
Policy Maker	(V)	Pragmatist	(V)
Ritualist	(V)		
Pragmatist	(G)		
Constitutional Defender	(G)		

* G = Glick, U = Ungs and Baas, and V = Vines

to cases while the appellate judges are more concerned with arriving at a "just settlement." [37] Thus, the trial judges are concerned with an immediate solution to the dispute before them within a context of law and precedent. The appellate judges, on the other hand, take a longer view of the case and attempt to reconcile the conflicting interests through some broad interpretation of justice.

The adjudicator regards himself as a policy maker, but he perceives his standards of decision making to be more narrow and objective than the standards of his personal philosophy and values. Accommodation and mediation provide the means by which the adjudicator weighs the demands of competing interests represented by the parties before him.

The role performance of the administrator ("task performer" according to Glick; "ritualist" according to Vines) is exemplified by an emphasis on procedure,[38] precedent, and administrative tasks in order to speed up and complete judicial tasks. The peacekeeper views his role "to include balancing contending principles, a task that requires legal ability, judgment, knowledge, social idealism, and

[37] Charles H. Sheldon, "Perceptions of the Judicial Roles in Nevada," *Utah Law Review*, MCMLXVIII (September, 1968), 358.
[38] Vines, p. 468, and Glick, p. 31.

integrity." [39] Through employing these norms of decision making, the judge will be able to function as a "keeper of the peace."

Some judges have viewed their role as intermediate between the precedent-oriented law interpreter and the policy function of the law maker. Glick and Vines labeled these judges as performing a pragmatist role.[40] It might be suggested that in fact these pragmatists, instead of adopting a distinctive role, are experiencing role conflict and thus fall between the law interpreter and the law maker. The constitutional defender, finally, is the protector of individual rights. Although conventional literature suggests such a role, none of the judges in Glick's study accepted this role.

Selection methods appear not to have any substantial impact on the role orientations of the judges and, at least in Vines's limited study, background characteristics were not statistically significant although religious background might have some impact on role. Liberal and conservative decisions seemed also not to be significantly associated with roles.[41]

Decisional roles vary according to the several perceptions held by the judges regarding the appropriate decisional norms to be adopted. The trial judge follows precedent and ascertains facts; and, for him, judging becomes the administration of justice in particular cases. His decisional horizons do not go beyond the immediate case. The mechanist views decision making as merely a process of "applying correct, readily apparent answers to legal questions." [42] The specialized and unique training lawyers and judges gain will provide the insight into what the correct answer is. The formalist feels that judges ought to arrive at a decision through a formal and well-established procedure, beginning with the initial filing stages of the process and leading to the final decision. The procedure provides the decisional guidelines. The realist makes his decisions on the basis of a wide variety of factors quite beyond the limits of legal training and procedures. The law interpreter does not decide issues committed to the other branches of the government; but what makes judicial decision making different for the interpreter is the institutional differences between courts and legislatures. Procedure, as with

[39] Ungs and Baas, p. 362.
[40] Vines, p. 476, and Glick, p. 41.
[41] Vines, p. 481.
[42] Glick, p. 72.

the formalist, becomes important. The law maker utilizes the same guidelines for decisions as the legislator. The public interest, general welfare, or the needs of society may constitute his decisional criteria. Thus, Vines's law maker would be very similar, if not identical, to Glick's realist. The pragmatist would use both interpreting and law-making approaches, depending upon the issue before him.

Vines found that judges who often accepted ritualist purposive roles also quite frequently assumed law interpreter decisional roles. The policy makers were also law makers, and adjudicators were likely to be performing a pragmatist decisional role, again according to Vines. Glick suggested that the task performers tended to accept formalist decisional norms and realists often played law maker purposive roles. Ungs and Baas combined decisional and purposive orientations to arrive at their classification, although the trial judge role in their classification seemed most concerned with decision making and the other roles cited with the purposes and goals of being a judge.

How are judicial role norms related to actual decisions and behavior? Theodore Becker found that law students accepted the norm of precedent to a greater degree than non-law students in judging a hypothetical case, indicating that law school training is somewhat responsible for socializing future judges into the *stare decisis* norm.[43] In a subsequent study, Becker asked judges in Hawaii to decide the same hypothetical case.[44] Those accepting precedent as an important norm often decided against their personal view of the case and, thus, decided "objectively." *Stare decisis* was a strong judicial role norm and the effect of the norm, at least in a hypothetical case, was more objectivity. It certainly cannot be denied that following precedent is an important norm for many judges.[45] Nonetheless, as we have

[43] Becker, *Political Behavioralism* (n. 3 above), p. 130.

[44] Becker, "A Survey Study of Hawaiian Judges" (n. 3 above), p. 677. See also his *Comparative Judicial Politics,* especially Chapter 1 (n. 3), and Victor E. Flango and Glendon A. Schubert, "Two Surveys of Simulated Judicial Decision-Making: Hawaii and the Philippines," in Schubert and David J. Danelski, eds., *Comparative Judicial Behavior* (New York: Oxford University Press, 1969), p. 197.

[45] Even Glendon A. Schubert, who has been accused of seeing all judicial behavior as flowing from ideology rather than institutional norms, grants importance to *stare decisis* as a decisional factor. See his "Civilian Control and *Stare Decisis* in the Warren Court," in Schubert, ed., *Judicial Decision-Making* (New York: The Free Press, 1963), p. 55.

seen from Dorothy James's study, following precedent is only a marginal norm—one that can be accepted or rejected by Supreme Court justices, at any rate. Kenneth Vines has also attempted to relate various roles with actual court decisions. In only two percent of the cases he reviewed were there references to roles, but these references indicated much consistency between role perceptions and actual behavior.[46]

In critically analyzing the data presented by scholars who had identified subgroups or cliques on the Supreme Court bench, Joel Grossman has suggested that court norms tend to restrain justices dissenting together against the majority. Dissenting blocs are a function of a coincidence of voting rather than of actual interaction among the justices leading to stable blocs. Of course a justice will dissent, but the norms of the court work against his dissenting together through time with other justices. Dissent, for Grossman, is an individual act.[47]

POSITION INTERACTION

The importance of position interaction to role is recognized by Glick:

> First, the principal actor (ego) has expectations concerning what his own behavior should be, especially regarding his relationships with the incumbents of other or counter positions (alter). Second, other actors (alters) have expectations concerning the proper behavior and attributes of the principal actors. Relations between the principal and other actors are particularly important because the expectations of others constitute potential sanctions which may affect the perceptions and behavior of the main actor, thus influencing individual orientations to roles.[48]

Although implied in their analysis, most role scholars of the judicial process have neglected to analyze directly the position interaction aspect of the role formula. They have identified an "ego," mentioned an "alter," and neglected the interaction between the two. Most of our comments on the effect of judicial interaction with other judges, litigants, and lawyers are largely speculative. The model suggests

[46] Vines (n. 3 above), p. 483.
[47] Grossman, "Dissenting Blocs on the Warren Court" (n. 3 above), p. 1068.
[48] Glick, *Supreme Courts* (n. 3 above), p. 7.

that roles could change with a change in role partners, but the empirical data concerning this interaction is sparse.

Glick's work on four state supreme courts contains a fine compilation of types of intracourt interactions, but the description neglects the "ego" and "alter" poles of the interaction process. For example, although persuasion is regarded as a form of interaction, we must know by and with whom does persuasion tend to be associated. Persuasion, compromise, and voting are regarded as methods of resolving disputes among the justices on the state high benches.[49] A pleasing personality, proper work habits, objectivity, ethical personal conduct, and scholarship are basic attributes which should be possessed by a judge.[50] Despite these consensual norms, factions are present on some of the state high benches and dissent is not an uncommon form of behavior. What we would want to know, then, is whether the law interpreter dissents more than the peacekeeper and whether the adjudicator persuades more than the administrator. More complex but equally important would be to know if the law maker dissents more often from the law interpreter and agrees more often with the pragmatist. The possible combinations are great but, nonetheless, demand our attention.

Not only does interaction dictate the nature of the role relationship but it is the process by which new judges are socialized into their roles. Carp and Wheeler's investigation of the various means by which new federal district judges cope with legal, administrative, and psychological problems indicates that the older judges within the jurisdiction provide most of the solutions. Consequently, each federal jurisdiction tends to develop and perpetuate its own characteristic norms as they are passed from one judge to another.[51]

Much has been written about the sentencing behavior of judges. Some of this literature has a direct bearing on role theory simply because it represents an important position interaction dimension of at least the trial court situation. In many jurisdictions, the judge has been granted a great deal of sentencing discretion. Ideology, societal values, public opinion, and political factors may all enter into a judge's choice of the degree of severity to be embodied in his sentenc-

---

[49] *Ibid.*, p. 90.
[50] *Ibid.*, p. 62.
[51] Robert Carp and Russell Wheeler, "Sink or Swim: The Socialization of a Federal District Judge," *Journal of Public Law*, XXI (1972).

ing. But, equally as obvious, the judicial norm of equality before the law may dictate the form of sentence. Race, sex, age, or appearance ought not to be considered as variables in the judge's decision. The judge is expected to conform to the norm of equal treatment and to reject whatever personal attitudes he may have regarding the offender. On his part, the offender is expected to grant deference to the judge and the court. As these two courtroom positions interact—offender and judge—within the courtroom and sentencing situation, these two norms of equal treatment and deference would appear to be binding. Jaros and Mendelsohn's study of a Detroit Traffic Court indicates indeed that the equality norm prevails even despite the violation of the offender deference norm: "Legally relevant criteria in fact do show the most highly significant relationship with judges' actual [sentencing] behavior. . . . Concomitantly, legally irrelevant criteria, which could enter the judges' decisional process as a consequence of personality . . . are found to be almost totally without effect." The courtroom demeanor of the offender "does not relate to jail sentence at all" and only slightly to severity of the fines imposed.[52] Edward Green reached somewhat the same conclusion as Jaros and Mendelsohn. Legally relevant factors (judicial norms) accounted for most of the sentencing disparities he discovered in the Philadelphia Court of Quarter Sessions.[53]

When the situation moves from courts of limited jurisdiction, the norm appears not to be as strong. Jaros and Mendelsohn suggest that this may well be the case: "lower-court judges—due to their relatively structured and routinized circumstances—are more influenced by role considerations than by personal factors." [54]

Ethnicity is a factor associated with the degree of severity in felony sentencing in the criminal courts of Hawaii. The further apart the judge and offender stand in terms of "social distance" (social status), the greater the possibility of more severe penalties being imposed.[55]

[52] Jaros and Mendelsohn (n. 3 above), p. 487.
[53] Edward Green, *Judicial Attitudes in Sentencing* (London: Macmillan, 1961), p. 10.
[54] *Ibid.*, p. 486.
[55] A. Didrick Castberg, "The Ethnic Factor in Criminal Sentencing," *Western Political Quarterly*, XXIV (September, 1971), 436. For simulated juror reaction, to race, see Kalman J. Kaplan and Roger I. Simon, "Latitude and Severity of Sentencing Options, Race of the Victim and Decisions of Simulated Jurors: Some Issues Arising from the 'Algiers Motel' Trial," *Law and Society Review*, VII (Fall, 1972), 87.

H.A. Bullock's study of 3,644 inmates of Texas State Prison at Huntsville, showed that "being black generally means one type of sentence while being white means another." [56] The death penalty is imposed on blacks more than on whites in rape cases.[57] The same ethnic trend is also evident in juvenile hearings in the South.[58] Age, sex, residence, and employment status also appear relevant to the severity of sentencing.[59] Although these studies on ethnicity and sentencing were not conducted within a role framework, they provide data that would suggest that judicial norms give way to judicial values or community norms. Perhaps Jaros and Mendelsohn have supplied one explanation for the mixed results concerning sentencing behavior: norms are important but the situation dictates the strength of the norm.

Sentencing behavior implies that as the judge's role partner changes (e.g., a white offender vs. a black offender), his perceptions of the demands of the role change. But can we ascertain more subtle changes within the courtroom context which we can attribute to a change in partner and also norms, rather than to a possible rejection of norms as illustrated by some studies of judge's sentencing behavior? Answers from questionnaires administered by Sheldon to 1,250 lawyers in several states indicate that, indeed, as the partner changes, the role perceptions alter. Respondents were asked to rate various role prerequisites (role potential) and decisional factors (decisional role) for the trial and the appellate benches in their state. Likert scale responses were weighted from five to one in terms of the degree of importance each item was to the respondent, resulting in the following scores.

[56] H.A. Bullock, "Significance of the Racial Factor in the Length of Prison Sentences," *Journal of Criminal Law, Criminology and Police Science,* LII (November–December, 1961), 412.

[57] Hans Zeisel, "Methodological Problems in Studies of Sentences," *Law and Society Review,* III (May, 1969); 622; and Donald Partington, "The Incidence of the Death Penalty for Rape in Virginia," *Washington and Lee Law Review,* XXII (Spring, 1965), 43.

[58] William Arnold, "Race and Ethnicity Relative to Other Factors in Juvenile Court Dispositions," *American Journal of Sociology,* LXXVII (September, 1971), 214. For a general discussion of racism, law, and courts, see Derrick A. Bell, Jr., "Racism in American Courts: Cause for Black Disruption or Despair?" *California Law Review,* LXII (January, 1973), 165.

[59] D.N. Atkinson and D.A. Neuman, "Judicial Attitudes and Defendant Attributes: Some Consequences for Municipal Court Decision-Making," *Journal of Public Law,* XIX (1970), 69.

TABLE 3. Judicial Role Potential: Trial vs. Appellate

	Lawyers' Perceptions of Role Prerequisites (Maximum n = 1250)	
	Trial Mean	Appellate Mean
Extensive Law Practice (at least 10 years prior to selection to bench)	4.40	4.33
Legal Training at a Major Law School	3.90	3.97
Extensive Trial Experience as a Lawyer (10 years)	3.70	3.60
Business Experience	3.29	2.33*
Defense Experience	3.16	3.09
Extensive and Varied Community Services (church, fraternal, etc.)	2.08	2.35*
Some Experience in Partisan Politics (party leadership, public office)	1.98	1.59*
Government Service (federal, state, and local— not including prosecuting departments)	1.98	1.88
Legal Scholarship (publication in legal journals or law review, etc.)	1.92	2.32*
Prosecuting Experience	1.79	2.09*
Prior Judicial Experience	1.77	3.03*
Extensive Bar Association Activity	1.66	1.58

* $P < .01$

When the same lawyers were asked the same questions about the role prerequisites for judges at two separate levels (thus, different role partners), significant differences resulted. The difference persisted when lawyers were asked to weigh the importance of several decisional role norms as they applied to trial and then appellate judges. The point, again, is that as the role partner changes, so do the norms regulating those two partners. More role studies must be directed toward the position interaction process.[60]

[60] For an explanation of analysis of variance and F test, see Hubert M. Blalock, *Social Statistics* (New York: McGraw-Hill, 1960), Chapter 16. The data are from Charles H. Sheldon, "State Judicial Roles: Trial vs. Appellate" (unpublished research report, Washington State University, 1972).

TABLE 4.   Decisional Role Factors: Trial vs. Appellate

	Lawyers' Perceptions of Decisional Role Factors (Maximum n = 1250)	
	Trial Mean	Appellate Mean
Interpretation of Law and Precedent	4.35	4.13*
Common Sense	4.60	4.46*
Concept of Justice	4.36	4.19
Highly Competent Advocate (written briefs)	4.30	4.50*
Highly Competent Advocate (oral arguments)	3.96	3.92
Community Values	3.62	3.92*
Community Needs	2.44	2.38
Community Demands	2.27	2.48
Public Opinion	2.89	3.42**
Political Factors	2.06	2.48**

* $P < .05$ and $> .01$
** $p < .01$

The application of role models to judicial behavior is just beginning. Agreement on definitions, classification, and methods is lacking. Nonetheless, as new studies build upon the earlier works, these problems should fade and our understanding of the relationship between judicial roles and behavior increase. Role behavior does not constitute all of judicial (nor human) behavior, but is certainly an important part thereof.

As the analysis of judicial models broadens from decision-making, small-group, and role approaches to macro-group schemes, the focus of scholarly concern moves away from the judge as a point of concentration to an analysis of direct and often indirect influences quite beyond the court or conference room. The judge, now, tends to be viewed as merely another variable among many which demand our attention. The broad sweep of the total judicial process becomes apparent.

CHAPTER FOUR

Macro-Group Models

DESCRIPTION AND ANALYSIS OF
LARGE-GROUP MODELS

Man is a social animal. Compelled by nature and necessity, he joins with others into groups in order to satisfy his needs and fulfill his desires. Indeed, to understand groups is to understand man, whose attitudes, values, roles, and opinions are largely a result of his group experiences. Moreover, the dynamism of politics is a result of conflict and competition among groups for the scarce values a society is able to provide its members.

Two approaches are evident in group models. The micro-group model views "groups as societies" and the macro-group model sees "societies as groups." [1] Micro-group models attempt to understand the many subtleties of interpersonal relations within a small group of people. Macro-group models seek knowledge in terms of the struggles between and among larger groups—for example, interest or pressure groups—within society. [2] The essence of politics is this conflict and competition between and among groups. However, despite the distinctions between the small- and large-group approaches, the common assumption underlying each is the social drive of man.

The seed for group theory in American political science was sown early; but, as is often the case, it was a long time in germinating and taking root. Arthur Bentley's *The Process of Government*, in which a theory of groups was postulated, was published in 1908. [3] Although

[1] S. Sidney Ulmer, ed., *Introductory Readings in Political Behavior* (Chicago: Rand McNally, 1961), p. 189.

[2] Earl Latham, "The Group Basis of Politics: Notes for a Theory," *The American Political Science Review*, XLVI (June, 1952), 376; Phillip Monypenny, "Political Science and the Study of Groups," *Western Political Quarterly*, VII (March, 1954), 183; and Harmon Zeigler, *Interest Groups in American Society* (Englewood Cliffs, N.J.: Prentice-Hall, 1964).

[3] Arthur Bentley, *The Process of Government* (Chicago: University of Chicago Press, 1908).

works by such authors as E. Pendleton Herring, Peter Odegard, and M. Louise Rutherford increased our understanding of specific groups or of lobbying activities, none attempted to develop further the theory postulated by Bentley.[4] Bentley's theoretical scheme was revitalized in 1951 with the publication of David Truman's *The Governmental Process*.[5] Truman gave expression to the basic assumption, if not conclusion, underlying group approaches:

> . . . group experiences and affiliations of an individual are the primary, though not exclusive, means by which the individual knows, interprets, and reacts to the society in which he exists. Their significance here is they produce in their participants certain uniformities of behavior and attitude that must be achieved by the individual if he is to be a completely accepted member of the group.[6]

Government is intimately involved in the group struggle. Again, in Truman's words:

> . . . even in its nascent stages government functions to establish and maintain a measure of order in the relationships among groups for various purposes. What a particular government is under these circumstances, its "form" and its "method," depends upon the character of the groups and the purposes it serves.[7]

It is with these government-group relationships that macro-group models are concerned.

The micro-group approach (Chapter 2) concentrates on the uniformities of behavior and attitude within the group. The interaction among the members of a small group can explain the nature of that group and, more importantly, the nature of the separate members. Broader in scope, the macro-group model views politics as the authoritative allocation of values in society "through the process of the

---

[4] E. Pendleton Herring, *Group Representation Before Congress* (Baltimore: The Johns Hopkins Press, 1929); Peter H. Odegard, *Pressure Politics: The Study of the Anti-Saloon League* (New York: Columbia University Press, 1928); and M. Louise Rutherford, *The Influence of the American Bar Association on Public Opinion and Legislation* (Philadelphia: The Foundation Press, 1937).

[5] David Truman, *The Governmental Process* (New York: Alfred A. Knopf, 1951).

[6] *Ibid.*, p. 21.

[7] *Ibid.*, p. 45.

conflict of groups." [8] According to this view, judges and those directly involved with them may be regarded as either referees over, or participants in, the politics of group struggle within the American political system. Policy outcomes are the result of the political give and take among political parties, pressure groups, businesses, labor, minority organizations, and ideological groups—all struggling for scarce political, economic, and social rewards. The courts can be viewed as scorekeepers in the game of politics or as contestants in the struggle or both. To understand, for example, the group dynamics of civil rights in the past score of years, the courts cannot be ignored. The Supreme Court and lower federal courts have not just refereed the white-nonwhite conflict; they have been direct participants in the group struggles involving desegregation.

Political groups are often not easily identified. However, shared interests or some common characteristic is one factor common to groups.[9] The degree and nature of interaction among those who have that common interest or characteristic further adds to the location of a group.[10] The macro-group model assumes a pluralistic society and that "the chief social values cherished by individuals in modern society are realized through groups." [11] Government agencies join the struggle often as one of the antagonists.

> The group struggle . . . is apparent in the universe of unofficial groups and in that of official groups. Furthermore, these are not sep-arate universes. They are one. Official groups are simply inhabitants of one pluralistic world which is an aggregation, a collection, an assem-blage, a throng, a moving multitude of human clusters, a consociation of groups, a plurality of collectivities, an interesting series of social organisms, adhering, interpenetrating, overlapping—a single universe of groups which combine, break, federate, and form constellations and coalitions of power in flux of restless alterations.[12]

The issue of whether the government acts as a referee among groups or is actively participating in the group struggle is easily met.

---

[8] Charles B. Hagan, "The Group in a Political Science," in Roland Young, ed., *Approaches to the Study of Politics* (Evanston: Northwestern University Press, 1958), p. 40.

[9] Truman, p. 23.

[10] *Ibid.*, p. 24.

[11] Latham (n. 2 above), p. 376.

[12] *Ibid.*, p. 383.

It does both when the judicial process is involved. In this situation the courts are governmental agencies which lend final authority to the law to which others appeal. But governments also institute cases and urge upon the courts certain allocations to be legitimated by the courts. Even courts, themselves, actively participate in the group struggle. When federal courts of appeal often disagree with each other or with district courts in similar cases, they force the Supreme Court to resolve the conflict. By its decision to intervene or not intervene, the Supreme Court assumes the role of an interested party or participant in the group struggle. This is so because: "A judge is in the political process and his activity is interest activity not as a matter of choice but of function. Judicial participation does not grow out of the judge's personality or philosophy but out of his position. A judge who defers to the legislature is engaging in interest activity just as much as the judge who avowedly writes his own preferences into his opinions." [13]

Groups are involved at all levels of the judicial process, including in the politics of judicial selection. Political parties are the most obvious example. Special interests attempt to gain access to the courts through test cases, and their support for litigants through "cooperating attorneys" is well known. The NAACP and the ACLU are the most common examples. Interest groups support research into legal problems. They utilize the *amicus curiae* brief to gain access. The federal and state governments also join the conflict within the courts by filing briefs supporting their causes. Following court decisions, groups may actively resist court rulings by advocating constitutional amendments, by bringing about change through lower courts, or by pressuring Congress or state legislatures to redefine the law in an acceptable manner. At all levels throughout the judicial process, groups are active and, according to the macro-group model advocates, are supplying the content of the law emanating from the courts. [14]

Access is the crucial concept for the macro-group model. Those who have access to the courts—when the courts exercise a crucial

---

[13] Jack W. Peltason, *Federal Courts in the Political Process* (New York: Random House, 1955), p. 3.

[14] As we have seen, political parties have an indirect access to courts by leading some judges to decide cases in directions consistent with their present or former party affiliations. See Chapter One.

role—are those who have success. Without access, a group's protestations against the authoritative allocation of values remains outside the judicial process. Thus, the measurement of a group's access to the courts partly measures the power of that group in the pluralistic struggle.[15] Access to the courts can be measured by studying (1) the organizational characteristics of the group (quality of leadership, discipline, morale, lines of communication and resources); (2) the status of the group within society (prestige and deference among the public and elites); and (3) the nature of the governmental agencies to which the groups are attempting to gain access (tactics of the group as they relate to the rules and practices of the agencies). It is in this third area that macro-group models have made their greatest contribution to an understanding of the judicial process.[16] In sum, the degree and content of interaction of individuals identifies the group and access indicates its power.

The macro-group model is graphically presented in Figure 9.

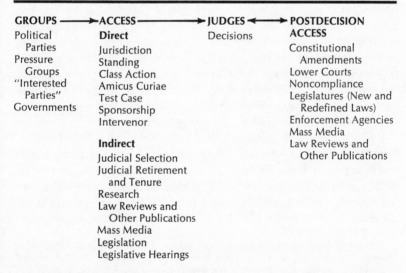

FIGURE 9.   Model of the Judicial Process from a Macro-Group
Perspective

[15] Truman, p. 264.
[16] *Ibid.*, pp. 265–69.

Assuming that the most meaningful, if not all, politics are generated by group conflict, the macro-group model views the various groups gaining access, directly or indirectly, through special methods characteristic of the courts. For example, rules of standing and jurisdiction define the limits of direct access; laws and custom prevent groups from pressuring judges with political threats or the letter-writing campaigns common to legislative lobbying activities. Following decision, the groups are still active and attempt to gain access to those agencies able to influence, change, or reinforce the decision. Again, we must be reminded that courts are unable to enforce their own decisions.

CRITIQUE

The macro-group model, which views the American political system as involving competition and conflict between groups, has been fruitful in placing the courts within the real world of the broader political system. Certain aspects of the judicial process have also been significantly explained through use of this model, such as the impact of groups on the selection process of judges [17] and the role of "friends of the court" litigants.[18] Although conflict, competition, and disagreement traditionally distinguish that which is political from other aspects of society, they may not go far enough in explaining the American political system, of which the courts are an integral part. Consensus, cooperation, and unity are important social circumstances which are ignored by the group model.

Perhaps more with the courts than with any other political institution, the individual who has a legal grievance has a chance, admittedly slight, to have an impact on a court. Besides more normal initiation of a suit, the use of *in forma pauperis* petitions allows individuals, quite isolated from groups or group membership, to have their day in court. *Gideon* v. *Wainwright* is an example, how-

---

[17] See Joel B. Grossman, *Lawyers and Judges: The ABA and the Politics of Judicial Selection* (New York: John Wiley, 1965); Richard A. Watson and Rondal G. Downing, *The Politics of the Bench and Bar* (New York: John Wiley, 1969); and Harold W. Chase, *Federal Judges: The Appointing Process* (Minneapolis: University of Minnesota Press, 1972).

[18] See Lucius J. Barker, "Third Parties in Litigation: A Systemic View of the Judicial Function," *Journal of Politics*, XXIX (February, 1967), 41; and Samuel Krislov, "The *Amicus Curiae* Brief: From Friendship to Advocacy," *Yale Law Journal*, LXXII (March, 1963), 694.

ever persistent and exceptional Clarence Earl Gideon may have been.[19] Certainly at the trial levels, the individual, even with limited financial resources, can give to the judicial process an impetus quite apart from groups.

The concept of *access*, however meaningful in explaining the political activities of groups, may have limited value in explaining judicial process, especially at the trial level. The accused in criminal cases, and the defendant in civil cases, gain automatic access to the courts quite apart from their group affiliation and, obviously, quite against their wills. And, yet, from their cases may come meaningful policy decisions. Also, the macro-group model, like the decision-making model, has been fruitfully applied to appellate courts, but the lower courts have been ignored. Perhaps the trial phase of the judicial process will not lend itself to group models simply because the vast majority of cases which ultimately come to trial—and the many, many more that fail to reach the courtroom but are still part of the process—involve individuals who have no group affiliations, half of whom want no access to the courts. At most, groups would be significant sources of study at this level in that they are responsible for attitudes held by the individual litigant, advocate, judge, or juror.

Many would argue that an undue emphasis on politics as a group struggle does much damage to the independent and unique aspects of judicial decision making. If policies emanating from courts are largely (if not exclusively) the result of group efforts, we are assigning to the judge a mechanical role which could better be assumed by a computer. In this view the group conflict is the stimulus and the decision is the response, with the judge acting only as a scorekeeper and contributing nothing significant of his own to the process. Probably most judges and political scientists would reject this oversimplified view of the judge's role. However, despite shortcomings, the macro-group models have added substantially to our understanding of the political role of courts.

MACRO-GROUP STUDIES

In what still remains the best single account of pressure activities before courts, Clement Vose has written:

[19] Anthony Lewis, *Gideon's Trumpet* (New York: Random House, 1964).

Analysis of the Negro victory in the *Restrictive Covenant Cases* forces the conclusion that this result was an outgrowth of the complex group activity which preceded it. Groups with antagonistic interests appeared before the Supreme Court just as they do before Congress or other institutions that mold public policy. Because of organization the lawyers for the Negroes were better prepared to do battle through the courts. Without this continuity, money, and talent, they would not have freed themselves from the limiting effects of racial residential covenants, notwithstanding the presence of favorable social theories, political circumstances, and Supreme Court Justices.[20]

However, the NAACP has certainly not been the only group attempting and succeeding in changing the allocations of values in society through the judicial process. The Watchtower Society has been most active in protecting the rights of the Jehovah's Witnesses.[21] The American Civil Liberties Union is active at all levels of the court system as a special group specifically concerned with utilizing the courts to further its interests.[22] The National Institute of Municipal Law Officers, American Trial Lawyers' Association, Emergency Civil Liberties Committee, Commission on Law and Social Action of the American Jewish Congress, American Committee for the Foreign Born, Congress on Racial Equality, and American Jewish Committee are but a few of the organizations which have been directly involved in court litigation.[23] A quick scanning of the current *U.S. Reports* indicates that less familiar groups (e.g., Youth Franchise Coalition, Classroom Teachers Association of the Charlotte-Mecklenburg School System, Adult Film Association of America, United Negro College Fund, Motor Bus Owners, Public Power Association, and The National Jewish Commission on Law and Public Affairs) are

[20] Clement Vose, *Caucasians Only* (Berkeley: University of California Press, 1959), p. 252.

[21] E.g., *Lovell* v. *Griffin,* 303 U.S. 444 (1938); *Saia* v. *New York,* 334 U.S. 558 (1948); *Niemotko* v. *Maryland,* 340 U.S. 268 (1951); and *West Virginia Board of Education* v. *Barnette,* 319 U.S. 624 (1943). See also David Manwaring, *Render Unto Caesar: The Flag-Salute Controversy* (Chicago: University of Chicago Press, 1962); and William J. Whalen, *Armageddon Around the Corner: A Report on Jehovah's Witnesses* (New York: John Day, 1962).

[22] Any issue of the ACLU newspaper, *Civil Liberties,* will cite cases at all levels of the court system in which the ACLU is involved. See also Charles L. Markamm, *The Noblest Cry* (New York: St. Martin's Press, 1965).

[23] Clement Vose, "Interest Groups, Judicial Review, and Local Government," *Western Political Quarterly,* XIX (March, 1966), 85.

attempting to influence the judicial process through petitions to file *amicus curiae* briefs with the Supreme Court. State and federal governments are also active in intervening in cases as interested parties.[24] It would appear that pressure groups are intimately involved in court decisions.

SPONSORSHIP

Sponsorship, *amicus curiae* participation, and intervention are the three major forms taken to gain direct access to the courts. In all forms, the groups must ultimately face the sometimes formidable obstacles to access: jurisdiction and standing. Given the dual nature of our court system, with both state and federal courts resolving disputes, jurisdiction can become an important question. A plaintiff often has a choice of courts in which he can institute his suit. Title 28 of the *United States Code* spells out the jurisdiction of the federal courts. Each state has comparable statutes defining the jurisdiction of its courts. Once the litigant who is backed by groups presents to the court a true "case or controversy" and the judge accepts jurisdiction, a further obstacle faces the parties to the dispute: standing. The question becomes: "Does the party bringing the issue before the courts have standing to sue?" The Supreme Court's answers to this question are reviewed admirably by Justice Douglas in his dissent to the Supreme Court's refusal to hear a case dealing with the constitutionality of the Viet Nam war and draft: *Commonwealth of Massachusetts* v. *Laird,* 400 U.S. 886 (1971). However, in state courts the barriers to standing or justiciability are not as formidable. With sufficient planning, persistence, and legal manipulation, sponsoring pressure groups can overcome the strictures of jurisdiction and standing.[25]

Any group contemplating access to courts as a means of furthering its interests must balance advantages with substantial risks; and of course the decision to litigate will certainly vary with the times, the

---

[24] Note, "Federal Intervention in Private Actions Involving the Pubilc Interest," *Harvard Law Review,* LXV (December, 1951), 319; and Note, "Protecting Civil Liberties through Federal Court Interventions in State Criminal Matters," *California Law Review,* LIX (November, 1971), 1549.

[25] Comment, "Taxpayers Suits: A Survey and a Summary," *Yale Law Journal,* LXIX (April, 1960), 895; and Vose, "Interest Groups," p. 85.

group, and the issue.[26] Through litigation, the group can gain greater acceptance with the public. People generally accept resolution before a judicial forum as a legitimate method of furthering interests, whereas the same activities carried on in the legislature are viewed as suspect. Lawsuits allow groups to educate the public as to their cause without appearing to propagandize them. Publicity, financial donations, and increased membership are often concomitants to court litigation. For weak and unpopular groups, the courtroom represents a neutral and possibly receptive forum for their causes not found elsewhere. Court litigation, although not inexpensive, is often an economical means of protecting and furthering interests when compared with the costs of lobbying legislators. Judges, especially on courts of last resort, make basic and enduring decisions—clearly worth the effort of the groups involved.

Groups may hesitate, despite the advantages, to achieve access to the courts for several reasons. Oftentimes, groups may leave the impression that their interests are largely of a constitutional nature necessitating court action and consequently delay, with the resulting decision limited only to the parties to the dispute. In the area of church-state relations this has clearly happened. People tend, then, to expect courts to settle these issues rather than legislatures or administrative agencies when a change in the law or bureaucratic rules would suffice. Legislators themselves may pass the buck to the courts rather than face the issue in the legislative arena. Groups must also consider that their case may be lost in the courts or that an apparently favorable ruling may involve some unanticipated or unwanted language or results. Court suits can also lead to constitutional amendments, legislation, or a public opinion which would place the group in a more disadvantageous position. Finally, courts can decide; but federal, state, and local officials will enforce, or neglect to enforce, these decisions. Thus the problem may be solved only legally—not politically and socially. Obviously, to sponsor, intervene,

[26] The advantages and disadvantages of gaining court access have been reviewed by Walfred H. Peterson, former Director of Research for the Baptist Joint Committee on Public Affairs. "Some Common Predispositions Affecting Church-State Relations" (unpublished mimeograph of a paper delivered to the Religious Liberty Conference, Washington, D.C., 1965). The BJCPA has been involved in lobbying before the courts. This account of advantages and disadvantages draws from Peterson's paper.

or file *amicus* briefs does not mean that the group's interests will always be furthered. Groups before courts have to take some very real risks.

Sponsorship of court cases involves a myriad of tactics which, singly or in combination, an interested party can utilize. Class actions lend themselves well to group efforts simply because the major goal of most groups is to develop long-range and broad policy changes through the court quite beyond the immediate concerns of the principals in the case.[27] For example, the NAACP was more concerned with the condition of blacks in segregated schools everywhere than with forcing the schools of Topeka, Kansas, to accept Oliver Brown's child.[28] By bringing an action on "behalf of other persons similarly situated" under Rule 23 of the Federal Rules of Civil Procedure for the United States District Courts, the group can achieve the goal of gaining a decision from the courts that will benefit all persons whose interests they represent. From the standpoint of the courts, some economy is gained as class actions allow one decision to substitute for a series of individual suits which would have to be filed. The groups sponsoring the case favor class actions simply because the problems of mootness can be easily overcome by substituting another litigant; and contempt proceedings can replace the bringing of further suits.[29]

Although looked upon with suspicion by courts, a prearranged controversy or "test case" may be instituted in order to settle a legal question:

Many suits are carefully planned and brought up to the Supreme Court as "test cases" to secure rulings on disputed constitutional issues. Organizations such as the American Civil Liberties Union and the

[27] L. Ashe, "Class Actions: Solutions for the Seventies," *New England Law Review*, VII (Fall, 1971), 1; Abraham L. Pomerantz, "New Developments in Class Actions—Has Their Death Knell Been Sounded?" *Business Lawyer*, XXV (April, 1970), 259; Note, "Expanding the Impact of State Court Class Action Adjudications to Provide an Effective Forum for Consumers," *UCLA Law Review*, XVIII (May, 1971), 1002; and Note, "Impact of Class Actions on Rule 10b-5," *University of Chicago Law Review*, XXXVIII (Winter, 1971), 337.

[28] Daniel M. Berman, *It Is So Ordered* (New York: W.W. Norton, 1966).

[29] Richard B. Wilson, "Massive Insistence or Massive Resistance? The Judicial Administration of the Civil Rights Revolution," *George Washington Law Review*, XXXIII (April, 1965), 831.

National Association for the Advancement of Colored People devote much effort to finding good test cases involving constitutional principles on which they hope to draw a favorable ruling from the Supreme Court.[30]

The Department of Justice often selects a test case to clarify some legal issues.[31] Questions of standing and of whether the issue is a true "case or controversy" must be answered by those bringing test cases. But courts allow some cases "even if the situation is somewhat contrived—provided there is a genuine disagreement and the indications are that both points of view will in fact be fairly and fully developed." [32] The problem is usually solved simply by a group finding a suitable case already instituted by private parties and then sponsoring that case in the courts.

Pressure groups concerned with litigation have provided advice to the principals in a case; supplied information pertaining to the legal and social problems presented by the legal issue; and donated services such as legal secretaries, clerks, office facilities, or an attorney or cooperating lawyer to assist planning for the trial or appeal. Expert testimony may also be provided by the interest group.[33] Actually, these activities of sponsorship are not altogether different from what lobbies do when before legislatures or administrative agencies.

Court costs are more than often barriers to an adequate defense at the trial level and certainly to appealing the case higher. Pressure groups can thus assist litigation which relates to their interests through financial assistance. David Manwaring, in his fine study of the efforts of the Jehovah's Witnesses to fight the issue of compulsory flag salute in school, illustrated the importance of financial support in court cases: "Immediately after the school board voted

[30] C. Herman Pritchett, *The American Constitution* (New York: McGraw-Hill, 1968), p. 169.

[31] *Ibid.*

[32] Samuel Krislov, *The Supreme Court in the Political Process* (New York: Macmillan, 1965), p. 45.

[33] Nathan Hakman, "The Supreme Court's Political Environment: The Processing of Non-Commercial Litigation," in Joel B. Grossman and Joseph Tanenhaus, eds., *Frontiers of Judicial Research* (New York: John Wiley, 1969), p. 199. Fine accounts of sponsorship tactics are found in Vose, *Caucasians Only* (n. 2 above), and Berman, *It Is So Ordered.*

for an appeal, the school superintendent seems to have sent out urgent appeals for financial aid to the various patriotic organizations which had expressed interest theretofore. The response was immediate and strongly favorable. . . ." [34] The costs of litigation for the school board in *Minersville School District* v. *Gobitis* (310 U.S. 586 [1940]) were financed by patriotic organizations.

Ultimately, the school board lost to the religious freedom demands of the Jehovah's Witnesses in *West Virginia Board of Education* v. *Barnette* (319 U.S. 624 [1943]). But certainly the court issue of compulsory flag salute would not have been continued had it not been for the persistence of the Watchtower Society's legal counsel, the ACLU, and the Bill of Rights Committee of the ABA on the one hand, and the financial and moral support of the patriotic groups on the other. It was groups that pushed the *Gobitis* and *Barnette* cases through the Supreme Court. Although legal-aid, OEO, public defender systems, and "storefront lawyers" have mitigated some of the financial bars to litigation, most principals would still benefit from financial assistance.

Interested parties may, in some cases, assume complete control of the litigation. Publicity, broadening of the issue, and a genuine concern for the interests represented by the principals in the case may motivate these pressure groups. [35] What heretofore had been a private legal issue, becomes a test case under the direct control of the pressure group.

Sponsoring litigation in alternative judicial forums provides pressure groups with greater opportunities to bring a timely and acceptable case to the Supreme Court, or to gain a favorable decision at least in one jurisdiction. Different issues can be tested in the various courts; conflicting decisions can be obtained, encouraging appellate review; and different precedents and procedures can be exploited. However, if this procedure is followed, great coordination and organizational efforts must be involved. What is more likely is that groups become aware of similar cases in different jurisdictions, and then concerted efforts are marshaled around the one case most likely

[34] Manwaring, *Render Unto Caesar* (n. 21 above), p. 107.
[35] An interesting and well-written account of conflicts between groups over the control of litigation is presented by Dan T. Carter, *Scottsboro: A Tragedy of the American South* (Baton Rouge: Louisiana State University Press, 1969).

to present their interests and most likely to receive favorable review by a court of last resort.[36]

Law reviews and scholarly publications are of value to sponsoring groups. The development of favorable legal theory which would be granted consideration by a court of law is crucial to groups hoping to achieve a change in the prevailing legal thought. New theories and developments of old theories are more often than not found in law reviews. It is through these journals that the legal profession communicates with one another. Charles Evans Hughes once wrote that "in confronting any serious problems, a wide-awake and careful judge will at once look to see if the subject has been discussed, or the authorities collated and analyzed, in a good law periodical." [37] Groups can commission or encourage research into the legal issue which concerns them and then hope for publication in a law review.[38] At least no alert group is going to ignore legal periodicals as a source for authority on its particular interest. To take one specific example, the role of Professor Dudley O. McGovney's article in the *California Law Review* was important in the NAACP's attack against restrictive covenants.[39]

Law review articles are used increasingly by Supreme Court justices, and, we can assume, by lawyers filing briefs and arguing cases before them. Between 1939 and 1943, for example, 17 percent of the written opinions of the Supreme Court contained references to law articles. By 1952, it had increased to 26 percent.[40] A quick review of the 1972 term of the Court indicates that law reviews are commonly cited. The Court can either accept law review arguments from the briefs filed by the principals or *amici*, or search out on its

[36] The Commission on Law and Social Action of the American Jewish Congress assists groups interested in test cases by publishing biannually an extensive list of pending cases in federal and state jurisdictions which affect state-church relations. Through this communication, groups can investigate the possibility of sponsoring a favorable case. See their "Litigation Docket of Pending Cases Affecting Freedom of Religion and Separation of Church and State," American Jewish Congress, 15 East 84th Street, New York, N.Y., 10028.

[37] Vose, *Caucasians Only* (n. 20 above), p. 71.

[38] Wright Patman, "Lobbying Through Law Reviews," in Walter F. Murphy and C. Herman Pritchett, eds., *Courts, Judges, and Politics* (New York: Random House, 1961), p. 310.

[39] Vose, *Caucasians Only*, pp. 68–71. See also Manwaring (n. 21 above), p. 111.

[40] Chester Newland, "Legal Periodicals and the United States Supreme Court," *Midwest Journal of Political Science*, III (February, 1959).

own for law review justifications. Of course, this practice is not always viewed with favor: "Today we are finding that an additional factor is creeping in to influence the thinking and action of the Supreme Court. . . . That factor is the Court's consideration of unknown, unrecognized and nonauthoritative text books, Law Review articles, and other writings of propaganda artists and lobbyists." [41]

Since the Supreme Court is called upon to decide issues of great social and political import, we would expect that its decision-making and opinion justifications would embody materials found in law reviews, which are not generally regarded as purely legal sources. But do groups utilize law review articles in other courts? Richard Daynard has suggested that little opportunity exists for the use of strictly nonlegal sources in lower courts. In only 4 percent of the cases heard in 1968 by Federal Courts of Appeals (the D.C. and Second Circuits) and the New York Court of Appeals was a large social issue involved that would lend itself well to use of law review materials by pressure groups. [42]

Despite these opportunities for sponsorship, it is not yet altogether clear that pressure groups commonly avail themselves of these tactics. Nathan Hakman has questioned the degree to which groups are involved in litigation. Data compiled from questionnaires and interviews sent to lobbyists and lawyers involved in Supreme Court litigation led Hakman to conclude that the view of extensive pressure activities existing before court was largely "political science folklore." [43] "Litigants in court cases are not pawns or symbols and are usually not manipulated by behind the scenes groups or organization," according to Hakman. Criminal cases most often involve individuals pushing their own "exclusively private claims and interests." The more prestigious and stable pressure groups "do not play a significant role in influencing the scope of conduct of courtroom controversies." The few lawyers who specialize in civil liberties litigation are not "in a theoretical strategic position to control a number of cases raising similar issues in different judicial forums." [44]

[41] Patman, p. 309.

[42] Richard A. Daynard, "The Use of Social Policy in Judicial Decision-Making," *Cornell Law Review*, LVI (July, 1971), 924.

[43] Nathan Hakman, "Lobbying the Supreme Court: An Appraisal of Political Science Folklore," *Fordham Law Review*, XXXV (October, 1966), 15.

[44] Hakman, "The Supreme Court's Political Environment" (n. 33 above), p. 245.

Supreme Court non-commercial cases, like most other litigation, are carried to the Supreme Court primarily to resolve the immediate disputes among private adversaries. Attorneys and their clients, more often than not, make no efforts to raise funds, secure additional representation, coordinate with other litigants, or employ research, publicity, or *amici curiae* activity to broaden the scope or political significance of their litigation efforts. Long range effects or policy changes resulting from the efforts of litigants and their supporters must still be considered in the realm of unanticipated and/or fortuitous circumstances.[45]

But even if Hakman is correct, if one considers the great decisions in which the NAACP, ACLU, and Jehovah's Witnesses have been directly involved, activities of groups are clearly seen to have been crucial in some landmark cases. Civil liberties issues clearly attract pressure group support. The attraction may be explained by the fact that minorities usually require financial support as well as encouragement to pursue their goals or to protect their position in a majoritarian society. In 1963, the *Yale Law Journal* conducted a survey of pressure groups involved in Supreme Court civil liberties litigation and discovered that the involvement was widespread. For example, of 318 selected cases between 1933 and 1963, the ACLU had participated in 120 cases, the NAACP in 51, American Jewish Congress in 29, American Committee for Protection of the Foreign Born in 25, Emergency Civil Liberties Committee and Jehovah's Witnesses in 17 each, and American Jewish Committee in 11—or a total of 270. In 32 percent of the total number of cases in the *Yale Law Journal* survey, the groups had provided financial or legal assistance. In 54 percent, these organizations not only provided financial or legal assistance, but also appeared as *amicus* or gave strategic advice.[46] Thus, gaining access to courts is not an uncommon practice among pressure groups concerned with the Bill of Rights. In addition, the potentials for group litigation at the state and local levels are great, although little research has yet been conducted in this area.[47]

[45] *Ibid.*, p. 246.
[46] Comment, "The South's Amended Barratry Laws: An Attempt to End Group Pressure Through the Courts," *Yale Law Journal*, LXXII (Summer, 1963), 1613.
[47] Vose, "Interest Groups" (n. 23 above), p. 85.

Amicus Efforts

Groups can and often do use *amicus curiae* techniques to gain access to courts. Either through permission from the parties to the dispute, or from the Court itself, interested parties are allowed to present their arguments although they are not directly involved in the immediate legal issue before the court. The reasons for granting or refusing to grant permission are not always clear but Rule 42 of the Supreme Court Rules reads: "[A motion for leave to file a brief of *amicus curiae*] shall concisely state the nature of the applicant's interest, set forth facts or questions of law that have not been or reasons to believe that they will not adequately be presented by the parties and their relevancy to the disposition of the case; . . . ." [48] Apparently, the Court has to be convinced, when parties to the dispute are not, that an *amicus* will add substantially to the resolution of the issue.

The *amicus curiae* or "friend of the court" role has a long and respected history in Western legal development which can be traced back to Roman law. Initially, an *amicus curiae* was a friendly bystander "without having an interest in the cause. . . . He acts for no one but simply seeks to give information to the Court." [49] The *amicus*, in other words, was merely a neutral friend helping the court to decide. By the twentieth century, the neutral friendship had changed to active advocacy. Today, "the *amicus* is no longer a neutral amorphous embodiment of justice, but an active participant in the interest group struggle." [50] When the legal issue is most important, *amicus* participation is assured: "Where the stakes are highest for the groups, and where the needs on the part of the judges for information and for sharing of responsibility through consultation are at a peak, access has appropriately, and almost inevitably, been at its greatest." [51]

In 1949, the Supreme Court changed its rules to discourage motions for leave to file an *amicus* brief, but through time little change has resulted. In 1949, 118 *amicus* briefs were filed in 53 cases and 11

[48] Rules of the Supreme Court, 388 U.S. 974 (1966).
[49] Samuel Krislov, "The *Amicus Curiae* Brief: From Friendship to Advocacy," *Yale Law Journal*, LXXII (March, 1963), 694.
[50] *Ibid.*, p. 716.
[51] *Ibid.*, pp. 703–04.

amicus oral arguments were presented. The Court turned down no requests for leave to file. In 1961, 107 briefs in 54 cases were presented along with 7 *amicus* oral arguments. Only two motions for leave to file a brief were denied.[52] Indeed, after an initial post-1949 decline, the Court's receptivity to *amicus* efforts increased.

The uses of the *amicus curiae* are varied. When principals to the case grant permission for support from groups, often the *amicus* brief is only a further endorsement of the leading arguments. For example, gaining of the endorsement of twenty-three states for an overruling of *Betts* v. *Brady* gave greater weight to Abe Fortas' arguments in *Gideon* v. *Wainwright* for a constitutional requirement of right to counsel in state felony cases.[53] *Amicus* briefs (and oral arguments) can introduce subtle variations of the basic legal arguments in which the principals wish not to indulge. Less common, but certainly a tactic used in *amicus* briefs, are the presentation of emotional and risky, if not provoking, arguments. The lawyers for the immediate litigants would not jeopardize their clients by using similar arguments. Utilization of new arguments with unique sources by the *amici* is often a group tactic.

Data indicates that the Supreme Court grants motions to file *amicus curiae* briefs quite commonly. The justices find them valuable supplements to their decision making; in particular, their fact finding is assisted by these briefs. For example, in *Baker* v. *Carr*, through the *amicus* briefs the court could be appraised of malapportionment conditions in states other than Tennessee. Through such briefs judges are allowed to give judicial notice to the broader social and political conditions pointed out by the *amici*. Actually, the courts are able to weigh social, political, and economic data in a judicial manner merely by being made aware of them by *amici* presentations. The justices are also able to develop some awareness of those who may support or oppose their decisions.[54]

[52] *Ibid.*, p. 716.

[53] Lewis, *Gideon's Trumpet* (n. 19 above). Two years after serving as court-appointed counsel for Gideon, Abe Fortas was nominated by President Johnson to the Supreme Court. The events leading up to his resignation from the high bench in 1969 are covered in Robert Shogan's *A Question of Judgment* (Indianapolis: Bobbs-Merrill, 1972).

[54] Lucius Barker, "Third Parties in Litigation: A Systemic View of the Judicial Function," *Journal of Politics*, XXIX (February, 1967), 41.

Lucius Barker argues that with the increased use of *amicus curiae* briefs and oral arguments the basic nature of the judicial process has been altered.[55] The triangulation of the adversary process has been changed to a multisided conflict. *Amici* now join the principals in the verbal battle before judges. Also, the judicial process has taken on a legislative function. Since the arguments presented by friends of the court are representative arguments, the collective interests of the pressure groups have permeated the judicial system as well as the legislature. Social, political, and economic data—similar to what is presented to legislative committees—constitute much of the *amici* presentations. When faced with a reluctant if not hostile legislature, governments utilize *amicus curiae* and intervention tactics to gain changes in the law. Thus in combination, groups before the courts have changed the nature of the judicial function. Barker states: "That our adversary system has been broadened to accommodate views of private groups and government reflects not only the political-social dimensions of issues brought for judicial determination, but it also reflects the important role of the judiciary in resolving such questions."[56] But, after all, it is the successful resolution of political-social issues for which governments (including courts) have been instituted.

GOVERNMENT AS INTERVENOR AND AMICUS

The intervention of state or federal governments into court cases illustrates two forms of group action. First, governments themselves are groups competing in the political give and take of the American system. Second, oftentimes government agents will participate as formal intervenors or as *amici curiae* in order to lend weight to litigants representing broader interests. The actions of the Attorney General and Solicitor General at the federal level bear directly on cases which have implications for groups.[57] Unlike other organiza-

[55] Lucius J. Barker reviews the change to a legislative role but lays the blame on the unwillingness or inability of the other branches of government to perform their constitutional and political function. *Ibid.*, p. 69.

[56] *Ibid.*, p. 42.

[57] Cf. Note, "Government Litigation in the Supreme Court: The Roles of the Solicitor General," *Yale Law Journal*, LXXXIII (July, 1969), 1442; and Luther A. Huston *et al.*, *The Role of the Attorney General of the United States* (Washington, D.C.: American Enterprise Institute, 1968).

tions, the federal government need not gain permission from the parties to the dispute or from the Supreme Court to participate as *amicus* (Rule 42 of the Supreme Court Rules). Thus, depending upon the initiative of the Attorney General or Solicitor General, the federal government has great opportunity to influence the course of Supreme Court litigation. It has increasingly taken advantage of this opportunity. In 1955, the federal government appeared as *amicus* in two Supreme Court cases, representing only 3 percent of the total cases in which the government appeared. By 1966, these *amicus* activities had increased to ten cases, totaling 13 percent of all cases in which the government appeared.[58] Many of these *amicus* appearances involved government support for civil rights actions backed by special interest groups.[59]

As an intervenor, the Attorney General must show an intimate involvement in the outcome of the case as outlined in the Federal Rules of Civil Procedures (28 U.S.C.A. 2072), but from time to time Congress has authorized further intervention beyond those outlined in the rules.[60] The federal government as intervenor becomes one of the parties to the dispute, with the same rights and liabilities as a defendant or plaintiff. As a friend of the court, the government cannot be such a "party" to the dispute. Both as intervenor or as *amicus*, the government must utilize the "public interests" as its justification for participation. Oftentimes, "the line between an intervenor . . . and *amicus curiae* is . . . blurred." [61]

Technically, intervention allows the Solicitor General more opportunities to influence the outcome of a case than does *amicus* participation.

> . . . the status of an *amicus curiae* [as opposed to an intervenor] does not give the Government sufficient freedom in developing its presentation. An *amicus'* function is limited by the discretion of the court. Rarely may he present evidence, and though he may generally submit a brief, the court may disregard it. The Government thus would

---

[58] Samuel Krislov, "The Role of the Attorney General as *Amicus Curiae*," in Huston, p. 91.

[59] Robert G. Dixon, Jr., "The Attorney General and Civil Rights," in Huston, p. 105.

[60] Note, "Government Litigation," p. 1442. See also A.K. Butzel, "Intervention and Class Actions Before the Agencies and the Courts," *Administrative Law Review*, XXV (Spring, 1973), 135.

[61] Krislov, "The Role of the Attorney General," p. 77.

be handicapped, for example, in any attempt to furnish the factual
. . . background . . . [necessary to its case].[62]

The government has no right to appeal the decision if it goes against
those it supported in an *amicus* brief, and the government is prevented from attacking the "good faith of either party" in the dispute
if it were deemed necessary. As an intervenor, both opportunities
are available. When presented with a choice as to whether to intervene or act as a friend of the court, certainly the government would
opt for the former, should the case warrant its support. It should be
recognized, however, that the government takes on greater responsibilities as intervenor, and its cause may be best served by the economical *amicus* route.

The Solicitor General maintains a unique autonomous role in
handling the concerns of the federal government before the Supreme
Court. He reviews the requests by government agencies for writs of
certiorari before they are filed, and he makes the decision to seek
certiorari. His role is important in resolving intergovernmental conflicts in real or potential litigation. The Supreme Court "relies upon
his ability to limit the number and guarantee the importance of cases
appealed by the government. It also depends upon him to present
the views of the Executive and often to inform the Court, for example, as to the content of barely legible *in forma pauperis* petitions.
. . . [The Court is confident that he] will aid . . . in finding the solution most conducive to the public interests." [63] But it is the *amicus*
and intervenor activities of the Solicitor General that allow the
government to become involved in the group conflict outside the
government.[64] According to the *Yale Law Journal:* "Amicus participation usually involves none of the theoretical limitations of an
adversary stance and allows the Solicitor General freer reign to point
the Court in directions he deems desirable." [65] It is in the area of

[62] Note, "Federal Intervention in Private Actions Involving the Public Interests," *Harvard Law Review*, LXV (December, 1951), 327; and Note, "Protecting Civil Liberties through Federal Interventions in State Criminal Matters,"
California Law Review, LIX (November, 1971), 1549.

[63] Note, "Government Litigation" (n. 57 above), p. 1443.

[64] The Supreme Court favors the federal government in granting petitions for
writs of *certiorari*. Joseph Tanenhaus *et al.*, "The Supreme Court's Certiorari
Jurisdiction: Cue Theory," in Glendon A. Schubert, ed., *Judicial Decision-
Making* (New York: The Free Press of Glencoe, 1963), p. 122.

[65] Note, "Government Litigation," p. 1479 .

constitutional litigation that the supporting role of government in group conflicts can best be seen. In civil disobedience, desegregation, and reapportionment cases the Solicitor General has become "a partisan advocate of a particular constitutional argument" in favor of NAACP, ACLU, or other groups and in opposition to some state and federal political institutions.[66]

The federal government itself, quite apart from its *amicus* participation, was involved as initial litigant or as intervenor in 34 percent of all the cases on the Supreme Court's docket in 1966, and in 51 percent of all cases that were argued on their merits.[67] If we are to view the government as one of the groups in the political group struggle, its activities in the judicial process are clearly extensive.

There is little doubt that group sponsorship, *amicus curiae* participation, and government intervention have an important impact on at least the Supreme Court. But as Hakman has pointed out, the group struggle does not permeate all that transpires in the judicial process and may account for only a small amount of the litigation when one considers all levels of the court system. Nonetheless, the great landmark decisions have involved the efforts of groups, and the broader concerns of these groups have often overshadowed the immediate dispute between the principal litigants in the case. What is needed is more research into lower federal courts and state courts at all levels within the framework of the macro-group model. The studies of Vose, Barker, Krislov, Hakman, and Newland must be replicated or redesigned and applied to the other levels of the American court system.

GROUPS AND JUDICIAL SELECTION

Political parties are major participants in the group struggle called politics. Quite apart from competing for the favor of the American voter and for control of the politician, the parties also wish to influence the judicial process. The impact of political party can be felt at two points in the judicial process. First, political party has been isolated as the single most important background characteristic

---

[66] Cf. *Green* v. *School Board of Virginia*, 391 U.S. 430 (1968); *Raney* v. *Board of Education*, 391 U.S. 443 (1968); *Griffin* v. *Maryland*, 378 U.S. 130 (1964); *Barr* v. *City of Columbia*, 378 U.S. 146 (1964); *Reynolds* v. *Sims*, 377 U.S. 533 (1964); and *Avery* v. *Midland County*, 390 U.S. 474 (1968).

[67] Note, "Government Litigation," p. 1442.

which can be associated with decision making of the judges. Although, political party as a decisional variable explains only a small part of the directions taken by judicial decisions. Second, in the macro-group model, political parties turn out to be most active in the selection of judges.

In the federal system, political party affiliation is the most important variable in the politics of selection. Federal judges have been predominately of the same political party as the appointing President. Roosevelt appointed 203 Democrats and only 8 Republicans; Truman's record was 129 Democrats and 13 Republicans; Eisenhower appointed 11 Democrats and 176 Republicans; Kennedy's record was 113 Democrats and 11 Republicans; Johnson appointed 170 Democrats and 11 Republicans; and President Nixon upheld the partisan pattern by appointing 12 Democrats and 166 Republicans in his first term in office.[68] Senatorial courtesy reinforces the party orientation of the selection at the federal level.[69]

Twenty states utilize partisan elections for the selection of state judges.[70] Obviously, the political party is crucial in the selection of judges under this system. Several states, although having a nonpartisan form of judicial selection, rely upon political party endorsement, nomination, and campaigning to recruit lawyers to the bench.[71] A federal analogy is used by some states in which the governor nominates and the legislature grants or withholds "advice and consent." As at the federal level, the party politics of the governor may

[68] John M. Burns and Jack W. Peltason, *Government by the People* (Englewood Cliffs, N.J.: Prentice-Hall, 1972), p. 394; and Robert A. Diamond, ed., *Nixon: The Fourth Year of His Presidency* (Washington, D.C.: Congressional Quarterly, 1973), p. 29.

[69] Joseph Harris, *The Advice and Consent of the Senate* (Berkeley: University of California Press, 1953); Richard K. Burke, *The Path to the Court: A Study of Federal Judicial Appointments* (Ann Arbor: University of Michigan Microfilms, 1958); and Harold W. Chase, *Federal Judges: The Appointing Process* (n. 17 above), p. 6.

[70] For a fine discussion of the influence of selection systems on the characteristics of state judges, see Bradley C. Canon, "The Impact of Formal Selection Processes on the Characteristics of Judges—Reconsidered," *Law and Society Review*, VI (May, 1972), 579.

[71] David W. Adamany, "The Party Variable in Judges' Voting: Conceptual Notes and a Case Study," *The American Political Science Review*, LXIII (March, 1969), 57; Malcolm Moos, "Judicial Elections and Partisan Endorsements of Judicial Candidates in Minnesota," *The American Political Science Review*, XXXV (March, 1941), 69; and S. Sidney Ulmer, "The Political Party Variable on the Michigan Supreme Court," *Journal of Public Law*, XI (1962), 352.

be crucial in his nominations.[72] The possibility of party influence is obvious in those states using legislative-appointment techniques for selecting judges. The majority party dominates. Even in those states that rely upon an executive council for judicial confirmation, the party makeup of the council may be influential.[73] Few studies have been directed toward a detailed study of formal and informal party influences on the selection of judges, although we are beginning to understand more about the influence of past party affiliations on judicial decision making.[74] For example, Martin A. Levin's comparative study of judges in Pittsburgh and Minneapolis indicates that those jurists who have a political background and who have been selected to the bench by clearly political means are better able to assimilate the contradictions presented by the law, which represents a middle-class culture, and defendants from a lower-class environment than are those jurists selected by nonpolitical methods. Political party considerations have, therefore, an impact on judicial decision making and Levin is at least implying that such political considerations are not altogether undesirable.[75]

Often the formal judicial selection system of a particular state is deceiving with respect to the influence of party on selection. For example, Bradley Canon has pointed out that 45.7 percent of state supreme court justices leave the court before the completion of their terms either through death or resignation, thus allowing the governor to appoint a candidate to finish out the term.[76] Seldom is an incumbent challenged and rarely is he defeated should the office be contested.[77] Thus, the governor may make a party decision to fill a

[72] John E. Crowe, "Subterranean Politics: A Judge Is Chosen," *Journal of Public Law*, XII (1963), 275.

[73] D.I. Hodgkin, "The Maine Executive Council: Representative of Whom," *Juncture—Where Ideas Meet* (Orono, Maine: Bureau of Public Administration, University of Maine, 1971); and Clement Vose, *The Executive Council of Maine in Decline* (Brunswick: Bureau for Research in Municipal Government, Bowdoin College, 1959).

[74] See Chapter 1.

[75] Martin A. Levin, "Urban Politics and Judicial Behavior," *The Journal of Legal Studies*, I (January, 1972), 193.

[76] Bradley C. Canon, "Characteristics and Career Patterns of State Supreme Court Justices," *State Government*, XLV (Winter, 1972), 37. See also James Herndon, "Appointment as a Means of Accession to Elective Courts of Last Resort," *North Dakota Law Review*, XXXVIII (January, 1962), 60.

[77] *Ibid.*; and Herbert Jacob and Kenneth Vines, *Politics in American States* (Boston: Little, Brown, 1971), p. 283.

judicial vacancy and the nonpartisan election merely confirms the decision.

The Missouri Plan for the selection of judges was designed to remove judges from the struggles of party and pressure politics as well as gubernatorial patronage. Judges are nominated by a special commission of lawyers, judges, and lay people. The governor appoints from those names submitted by the commission and, after serving on the bench for a short time, the incumbent must go before the people in an election.[78] However, the plan has merely made partisan and group pressures less obvious. For example, business executives have attempted to influence judicial nominations by writing to the nominating commission in behalf of particular candidates. Also, business groups attempt to influence the governor when he makes his selection from the list of nominees sent him by the commission. Watson and Downing have concluded that " . . . the business community, year in and year out, has continued to have an important voice in the overall selection process" in the State of Missouri.[79] Divisions in the Missouri state and municipal bar associations are reflected in the campaigns for election of lawyer and lay members to the nominating commissions. The governor often appoints lay members to the commission who are predominantly of his party.[80] It seems clear that political parties as groups have been active in gaining indirect access to the courts through the selection process of the Missouri Plan despite its design to the contrary.

In addition to political parties, other interested parties and groups are also competing for the privilege of having their favorites selected to the federal and state benches. For example, the American Bar Association plays an important role in the selection of federal judges

[78] The literature on the Missouri Plan for the selection of state judges is extensive. E.g., Glenn R. Winters, ed., *Selected Readings on Judicial Selection and Tenure* (Chicago: American Judicature Society, 1967); Jack W. Peltason, "The Missouri Plan for the Selection of Judges," *The University of Missouri Studies,* XX (Columbia, Mo.: University of Missouri Press, 1945); Lloyd E. Roberts, "Twenty-five Years Under the Missouri Plan," *Judicature,* XLIX (October, 1965), 92; and Glenn R. Winters, "Selection of Judges—An Historical Introduction," *Texas Law Review,* XLIV (June, 1966), 1081. The American Judicature Society in Chicago has been instrumental in furthering the cause of the Missouri Plan. Consult *Judicature,* the society's fine journal.

[79] Richard A. Watson and Rondal G. Downing, *The Politics of the Bench and Bar* (n. 17 above), p. 131.

[80] *Ibid.,* especially Chapter 1.

although the ABA must act at the pleasure of or through the Attorney General's office,[81] the Senate Judiciary Committee, and individual senators. In the period from 1951 to 1958, bar associations opposed in any one year up to 20 percent of the candidates being considered by the Judiciary Committee. Non-bar group and individual opposition varied from 8 percent to 20 percent during that period.[82] These figures of course do not indicate the degree to which groups were involved in *support* of judicial candidates. Moreover, the figures are not entirely indicative of group activity simply because by the time the Senate Judiciary Committee receives the President's nomination, much of the group conflict has been resolved.

President Nixon's nominees to the U.S. Supreme Court have fostered group opposition. Clement F. Haynsworth, Jr., was opposed by the Urban League, Americans for Democratic Action, Leadership Conference on Civil Rights, and AFL-CIO.[83] In 1970, the NAACP urged the Senate to reject G. Harrold Carswell. George Meany of the AFL-CIO, National Urban Coalition Action Council, and the Democratic Policy Council joined the NAACP.[84] The American Civil Liberties Union, in departure from long-established policy not to oppose a candidate for public office, campaigned against William Rehnquist. The National Bar Association and NAACP also publicly opposed the nominee.[85] The various groups succeeded in preventing Haynsworth and Carswell from being confirmed by the Senate, but Rehnquist assumed his seat on the high bench in January, 1972.

The Attorney General, who has prime responsibility for recommending potential nominees to the President, must account for the interests of many groups concerned with court personnel: "The Attorney General must choose persons for federal judgeships who will not seriously offend the sensitivities of any of the major interest groups on whom the administration must rely for political support or

[81] Joel B. Grossman, *Lawyers and Judges;* and his "Federal Judicial Selection: The Work of the ABA Committee," *Midwest Journal of Political Science,* VIII (August, 1964), 221.

[82] Grossman, *Lawyers and Judges,* p. 168.

[83] *New York Times,* August 19, 1969, p. 27; August 21, 1969, p. 24; October 6, 1969, p. 29.

[84] *Ibid.,* January 22, 1970, p. 22; January 27, 1970, p. 1; February 5, 1970, p. 22; and February 11, 1970, p. 26.

[85] *Ibid.,* December 6, 1971, p. 35; November 18, 1971, p. 33; and December 4, 1971, p. 20.

who have established a legitimate claim to participate in the judicial selection process." [86] The same statement applies to the demands upon individual senators as they exercise their senatorial courtesy prerogative regarding judicial selection. Thus, similar and continuing cross-pressures are felt by all administrations, giving them little freedom in their selection of judges at, certainly, the lower levels of the federal bench. Harold W. Chase's study of judicial selection concludes that despite the political contrasts between the Eisenhower, Kennedy, and Johnson administrations, the dynamics of the selection process lead to similar kinds of lawyers being elevated to the bench. Chase is optimistic about the results of such a process and feels that it could be improved by downgrading the force of senatorial courtesy.[87]

In sum, indirect access through the selection process provides a meaningful channel for political parties and pressure groups to have an impact on the judicial process. Politics cannot be eliminated from the selection of judges and perhaps ought not to be. Changing the means of selection only changes the points at which the parties and groups exert most of their efforts, with some mitigating influences on the crassness of the pressure. However, in a pluralistic democracy—a democracy postulated by the group theorists—direct and indirect pressures will remain and, in fact, must remain for the system to continue to function.

POSTDECISIONAL ACCESS

Postdecisional access is clearly indirect in that groups pressuring for changes in court decisions must lobby with other political and administrative agencies. Nonetheless, what happens at this postdecisional level may affect subsequent litigation, pressure group activities, and judicial decisions.[88] The Eleventh, Thirteenth, Sixteenth, and Twenty-Sixth Amendments to the U.S. Constitution

[86] Grossman, p. 120.
[87] Chase, *Federal Judges: The Appointing Process* (n. 17 above). Chase does suggest that the best institution for choosing federal judges would be the U.S. Supreme Court. Unfortunately he fails to pursue fully the implications of his suggestion.
[88] The postdecisional aspect of the macro-group model is covered by the discussions in Chapter 5 dealing with the impact models.

were the results of Supreme Court decisions.[89] Recent segregation, prayer, and reapportionment amendments, although not proposed by Congress, were reactions to the Court's rulings.[90] Groups were involved in those efforts.

Lower courts, possibly under the pressures of real and potential group activity, can alter the impact of higher courts' rulings.[91] Legislatures can pass new laws or redefine the interpretation given laws by courts as a reaction to judges.[92] Enforcement agencies can ignore, evade, or vigorously observe court guidelines.[93] Finally, people can, at some peril, fail to comply with the provisions of a court decision. Desegregation and prayers are two areas where, in some regions, compliance has been spotty.[94] The point is that although groups may win or lose in court, they need not, and do not, discontinue their efforts. These efforts in turn may necessitate further court action. Such postdecisional access is beyond the discussion of this review since in such cases groups tend to fall back on traditional tactics appropriate for legislative or administrative agencies. For the macro-group theorist, the group struggle goes on and on—providing him with an unending source of study.

[89] *Chisolm* v. *Georgia*, 2 Dallas 419 (1793); *Dred Scott* v. *Sandford*, 19 How. 393 (1857); *Pollock* v. *Farmers Loan and Trust*, 158 U.S. 601 (1895); and *Oregon* v. *Mitchell*, 400 U.S. 112 (1970).

[90] Talmadge Amendment (1960) attempted to reverse the *Brown* decision; *Congressional Record*, January 28, 1960, pp. 1499–1500. The Becker Amendment (1963) attempted to undo the *Engel* and *Schempp* prayer cases; House Joint Resolution 9, January 9, 1963. The Dirksen Amendment (1965) was proposed to allow states to apportion upper-house as they saw fit (*Reynolds* v. *Sims*, 377 U.S. 533 [1964]); *Congressional Record*, August 11, 1965, p. 19375.

[91] Walter F. Murphy, "Lower Court Checks on Supreme Court Power," *The American Political Science Review*, LII (December, 1959), 1017; Note, "Evasion of Supreme Court Mandates in Cases Remanded to State Courts Since 1941," *Harvard Law Review*, LXVII (May, 1954), 1251; and Jack W. Peltason, *Fifty-eight Lonely Men* (New York: Harcourt, Brace and World, 1961).

[92] Walter F. Murphy, *Congress and the Court* (Chicago: University of Chicago Press, 1962); C. Herman Pritchett, *Congress vs. the Supreme Court* (Minneapolis: University of Minnesota Press, 1961); and A.C. Breckenridge, *Congress Against the Court* (Lincoln, Nebraska: University of Nebraska Press, 1970).

[93] Jerome H. Skolnick, *Justice Without Trial* (New York: John Wiley, 1967); and Michael S. Wald *et al.*, "Interrogations in New Haven: The Impact of *Miranda*," *Yale Law Journal*, LXXVI (July, 1967), 1521.

[94] E.g., Charles H. Sheldon, ed., *The Supreme Court: Politicians in Robes* (Beverly Hills: Glencoe Press, 1970), pp. 83–87.

CHAPTER FIVE

Impact Models

DESCRIPTION AND ANALYSIS OF IMPACT MODELS

Two revolutions are responsible for the recent development of impact studies.[1] One occurred quite outside the scholarly world of political science and one involved the profession directly. In 1954, the Supreme Court decided *Brown* v. *Board of Education*, 347 U.S. 483 (1954), striking down the "separate but equal" doctrine in public schools. The justices delayed immediate implementation until they were informed of the impact of their decision. The "with all deliberate speed" of the second *Brown* decision, 348 U.S. 294 (1955), was the result. The justices were thus aware of the magnitude of the desegregation issue but could they have anticipated that, nineteen years later, the debate over the issue would still rage? Few anticipated the long-range impact of the desegregation decisions; and scholars, realizing the need for more knowledge, moved to fill the gap.

Quite apart from the real world of Supreme Court litigation, another revolution was taking place within the political science profession. Political scientists were undergoing an agonizing reappraisal of their discipline. One of the results (discussed later in Chapter 6) was the behavioral approach to the study of political phenomena, in

---

[1] The number of impact studies has increased steadily in the past few years. Some of the general works are Stephen L. Wasby, *The Impact of the United States Supreme Court: Some Perspectives* (Homewood, Ill.: Dorsey Press, 1970), which contains an excellent bibliography; Theodore Becker, ed., *The Impact of Supreme Court Decisions* (New York: Oxford University Press, 1969); Richard Johnson, *The Dynamics of Compliance* (Evanston: Northwestern University Press, 1967); and Kenneth M. Dolbeare and Phillip Hammond, *The School Prayer Decisions: From Court Policy to Local Practice* (Chicago: University of Chicago Press, 1971).

which scholars came to give greater concern to the "science" of political science. The behavioral revolution succeeded, but some scholars then wanted to move beyond behavioralism to policy analysis. The questions of these scholars centered on the analyses and explanations of actual policy outcomes of the political process. Many of those interested in the judicial process posed questions concerning the intended and unintended effects of court decisions: "The court may decide, but what impact, if any, does its decisions have on society and why?" The behavioralist insists upon a rigorous adherence to the scientific method to measure political phenomena; the policy-oriented scholar agrees but argues that we must know more about the social, governmental, and economic repercussions of political phenomena. Perhaps the "behavioralist" vs. "postbehavioralist" debate is largely an artificial creation of those wishing merely to generate discussion within the profession. Nonetheless, if the debate is meaningful, the author suggests that impact analysis can provide a common meeting ground for the factions. Certainly the development of this area of study is partially due to the demand, by some political scientists, that we must become more concerned with policy and its consequence.[2]

Not only are impact studies of value to the political scientist but, as the aftermath of the *Brown* cases illustrates, judges would benefit greatly from an understanding of where their decisions may lead society.[3] If the justices had known of the long-range consequences of the *Brown* decision, would they have ordered desegregation at once rather than "with all deliberate speed"? The need for more knowledge of the effects of court decisions is clearly evident.

One of the major problems with impact studies is that no theory of impact has yet been posited which would guide the many diverse case studies common to the impact literature. James Levine phrased the problem as follows: "My contention is that the low yield of these studies is partially the result of their methodological inadequacy. In scrutinizing conclusions about Supreme Court efficacy, irrelevance, or impotence which are suggested by researchers, we are usually at

[2] See Austin Ranney, ed., *Political Science and Public Policy* (Chicago: Markham, 1968); and David Easton, "The New Revolution in Political Science," *The American Political Science Review,* LXIII (December, 1969), 1051.

[3] Arthur S. Miller, "On the Need for 'Impact Analysis' of Supreme Court Decisions," in Theodore Becker, ed., *The Impact of Supreme Court Decisions,* p. 7.

a loss to understand the meaning or assess the validity of the propositions being advanced." [4] This does not mean that impact scholars are not trying to agree upon some comprehensive approach which would lead to a consensus on models to investigate the short- and long-range consequences of judicial decisions. Quite the contrary, Levine suggests that theories of utility, dissonance, learning, organization, and communications may provide an outline for impact models. Stephen Wasby feels that macro-group, systems, and communications theories may be of use to the scholar. But the fact remains that we are still moving toward a theory of impact. Presently, the efforts in impact scholarship can best be described as models in search of a theory rather than a theory in search of models.

INDEPENDENT VARIABLES

Several variables may account for degrees of compliance or noncompliance with court decisions. The Supreme Court pronounces the "supreme law of the land" but not all will adjust their behavior accordingly. Why not? The variables are hypothesized answers to this question. The independent variables are associated with the decision or decisions of the court. The intervening variables may reinforce, change, or mitigate the force of the decisions. The dependent variables, of course, are the degree of compliance or the variance in impact of the decision or decisions.

Independent Variables [5]

Decision(s)
　　Characteristics of Decision(s)
　　　　Facts
　　　　Time Sequence of Decision(s)
　　　　Degree of Unanimity
　　　　Statutory or Constitutional Basis
　　　　Ambiguity of Decision(s)
　　　　Completeness of Decision(s)
　　　　Statutory or Constitutional Basis

[4] James P. Levine, "Methodological Concerns in Studying Supreme Court Efficacy," *Law and Society Review*, IV (May, 1970), 584.

[5] These and the following variables are based upon Stephen Wasby, *The Impact of the United States Supreme Court*.

Impact studies begin with the decision of the courts. The characteristics of that decision or decisions may dictate the degree of compliance. The facts of the case cause impact variance in a variety of ways. If the decision in the case is confined only to its facts and the immediate litigants, compliance may be more likely than when the facts are broad and the case is a class action in which all of those "similarly situated" will be affected by the decision. Unique factual matters may prevent a particular case from becoming a precedent simply because few analogous factual situations will arise in the future. Decisions also have a cumulative impact. The direction of a series of cases may be changed by one later decision resulting in varying degrees of compliance. A series of cases which gradually develops a legal principle may lead to more compliance than a single case that establishes the principle at that moment. Stephen Wasby notes: "Important doctrinal developments may not be apparent except over the long run, until after several cases have been decided." [6] Cases that are bunched together may have important consequences. If one decision is greeted with hostility by the public, but is followed immediately with an acceptable decision, the impact of the original decision may change.

The degree of unanimity on the bench is an important characteristic of the case having impact consequences. Five-four decisions are more amenable to change and to noncompliance than eight-one or nine-zero decisions. Chief Justice Earl Warren's efforts for unanimity in the *Brown* case illustrate the importance of unanimous agreement. When the case is based on constitutional rather than statutory grounds, greater compliance is likely. How well did the justices explain their rationales in the Court opinions? Is the ruling clear or ambiguous? An ambiguous opinion allows greater leeway for administrators and lower courts to interpret. Finally, the impact may vary according to the degree to which justices faced up to the issues presented by the case.

INTERVENING VARIABLES

Intervening variables can change the impact of particular decisions. Although we may have isolated the characteristics of a de-

[6] *Ibid.*, p. 44.

cision, our speculations about the probable consequences of that decision must be tempered with an appraisal of the intervening conditions.

Intervening Variables

Communications Process
    Character of Message Transmitted
    Character of Transmitters and Receptors
    Means of Communication

Political, Economic, and Social Environment
    Nature of Public and Elite Opinion
    Pressure Group and Political Party Characteristics
    Geographical Scope of Decision(s)
    Economic Structure of System
    Kind of Intensity of Crises
    Belief Systems of Community

Follow-Up Factors
    Enforcement Provisions and Timing
    Numbers Needed and Enthusiasm for Enforcement
    Characteristics of the "Enforcers"

The character of the message transmitted is largely a function of the degree of ambiguity of the court opinions. If the opinion is clear, written in a nontechnical manner, and the result of a substantial majority of judges on a multimember court, the message transmitters are less likely to distort what the court meant. Despite the judges' efforts to clarify their decision, most of the ultimate receivers of the decisional message rely upon others for translation. Few of the journalists covering courts have had legal training. Lawyers and law professors often function, not only for the public but also for professionals, as the expert transmitters of court messages. Radio, TV, newspapers, and popular magazines are the means by which most of the public hears about court rulings. Distortion of the message is possible because of the inadequate time or space the media are willing to give to court decisions, and because of the oversimplification and sensationalism often present in the mass media.

Law reports, reviews, digests, bulletins, and subsequent legal arguments and briefs submitted to courts constitute the means of communicating decisions among the professionals in the legal system. But it may not be the lawyers and judges who most need immediate access to undistorted information. After the *Miranda* decision, 384 U.S. 436 (1966), in which it was decided that the accused must be informed of his rights, the degree of compliance to the policy may well have been in direct proportion to the arresting officer's understanding of the specific requirements of the decision. His attitude toward the decision might depend on whether he was given the requirements of the decision initially by his immediate superior, by a defendant's lawyer, or through reading it in the newspaper.

The nature of a court decision's impact may be dictated by the character of the opinion of the general public and of several elites or opinion leaders.[7] If the public remains split into many diverse groups with competing interests, a court decision can often achieve more compliance than when some issue unifies diverse groups. For example, in the early fifties and sixties, the Supreme Court came under attack for its alleged pro-Communist decisions. Segregationists, rural groups, big business, FBI, states' rightists, law enforcement officers, and church groups all agreed on only the one issue—the threat of communism—and centered their attacks on that issue. They may have hoped that their attacks would lead to a general relaxation of compliance, benefiting their particular interests.

The reaction of opinion leaders is, of course, crucial to the impact of a decision. Reverend Billy Graham's immediate reaction to the Court's prayer and Bible-reading decisions contributed to problems of compliance. At presidential press conferences, questions are often directed toward the President's attitude regarding Court decisions, which, in turn, will influence general public opinion. Supportive or critical statements from the political elite set the general tone of the public response, having consequences, often grave, for the outcome of a decision or a series of decisions. As we have seen, pressure groups and political parties have their influence on the outcome of a decision. Statements of their leaders influence the group and party membership and the vote in elections. The law-and-order issue of

[7] E.g., Dolbeare and Hammond, *The School Prayer Decisions.*

past elections is clearly a group and party response to Supreme Court decisions.

The more limited the geographical scope of a court decision, the less will be the resistance in a national sense but the greater the non-compliance in that particular area. The *Brown* decision, it could be argued, succeeded, however slowly, to desegregate the South simply because it was limited to that area. Had the Court also required desegregation in those areas of the North where *de facto* separation existed (and exists) because of the residential patterns, compliance would have been much more difficult. At the same time, because the decision did not deal with the North, the southern states expressed concern over the lack of fair and equal treatment. For example, the 1970 debates in the Congress on the extension of the 1965 Voting Rights Act were exactly in terms of whether the act should be extended to cover the North as well as the South.

The structure of the national or local economy also influences impact. As Wasby points out: "Certainly the large impersonal organization and a large, computer-run economy appear to decrease an individual's freedoms in some respects, and technology has made it easier for some to invade the privacy of others." [8] Compliance with wiretapping decisions of the Court may be high simply because more sophisticated "bugging" techniques are available. Also, the impact of decisions by a court on whether a large local industry has met the environmental requirements of antipollution legislation may vary according to the degree to which the locale is reliant on that industry.

Decisions that are announced during a crisis may have an immediate impact and change the direction of compliance. If the decision pertains to the crisis, compliance may vary; or if an otherwise controversial decision is handed down when the attention of the public elites and government is directed toward a crisis elsewhere, its impact may be postponed if not ignored. The Supreme Court's refusal to sustain an injunction enjoining the publication of the "Pentagon Papers" by the *Washington Post* and *New York Times,* in 1971, was interjected into a crisis situation. The reaction was that the decision struck a great blow for freedom of the press. But after the crisis waned, clearer heads began to realize that the decision may well have provided opportunities for more government controls of the

[8] Wasby, p. 49.

press than prior to the crisis. Civil rights and peace riots as crisis situations may have changed the attitudes of many police regarding compliance with the series of decisions dealing with the rights of the accused.

Wasby states: "Much of the impact of Supreme Court decisions, particularly with respect to cases involving civil rights and civil liberties, takes place in the local community." [9] The belief system, degree of homogeneity, and size of dominant interests within the community bear directly on the reaction of that community to decisions. The school prayer and Bible decisions had very little impact on communities with diverse religions; but in those communities dominated by one religion in which religious practices in schools were quite common, compliance became a serious question. At an individual level, as Wasby points out, a person's perceptions, expectations, and general value orientation have influence on his reactions to court decisions. [10]

The impact may vary with the nature and timing of follow-up efforts. A decision which is quickly backed up by legislation, providing rewards and punishments, will lead to more compliance than if follow-up is delayed. The Court itself may follow up earlier decisions with a ruling explaining standards to be applied and describing situations warranting the application of certain standards. The problems of follow-up were important in the Supreme Court's recent decisions relating to public support at that point where government becomes "excessively entangled" in church concerns. Supplementing the salaries of teachers in parochial schools would require constant administrative checks to assure there was no support for religious training in those schools. The task, according to the Court majority, would be too great, thus barring this kind of support; follow-up by government would involve excessive entanglement. [11]

Also, if those responsible for follow-up are members of the community, compliance is more likely than if the check on compliance comes from the outside. For example, it could be argued that when the Supreme Court relied on the local district courts to supervise desegregation and reapportionment, the Court was motivated by what it saw as a problem of compliance in many communities.

[9] *Ibid.*, p. 53.
[10] *Ibid.*, p. 55.
[11] *Lemon* v. *Kurtzman*, 403 U.S. 602 and companion cases (1971).

DEPENDENT VARIABLES

The dependent variables of impact usually fall within a compliance or noncompliance framework. However, the degree of compliance may not be the only impact we wish to explain in this area. Many unintended consequences may develop quite apart from compliance. For example, to what degree can we attribute the change of certain social attitudes to Supreme Court decisions? A law-abiding citizen can disagree with a court decision and still comply, or possibly he may comply because he has been "convinced" by the Court's justifications through his own study, or by his response to the media and opinion leaders. The degree of compliance in both cases is equal, but obedience because of the authority of a court and because of agreement with the Court are two different things. James P. Levine suggests three types of outcomes from Supreme Court decisions which include more than just degree of compliance and are based upon their "causal distance" from the Court.

Dependent Variables [12]

Legal Impact on Lower Courts

Political Impact on Congress, President, State and Local Governments

Social Impact on Behavior, Allocation of Costs and Benefits, Court's Legitimacy and Prestige, Second-Order Behavior, and Feedback

Lower courts are closest to the Supreme Court in terms of causal distance. They are first to feel the impact as well as being the agencies most susceptible to direct control by the high court. A court of last resort often issues specific orders and directives to lower courts having, obviously, a direct impact on those judges at the lower levels. A high court can simply reverse or affirm a lower-court decision. Not uncommonly, the cases are remanded to the lower court for "further proceedings not inconsistent with this opinion." Specific cases which constitute precedents may be cited by the high court

[12] Levine, "Methodological Concerns," p. 586.

as a guide to the lower court in the remand. Decisions may be reversed in part and affirmed in part, and remanded to the lower courts for further proceedings. More specific directives may accompany a decision ordering what is to be done with a particular litigant, allocating court costs, and posing questions which the lower court must answer in the rehearings. The courts of last resort establish the precedents to be followed by lower courts. Although the degree of observance of precedent by lower courts varies, this "hierarchical control" has an impact on the behavior of lower-court judges. Precedent must still be given prime consideration by judges.

However, the lower courts are not helpless should political and social factors require alteration in the higher court's rulings. The lower courts make findings of fact which largely limit the scope of the appellate court's review. Lower courts can distinguish cases to avoid precedent since identical facts in two cases are virtually impossible. Manipulating a high-court opinion relegating the holding to *dictum* and elevating irrelevant reasons to *ratio decidendi* is not an uncommon tactic of lower courts if they wish to avoid the thrust of a particular precedent. Reapportionment and desegregation cases are examples. State court judges may tie their decision to state law and thus isolate themselves from the supervision and review of the Supreme Court.[13] Explanations for the use of these tactical alternatives would be a goal of impact studies.

Levine suggests that the next groups experiencing impact are the various political agencies of government. Presidents, congressmen, senators, administrators, local school boards, and state officials have felt the impact of Supreme Court decisions and their actions can thus be seen as expressions of decisional consequences. Constitutions may be amended; laws written and changed; elections, appointments, or legislative votes won or lost as a result of reactions by political leaders to decisions of courts. A President returns a steel mill to private ownership; an ex-congressman is granted his back salary; a National Presidential Nominating Convention determines applications of its own rules; a school superintendent fashions desegregation plans; or the Atomic Energy Commission ignites a nuclear device—

[13] James P. Levine and Theodore Becker, "Toward and Beyond a Theory of Supreme Court Impact," *American Behavioral Scientist*, XIII (March–April, 1970), 562.

all of these are forms of behavior resulting from court decisions. Clearly, political impact is an important dependent variable.

Social consequences "are the broadest and most diffuse of all effects, but in the final analysis, they are the most important." [14] To what degree does the Supreme Court change the moral character of the South or the North through its decisions based upon the "due process" or "equal protection" clauses of the Fourteenth Amendment? One of the major functions of the law, according to Harold J. Berman, is to teach "right behavior." [15] As courts apply, interpret, and make the law, how effective have they been in changing behavior?

The economic costs and benefits flowing from Supreme Court decisions are not altogether understood. As yet no impact studies have centered on this question. Antitrust, taxation, welfare, school funding, and reapportionment decisions have their economic consequences. Variations in costs and benefits must result from these decisions over a long run. More attention must therefore be reserved to economic consequences.

Among the values that are allocated in society are those that involve no tangible benefit or cost but have a psychological dimension. Courts allocate "symbols."

> In this secular age, political symbols are fast replacing religion as both the opiate and intoxicant of the masses, and it may well be that the symbolic outcomes of Supreme Court decisions are an important input into other policy-making processes. Since men do *not* live by bread alone, the blessings, damnations, and graces which they receive from the preachers on the bench may be significant in determining how they ultimately feel, think, and act as political animals.[16]

The legitimacy and prestige of the Supreme Court, for example, is placed often on the side of minorities, poor, and persecuted. Quite apart from the immediate benefits to those "winners" in litigation, their stature and honor increases, both in their minds and in the minds of those outside their classifications. To be "right" is an im-

[14] *Ibid.*, p. 586.
[15] Harold J. Berman, *The Nature and Functions of Law* (Brooklyn: The Foundation Press, 1958), p. 37.
[16] Levine, "Methodological Concerns" (n. 4 above), p. 587.

portant value. The courts allocate this intangible value with varied consequences.

Many of the effects of court decisions are unintended, unforeseen, and far removed from the subject of the original litigation. Some have argued that a major impact of the Warren Court's rulings on the rights of the accused has been an increase in the crime rate. Others contend that the liberalization by the Court of laws regulating pornographic materials has led to more antisocial behavior. More must be known about the second-order consequences of court decisions.

Finally, to what degree are judges aware of the impact of their decisions? The nature, form, and intensity of feedback for the impact approach is similar to the feedback discussed in Chapter Six, on systems models. But impact scholars have pointed out that we must not only know about how judges react to their prior decisions, but we must know about the relationship of the variance in impact to the kinds of feedback (e.g., political as opposed to social), the forms feedback take (new litigation as opposed to new appointments to the bench), and the intensity of feedback (highly critical vs. mixed responses of elites).

Both time and space are important to an understanding of impact. The variables all work within these two dimensions so that they become general boundary variables for the entire impact model described above. Levine's typology of impact variables is clearly based upon what he calls the "causal distance" of the impact from the court. The space variable refers to the degree of direct control a court has over the group, agency, or individual which has been affected by the impact. The time variable pertains, of course, to the time span between when the court decides and when the impact is felt, and when the feedback, if any, is generated.

CRITIQUE

Perhaps the most telling criticism of the impact approach (although it is more a comment on the state of the scholarship in this area than on the possible inadequacies of the approach) is well expressed by Wasby: "If we had a more well-developed theory of impact, perhaps we could prescribe more specifically the exact steps to be taken to complete our task. Perhaps we have made more progress toward our real goal than we realize, but it seems, at least from where we now stand, that we have a long way to go and are not able to prescribe specific directions for our researchers."[17]

The high-court myth is still prevalent among impact scholars. The Supreme Court has remained the center of their concern, with only a few references to lower courts and none to trial courts. Some research of the impact *on* lower courts exists but none concerning the impact *of* lower-court decisions on society.

With extremely rare exceptions, all of the case studies on impact have been after the fact. After the Supreme Court has ruled on school prayers and Bible reading, for example, the student of impact attempts to measure how the decision has influenced behavior. Not only do case studies lack the before-and-after data, they lack other controls necessary for meaningful comparisons. If our concern, for example, is the impact of obscenity rulings on high school literature classes, we must take the same class before *A Book Named "John Cleland's Memoirs of a Woman of Pleasure"* v. *Massachusetts*, 383 U.S. 413 (1966) and compare it to the same class after the decision; or we should look at two classes after the decision that are identical in all respects except the one variable we wish to investigate. We could look at analogous classes in a Catholic school and in a public school in terms of attitudes, curriculum, texts, etc., and see if any variance was due to religion. But controlling for several variables is not ordinarily the method of case studies.

If impact studies are to be of value to policy makers, more effort must be made to measure the degree and nature of court impact as contrasted with legislative or executive impact. Comparative studies at this level are essential but, as yet, missing.[18] Also, cross-national comparisons are lacking. For example, in order to understand adequately the consequences of the federal-state structure of our court system, we need some comparisons with unitary countries.

Impact studies have, thus far, ignored comparisons between the responses of parties and nonparties to the dispute. Some school districts which were not parties to litigation desegregated soon after the *Brown* case but one of the litigants delayed action for years. Prince Edward County, Virginia, one of the original plaintiffs, abolished all

[17] Wasby, p. 266.
[18] An exception is C.T. Dienes, "Judges, Legislators, and Social Change," *American Behavioral Scientist*, XIII (March–April, 1970), 511.

public schools to avoid compliance. After ten years, the Supreme Court finally ruled such action as unconstitutional in *Griffin* v. *County School Board of Prince Edward County,* 337 U.S. 218 (1964).

Most of the impact studies have concentrated upon dramatic issues which have led to a great deal of noncompliance. Little attention has been paid to the responses to antitrust, taxation, regulation of industry, and environmental cases. And if the emphasis on noncompliance continues, we may discover what causes defiance to court decisions but not know what causes obedience. It is likely that compliance and noncompliance are not the two sides of one coin. Finally, no attention has been paid to the consequences of memorandum decisions. Clearly, the tasks facing the impact scholars are fascinating and numerous. The problem seems not to be the lack of adequate models but, rather, the limited application of those models.

IMPACT STUDIES

The Supreme Court, or for that matter any high court, begins the impact process with announcement of its decision. The consequences of the decision, as we have seen, are both immediate and remote. The immediate impact is felt by the principal litigants, usually through the hierarchy of the court system. Lower courts are generally given the responsibility for administering the directives of the appellate court. The political and, finally, the social consequences are not immediately evident, although sharp reactions from opinion leaders may have long-range political and social consequences. The following review of impact materials is organized around this idea of causal distance, in which the responses of lower courts are in time and space most directly related to a high court's decision, followed by agencies further removed from the courts (see discussion of "causal distance" in preceding section).

LEGAL IMPACT

The formal channels through which a high-court decision is transmitted to the lower courts do allow for some distortion and variance in impact. For example, in the *McCollum* case, 333 U.S. 203 (1948), the Supreme Court overruled the Illinois State Supreme Court by declaring released-time religious practices in public schools to be in violation of the Constitution. The case was remanded to the Illinois high court for further proceedings "not inconsistent with the opinion." The state court then transmitted to the court of original jurisdiction, the Sixth Circuit Court of Champaign County, the full text of the Supreme Court's opinion along with the following order:

> It is Hereby Ordered by this Court that the judgment of the Circuit Court of Champaign County, Illinois be reversed and the cause remanded to said circuit court for proceedings not inconsistent with the opinion of the Supreme Court of the United States, a copy of which opinion is annexed hereto and transmitted herewith.
> [The circuit court then issued a writ of *mandamus* ordering the school board to] immediately adopt and enforce rules and regulations prohibiting all instruction in and teaching of religious education in the manner heretofore conducted by said School District . . . ; and . . . to prohibit within said original School District . . . the use of the State's public school machinery to help enroll pupils in the several religious classes of sectarian groups.[19]

Finally, the school board issued directives to superintendents, who in turn informed their teachers. The opportunity therefore for distorting the original message through the many steps of the formal channels is great.

The response of many lower courts to the *Brown* decision illustrates further the direct control the Supreme Court has over lower courts. In 1956, the South Carolina Supreme Court reluctantly followed the *Brown* precedent and felt compelled to record its dissatisfaction:

> Our deep conviction is that the interpretation now placed on the Fourteenth Amendment, in relation to the right of a state to determine whether children of different races are to be taught in the same or separate public schools, cannot be reconciled with the intent of the framers or ratifiers of the Fourteenth Amendment, the actions of Congress of the United States and of the state legislatures, or the long and consistent judicial interpretation of the Fourteenth Amendment. . . . In the interpretation of the Constitution of the United States, the Supreme Court of the United States is final arbiter. . . . Recognizing

[19] The description of the formal channels involved in the *McCollum* case is found in Johnson, *Dynamics of Compliance* (n. 1 above), pp. 60–61.

fully that its decision is authoritative in this jurisdiction, any provision of the Constitution or statutes of North Carolina in conflict therewith must be deemed invalid.[20]

But lower-court responses are not always consistent with appellate court decisions. Richard Johnson has said that the "formal legal channels through which decisions are transmitted are not necessarily neutral ones which would ensure the application of a rule substantially similar to that enunciated by the Supreme Court." [21]

Lower-court judges can rule according to their perceptions of the direction a series of high-court cases may be going. The lower-court judge may ask not, as is often the question at the Supreme Court level, "What was the intent of the framers?" but "What would be the Supreme Court's view of the intent of the framers?" Of course, as Murphy points out, "This kind of speculation comes close to giving oneself a blank check." [22]

A lower-court judge may follow the trend he perceives as developing in higher-court rulings or he may defy precedent in anticipation of the higher court following suit. Judge John J. Parker anticipated that the Supreme Court would overrule its earlier flag salute case (*Minersville School District* v. *Gobitis*, 310 U.S. 586 [1940]) and held school flag salute requirements invalid when a question of religion is involved. His prophecy proved correct although other lower-court judges have practiced second guessing and found themselves overruled.

Forms of defiance to high-court rulings is not uncommon in cases involving sensitive issues. The "special circumstances rule" of *Betts* v. *Brady*, 316 U.S. 455 (1942), requiring court-appointed counsel, when applied by state appellate courts, resulted in only eleven of 139 defendants receiving right to counsel in noncapital cases. In Pennsylvania, an eighteen-year-old boy with an IQ of fifty-nine was denied counsel although clearly the case fell within the special circumstances rule. Levine and Becker commented: "Since *Betts* v. *Brady* was a landmark case, this smacks of outright defiance of the Supreme Court." [23]

[20] *Constantian* v. *Anson County*, 244 N.C. 228–9 (1956).
[21] Johnson, *Dynamics of Compliance*, pp. 62–63.
[22] Walter F. Murphy, "Lower Court Checks on Supreme Court Power," *The American Political Science Review*, LIII (December, 1959), 1026.
[23] Levine and Becker, "Toward and Beyond a Theory," p. 562.

In no area of recent Supreme Court litigation have the lower courts displayed greater defiance or response variance than in the area of school desegregation. The Supreme Court is somewhat responsible for creating the opportunity for impact variance in this area through its unwillingness or inability to set strict standards and deadlines and through its granting to the lower district courts the responsibility of supervising school desegregation. Jack Peltason has documented the slow and painful progress (or lack of progress) toward desegregation in the South. Even though the law was clear and the authority available,

> . . . six years of litigation produced negligible results. There were exceptions, but by and large federal judges applied the law adversely to the claims of Negroes. Some judges were so opposed to integration that they believed the safety of the nation depended upon their minimizing the scope of the Supreme Court's decisions. Others were affected by the "go slow" philosophy cultivated by President Eisenhower and the segregationists.[24]

To balance the ledger, Peltason points out that the lower-court judges were victims of their social and political environment, and to defy community mores was extremely costly. Judge J. Waties Waring, after he dissented in a case that continued segregation, received threats on his life, and he and his family suffered slander and abuse. As a consequence, he felt compelled to retire from the bench to move to the North. Very few judges would wish to submit themselves to such abuse. What little integration was achieved during the first six years following the 1954 *Brown* decision, however, was due directly to lower-court judges. Certainly, the state legislatures, governors, Congress, and the President did little to assist.

The impact on lower federal judges of the Supreme Court's decisions in reapportionment is analogous to the involvement of lower courts in desegregation. Again, guidelines from the Supreme Court were not altogether clear, making lower-court supervision of reapportionment difficult. The mathematical variations of the "one man-one vote" standard were wide. Robert Dixon commented that between 1964 and 1966, "A truly surprising range of mathematical

---

[24] Jack W. Peltason, *Fifty-Eight Lonely Men: Southern Federal Judges and School Desegregation* (New York: Harcourt, Brace and World, 1961), p. 93.

variation developed in judicially ordered or judicially approved plans. . . ."[25]

Evasion of high-court rulings by state judges is not uncommon. The *Harvard Law Review* studied 175 cases that had been remanded to state courts from 1941 through 1951 and discovered that in "slightly less than half [of those cases involving further litigation] the party successful in the Supreme Court was unsuccessful in the state courts following remand."[26] Some, but not all, of the evasive actions were regarded by the *Review* as legally questionable. According to the article, state courts ought not to reject the Supreme Court's definition of its own jurisdiction and what constitutes a federal quesion. Narrow interpretation of the high-court mandate was considered improper, as was also the practice of a lower court ordering a new trial in order to sustain the original decision on some theory not in the record. Nonetheless, state courts were considered to be acting quite appropriately if a change of the Supreme Court's ruling was based on nonfederal grounds. Evasion was acceptable also when the state court found some new facts in the remanded trial. To avoid the issue of what are proper and improper evasion tactics, some state attorneys have purposefully kept any mention of a federal constitutional claim out of their arguments before state courts. To appeal such a case beyond the state supreme court becomes, then, extremely difficult.[27]

Obviously, the impact of Supreme Court decisions on lower federal and state courts varies. The impact model is designed not only to compile data on variance, but also to relate the independent and intervening variables to the diverse inferior court responses. Peltason's study of the implementation problems of the *Brown* decision documents the strong pressures on lower federal courts to vary from the Supreme Court mandate. The ambiguity of the second *Brown* case allowed much diversity, especially in terms of the amount of

[25] Robert G. Dixon, Jr., *Democratic Representation: Reapportionment in Law and Politics* (New York: Oxford University Press, 1968), p. 442.

[26] Note, "Evasion of Supreme Court Mandates in Cases Remanded to State Courts Since 1941," *Harvard Law Review*, LXVIII (May, 1954), 1251. See also Note, "State Court Evasion of United States Supreme Court Mandates," *Yale Law Journal*, XXXVI (March, 1947), 574.

[27] W.P. Armstrong, "The Increasing Importance of State Supreme Courts," *American Bar Association Journal*, XXVIII (January, 1942), 3; reprinted in J. Schmidhauser, ed., *Constitutional Law in the Political Process* (Chicago: Rand McNally, 1963), p. 101.

time granted to local school boards for compliance. The political and social characteristics of the areas concerned also explains the responses of low-court judges. However, the prosegregation attitudes of district judges were a factor which might have been balanced somewhat by the judges' commitment to precedent. Peltason felt, nevertheless, that the ambiguity of the decision allowed the pressures of the southern culture to play a great role in lower-court responses.

> What the district judges need—and what most of them want—is not responsibility for making choices, but rigid mandates that compel them to act. The Supreme Court appears to have made a serious mistake when it delegated so much discretion to the district courts. It was, and is, politically unrealistic to think that a southern judge could, or would, cut through the Supreme Court's vague instructions to initiate action hostile to segregation.[28]

Kenneth Vines also has emphasized the importance of social and political influences as explanations for lower-court responses. The backgrounds of federal district judges who tended to resist integration rulings identify them more closely with southern culture than the backgrounds of more moderate or liberal judges. The segregationist judges held more state political offices prior to selection to the bench than the integrationist judges, who tended to be recruited from federal jobs. The segregationists' religion and political party affiliations paralleled southern culture to a significant degree. At least in race-relations cases in the South, environmental variables intervene between high-court rulings and inferior-court responses, and supply explanations for legal impact.[29]

POLITICAL IMPACT

The alternatives available to Congress to circumvent or change specific court decisions are many. The means to support or attack the Supreme Court (and other courts) as an institution are also by no

---

[28] Peltason, p. 245. It was not until 1969 that the Supreme Court dropped its "with all deliberate speed" formula and ordered desegregation in public schools "at once." *Alexander* v. *Holmes County Board of Education*, 396 U.S. 19 (1969).

[29] Kenneth Vines, "Federal District Judges and Race Relations Cases in the South," *Journal of Politics*, XXVI (May, 1964), 357.

means lacking. Decisions become susceptible to statutory changes and to constitutional amendments. The Court itself can be punished by withholding funds, threatening impeachment, influencing appointments, and changing staffing and organization.

Specific decisions have frequently been altered by Congress. For example, portal-to-portal pay provisions were excluded from legislation even though the Supreme Court had ruled that they should be included. State fair-trade laws were revitalized after the Court had made them useless. Congress excluded some personnel from coverage by the Administrative Procedures Act after the Court said they should be included. Congress gave the states the offshore oil rights after the Court had ruled the undersea land was under national control. Some workers were denied certain rights under the Fair Labor Standards Act after the justices had ruled otherwise.[30] From 1944 to 1957, Congress "reversed" Supreme Court decisions at least nineteen times. From 1957 through 1962, Congress considered forty-four reversal proposals to twenty-seven decisions. Forty of them achieved passage.[31] Since the bulk of the high court's work involves statutory interpretation, the rulings of the justices are susceptible to these congressional "reversals."

Although amending the Constitution is a laborious process, senators and representatives introduce proposals to change the Constitution with repeated abandon. In recent times, the Court's reapportionment, desegregation, and prayer and Bible-reading cases have evoked considerable amendment response from Congress. Eighty-five amendments were introduced in one single session of Congress to allow for prayers in public schools. One-hundred and sixty-four were introduced between 1963 and 1964, designed to reverse the *Engel*, 370 U.S. 421 (1962), and *Schempp*, 374 U.S. 203 (1963), decisions.[32] The Talmadge Amendment and the several Dirksen Amendments

[30] Jack W. Peltason, *Federal Courts in the Political Process* (New York: Random House, 1955), pp. 59–60.

[31] Harry Stumpf, "The Political Efficacy of Judicial Symbolism," *Western Political Quarterly*, XIX (June, 1966), 1. See also Note, "Congressional Reversals of Supreme Court Decisions, 1945–1957," *Harvard Law Review*, LXXI (May, 1958), 1324.

[32] W.M. Beaney and E.N. Beiser, "Prayer and Politics: The Impact of *Engel* and *Schempp* on the Political Process," *Journal of Politics*, XIII (August, 1964), 473; reprinted in Becker, *The Impact of Supreme Court Decisions* (n. 1 above), p. 20. In these two cases the Supreme Court declared prayers and Bible reading in public schools in violation of the First Amendment.

of the sixties were typical responses to *Brown* and *Baker,* 369 U.S. 186 (1962).

The vast majority of the proposed amendments were given little consideration. However, some of the amendment efforts persisted. Prayers and Bible reading was still a serious political issue in 1972. Governor George C. Wallace of Alabama attempted, without success, to add a plank in the National Democratic Party Platform that would call for a constitutional amendment to allow prayers in public schools. By 1969, the Dirksen Amendment, failing in Congress, had received all but one of the required resolutions from state legislatures calling for a constitutional convention to "correct" the reapportionment decisions. Even though Congress has sometimes approved a proposal, few ultimately become part of the Constitution. The Eleventh, Thirteenth, Sixteenth, and Twenty-Sixth Amendments have been the only additions to the Constitution in which Congress and the states joined to overrule the Supreme Court.

Studies directed toward explanations for successes and failures of congressional responses to Court rulings within the framework of the impact model have been very limited. Harry Stumpf investigated the importance of the prestige of the Supreme Court as a form of protection from congressional intervention. According to his findings, legislative bills designed to change specific decisions of the Supreme Court did not seem to succeed or fail because of the presence or absence of arguments that evoked the sacrosanctity of the Court. The prestige of the Court may protect the justices from general anti-Court legislation, but little or no variance in congressional response was evident in specific legislation.[33]

Stumpf's findings were substantiated by Schmidhauser and Berg. They found that Congress tended to vote more for the Supreme Court when it was under attack as an institution than when one of its cases was being "corrected" through legislation. The prestige of the Court was not an important variable in the congressional reactions, however. Lawyers, who through the professional socialization process should have a greater respect for the Court, failed to vote accordingly. When compared with nonlawyers in Congress, they, in some cases, were even more critical of the justices. Further, if the reverence for the high court was important, senators and representa-

[33] Stumpf, "Political Efficacy," p. 303.

tives should vote differently in anti-Court issues than in other legislation not relating to the courts; they do not. Party affiliation, ideology,
and region were, for Schmidhauser and Berg, more important in explaining the voting behavior of senators and representatives than any
reverence for the high court. They suggested that a study of the
reasons for the conservative coalition of Southern Democrats and
Republicans in Congress might help explain much of the Court's
impact on the national legislature.[34]

Beaney and Beiser found that the failure of the Becker Amendment, which was to "correct" the prayer and Bible-reading cases,
was, to a significant degree, due to the public hearings held by
Representative Emanuel Cellar's House Judiciary Committee. Not
only did those hearings influence waivering legislators, but they also
changed attitudes of opinion elites.[35]

During the fifties, the Supreme Court placed itself in direct conflict with Congress with respect to its national security rulings. On
June 17, 1957—"Red Monday"—the Supreme Court announced four
decisions that were to set off Congressional reactions comparable to
major Court-curbing efforts of the past. *Yates* v. *U.S.*, 354 U.S. 298
(1957); *Sweezy* v. *New Hampshire*, 354 U.S. 234 (1957); *Service* v.
Dulles, 354 U.S. 363 (1957); and *Watkins* v. *U.S.*, 354 U.S. 178
(1957), were all viewed by many members of Congress as pro-
Communist decisions which would threaten the internal security of
the United States. Congressional reactions in this case were aimed
at changing the specific decisions as well as at the Supreme Court
as an institution. Segregationists, law enforcement officers, members
of the legal community, states rightists, business, and radical right
groups backed the anti-Court legislators' proposals for constitutional
amendments, corrective legislation, and impeachment proceedings.[36]

[34] John Schmidhauser and Larry L. Berg, *The Supreme Court and Congress:
Conflict and Interaction, 1945–1968* (New York: The Free Press, 1972), pp.
183–84.

[35] Beaney and Beiser, "Prayer and Politics," p. 503.

[36] For excellent descriptive accounts of the political impact of the Court's
rulings during this period, consult C. Herman Pritchett, *Congress Versus the
Supreme Court* (Minneapolis: University of Minnesota Press, 1961); and Walter F. Murphy, *Congress and the Court* (Chicago: University of Chicago Press,
1962). The political implications of impeachment are described by Phillip B.
Kurland, "The Appointment and Disappointment of Supreme Court Justices,"
Law and Social Order, MCMLXXII (1972) and Raoul Berger, *Impeachment:
The Constitutional Problem* (Cambridge, Mass.: Harvard University Press,
1973).

Congress succeeded in changing only one minor aspect of the Court's decisions of the period, but the struggle illustrates the influence of several variables of the impact model.

The initial lineup for and against the Court followed conservative-liberal divisions in Congress. This dichotomy overlapped with the Republican-Democrat composition of the national legislature, thus placing party leadership in Congress in a good position to influence the legislative responses. Senate Majority Leader Lyndon Johnson was instrumental in defeating the foes of the Court, although his personal sympathies may not have been entirely with the justices.[37]

Contrary to what Schmidhauser and Berg concluded, C. Herman Pritchett felt that the pro-Court forces were assisted in their arguments by the general prestige of the Supreme Court as an institution: "[The] Court was protected by the respect which is so widely felt for the judicial institution in the United States." [38]

The foes of the Court were not a tightly disciplined core of legislators but a conglomerate of senators and congressmen who, for a variety of reasons, wished to strike back at the high court. For example, many southern senators were motivated by the Court's desegregation rulings more than by its "pro-Communist" rulings. Some senators may not have wished to be allied with segregationists although they may have been genuinely concerned for problems of internal security.

Finally, the Supreme Court itself disarmed many of its critics by responding with the *Barenblatt,* 360 U.S. 109 (1959), and *Uphaus,* 360 U.S. 72 (1959), decisions, in which the thrust of some of the earlier libertarian rulings was blunted. This indicates that the justices clearly are, or are becoming, aware of the political consequences of their decisions and do defend themselves by pulling back from earlier decisions.

Murphy's and Pritchett's reviews of past Court-curbing efforts convinced them that the struggles between Congress and the Court in the late fifties were fairly unique. Nonetheless, some impact patterns have persisted through time. Stuart Nagel studied the history of Court-curbing activities from the beginning of the Republic to

---

[37] See Murphy, *Congress and the Court,* Chapter 9.

[38] Pritchett, p. 19. For an appraisal of lawyer-Congressman responses see J. J. Green et al., "Lawyers in Congress: A New Look at Old Assumptions," *Western Political Quarterly,* XXVI (September, 1973), 440.

1960. During that period, 165 bills were introduced in Congress with the specific purpose of limiting the power of the Supreme Court. (Constitutional amendments, joint resolutions, or bills designed to change specific Court decisions were not included among the 165 bills.) Only nine serious limiting bills of the total passed both houses of Congress, but all were regarded as serious attempts to resolve "politically" the problems the justices had created. Nagel found that the Court had caused most of the curbing attempts through its exercise of judicial review. The subject matter of the issues was also a factor during the periods of intense Court-curbing activities. Federal-state and separation-of-powers issues have generated the most intense anti-Court activities. When the unanimity in Court voting is lowest, the Court's opponents are more likely to introduce legislation to control the Court than when the justices agree.

Nagel discovered that the types of curbing bills introduced generally fall into four categories. About 30 percent were aimed at abolishing or changing the Court's power of judicial review; 29 percent proposed changes in the qualifications for appointment to the high bench, or dealt with increasing or decreasing the size of the Court; and, finally, about 28 percent were designed to change the appellate jurisdiction of the Supreme Court.[39]

As Nagel's study illustrates, Court and congressional conflict are inherent in a government of separate but coequal branches. Separation of powers almost guarantees conflict. The Congress, the President, and the Court will continue to disagree. The issues will change but the struggle will remain.

The Court's conflicts with the President have been rare when compared with the disputes between Congress and the justices. In only fourteen cases, from 1804 until 1957, has the Supreme Court declared presidential orders to be unconstitutional.[40] The powers of the President in foreign affairs and as commander-in-chief have remained untouched by the courts; and the justices have, in fact, greatly enhanced the President's power. Thus, with few exceptions,

[39] Stuart Nagel, "Court-Curbing Periods in American History," *Vanderbilt Law Review*, XVIII (June, 1965), 925; reprinted in Becker (n. 1 above), p. 35.

[40] Glendon A. Schubert, *The Presidency in the Courts* (Minneapolis: University of Minnesota Press, 1957), p. 355. An important exception is the courts' involvement in questions of Presidential immunity and privilege surrounding the "Watergate tapes" case in 1973. See *Nixon* v. *Sirica*, 42 U.S. Law Week 2211 (October 23, 1973).

the impact of the courts on the presidency has been to legitimate presidential actions. Marshall and his Court had its differences with Presidents Jefferson and Jackson.[41] More recently, President Franklin Roosevelt, piqued at the "Nine Old Men" who were thwarting the New Deal programs, proposed expanding the Court beyond the traditional nine members if opponents of his program did not retire. His Court-packing plan failed, but the Supreme Court had already retreated from its earlier decisions, making curbing attempts superfluous.[42] Harry Truman relinquished federal control of steel mills upon order from the Supreme Court in 1952, and thereby avoided a prolonged confrontation.[43] Richard Nixon's conflict with the Supreme Court has been largely fought out in the Senate chambers. Campaigning on a law-and-order issue, Nixon promised the American people he would appoint "strict constructionists" to the high bench who would no longer "coddle the criminal" or "handcuff the police." By 1972, he had succeeded, after two Senate rejections, in appointing four new members to the Supreme Court, who joined with conservative Warren Court holdovers to check, if not change, the liberal trend of the decisions of the sixties.

With the exception of a few notable political struggles, we know precious little about the nature of the impact of court cases on the presidency. Court controls of administrative agencies would be a rich source of empirical studies applying the impact model (see Chapter Seven for studies of the thirties on the courts vs. the President). The reasons for the paucity of Court-President struggles—a paucity not evident in the judicial relations with Congress—flow from the Constitution and form the nature of the subject of many presidential policies. The Constitution grants to both the President and the Supreme Court powers which complement each other. Both are responsible for the "execution and the expounding of the law." The Constitutional Convention succeeded in granting power to the courts and to the President in order to provide a meaningful check on Congress. The "tyranny of the majority" expressed through Congress would thus be balanced by the two other branches of govern-

[41] Donald O. Dewey, *Marshall Versus Jefferson: The Political Background of Marbury v. Madison* (New York: Alfred A. Knopf, 1970).

[42] A.H. Cope and Fred Krinsky, eds., *Franklin D. Roosevelt and the Supreme Court* (Boston: D.C. Heath, 1952).

[43] Alan F. Westin, *The Anatomy of a Constitutional Law Case* (New York: Macmillan, 1958).

ment. Finally, the President has the specific responsibility to appoint Supreme Court justices and he attempts to select those who share his political views. The justices therefore tend to be more sympathetic toward the President than toward Congress. Separation of powers makes conflict between Congress and the Court natural; between the President and the high court, less typical.[44] The relative degree of agreement between the executive and the courts filters down to administrative agencies. The Supreme Court rarely checks, often approves, and most likely ignores what the upper levels of the bureaucracy do.[45] The President is commander-in-chief, chief diplomat, and the voice of the people.[46] Issues with which the President must deal often involve crucial matters in war, foreign, and national affairs. Intervention by the Supreme Court in these subject areas is perceived by most to be quite inappropriate if not dangerous. Conflicts between the President and the Court are therefore rare.

Impact studies of state and local governments have centered on four controversial areas: desegregation, prayer and Bible reading in public schools, police practices, and reapportionment cases. The impact in these four areas has been substantial and compliance has varied from violent resistance to quiet observance. The school boards of local governmental units have felt the impact of the prayer and desegregation cases; the state legislatures "suffered" from the reapportionment rulings; and local police departments were required by the Court to change many of their arresting and investigating practices. Some school boards, legislatures, and police departments changed quickly; others ignored the Supreme Court mandate; and still others defied the Court. Impact studies should provide the "whys" for the variance in compliance.

The struggle over desegregation, the wide variance in compliance, and the alternatives chosen by those who would resist the *Brown*

[44] Robert Scigliano, *The Supreme Court and the Presidency* (New York: The Free Press, 1971). For a discussion of the impact of court decisions on state governors, see James Galen Dickson, Jr., "Decision-making in a Restrictive Constitutional Environment: Impact on the Texas Governor of High Court Decisions and Attorney General Opinions," *The Rocky Mountain Social Science Journal* X (January, 1973), 51.

[45] Martin Shapiro, *The Supreme Court and Administrative Agencies* (New York: The Free Press, 1968).

[46] Clinton Rossiter, *The American Presidency* (New York: Signet Key Books, 1956).

ruling have been ably described in dozens of scholarly works.[47] But what is of greater interest to impact studies are the reasons for the acknowledged disparities in compliance. Although the problems facing each school district were likely different, some general trends are evident. Geography was an important factor. Implied in the term "geography" would be the myriad of historical and cultural variables which distinguish one area from another. The border states, for example, were the first to comply and, for the first few years, were the only states to observe the mandate of the *Brown* decision.[48] Some areas had already moved toward elimination of dual school systems prior to the decision. Consequently, in these areas the impact had little or no effect.

Rural areas resisted desegregation more than some urban areas for economic reasons. Rural areas depended upon cheap black labor, whereas urban areas needed skilled and educated labor. Keeping the blacks out of good white schools in rural areas meant they would be available for menial farm jobs. On the other hand, desegregation was encouraged by some school officials because of the costs of separate-but-equal facilities under the law prior to *Brown*.

The personal ideologies of school board members dictated the degree of compliance in many areas. Most board members accepted the inevitability of mixed schools, but their reluctance to prepare for the inevitable was a factor contributing to many community conflicts. Some school boards waited, submitted unacceptable plans, or asked for delay simply to create a situation which would make mixed schools, in their view, impossible under the circumstances. Whether integration would begin in either the elementary grades or in high school often was dictated by the school board's ideologi-

[47] For the best descriptions of desegregation, consult Albert P. Blaustein and Clarence C. Ferguson, Jr., *Desegregation and the Law: The Meaning and Effect of the School Segregation Cases* (New Brunswick, N.J.: Rutgers University Press, 1957); Robert L. Crain *et al.*, *The Politics of School Desegregation: Comparative Case Studies of Community Structure and Policy-Making* (Chicago: Aldine Publishing Company, 1968); Benjamin Muse, *Ten Years of Prelude: The Story of Integration Since the Supreme Court's 1954 Decision* (New York: Viking Press, 1964); Peltason, *Fifty-Eight Lonely Men* (n. 24 above); and Reed Sarratt, *The Ordeal of Desegregation: The First Decade* (New York: Harper and Row, 1966).

[48] Wasby (n. 1 above), p. 182. This summary of desegregation impact generally follows Wasby's fine review.

cal perception of the evils of mixed schools. Finally, as Robert Crain observed, many of the school boards failed to accept the responsibility for creating conflict in their community. Liberals and conservatives on boards could meet on this common ground: they were unwilling to make the hard decision in the face of community opposition.[49]

Crain has shown that the degree of acquiescence in the *Brown* decisions was correlated with several characteristics of local school boards. A cohesive board tended to work toward compliance more than a board which could not present a united front to the public. Dissenters became leaders for the opposition. The more liberals on the board, the more likely it was that compliance would result. And, finally, the appointed school boards tended to accept the inevitability of integration more readily than elected members.[50]

Education officials were also at the center of the prayer and Bible-reading controversies prompted by the Supreme Court. Richard Johnson attributed the compliance of the two communities he studied to the decision of the superintendent of schools. Because of his agreement with the Supreme Court ruling and because of his expertise, the school head was able to discontinue religious practices without much conflict. The school board, the local elites, and the parents had hired the superintendent because of his expertise in education. They, then, did not intervene when the superintendent ordered the schools to comply with the law simply because of the deference granted him as an expert in educational matters. The superintendent was also separated from the social life of the community, and, thus, was not a "victim" of its values and attitudes.[51]

Dolbeare and Hammond's study of five communities that did not comply with the prayer decision indicated that the superintendent also played a crucial role. Their lack of observance of the mandate of the Court was due to (1) commitment to "voluntarism" in educational matters and to (2) a feeling that the costs of complying would be too great in terms of their educational goals in other areas. All of the superintendents and all but a few members of the school boards did not appear to criticize or disagree strongly with the Supreme Court's decisions. They did, however, appear to interpret, or wish to

[49] Crain, Chapter 12.
[50] *Ibid.*, p. 176.
[51] Johnson (n. 1 above), pp. 144–45.

interpret, the rulings to mean that only coerced religious practices were outlawed. As long as prayers and Bible readings were strictly voluntary, they had a rationale for continuing the practices. A rationale was needed, for they felt that compliance might create conflicts that could lead to opposition to their building, athletic, and curricular programs. The risk was not worth taking.[52]

Robert Birkby found in his study of Tennessee school districts little correlation between responses of local school boards to the religious-practices cases, degree of urbanization and socioeconomic backgrounds of the board members, and degree of religious pluralism. The complying districts in his study admitted to no overt pressures from the community for dropping religious practices in public schools. Birkby postulated that the explanation for the differences between complying and noncomplying school boards may lie in a generally favorable (or at least not unfavorable) attitude of the public toward the Supreme Court as an institution and that those districts that did change their policy did so only in form—changing procedures but in practice allowing voluntary Bible reading in classes.[53]

The impact of the prayer and Bible-reading decisions on the individual teachers led to wide variance in the degree of compliance. Many school districts changed their official policy (a procedural change) to allow teachers to determine whether religious practices should be continued on a voluntary basis. H. Frank Way, Jr., surveyed over 1,700 school teachers throughout the nation in order to isolate reasons for compliance-noncompliance at the classroom level. The average teacher did feel the impact of the high court's decisions. Prior to the *Engel* and *Schempp* rulings, 60 percent of the classrooms had devotional practices. By 1965, only 28 percent continued religious exercise. Way found that church attendance was an important variable in noncompliance. Those teachers who attended church fairly regularly tended to continue the religious exercises. Roman Catholic and Jewish teachers accepted, to a greater degree than Protestants, the ban on classroom religious exercises. Age and experience of the teacher and the size of city in which the school

[52] Dolbeare and Hammond (n. 1 above), p. 86.
[53] Robert H. Birkby, "The Supreme Court and the Bible Belt: Tennessee Reaction to the *Schempp* Decision," *Midwest Journal of Political Science*, X (August, 1966), 304.

was located had some impact on compliance. Older experienced teachers in rural areas tended to ignore the ban. As we would expect, geography (culture) was extremely important. The South and, to a lesser degree, New England displayed the greatest degree of non-compliance. Way discovered that when all the variables are considered together, region becomes the most telling factor "explaining" noncompliance. He postulates, but was unable to isolate, the uniqueness of the southern culture as an explanatory variable for variance in classroom religious practices after *Engel* and *Schempp*.[54]

The impact of the *Baker* and *Reynolds* v. *Sims*, 377 U.S. 533 (1964), reapportionment cases was felt directly by state legislators and political party officials. The prime responsibility for applying the one man-one vote principle fell exactly upon the representative bodies of the states. Either the legislatures changed, or the courts would accomplish the task for them. Some of the variance in responses by state legislatures can be attributed to the lack of specific standards in the Court decisions. When lower courts continued to push for compliance, the legislators responded. This supervision of reapportionment by lower courts created a problem contributing to variance in compliance: lower courts failed to share their particular experiences with one another, resulting in a "patchwork" of standards.

Wasby summarized several long-range outcomes of the reapportionment cases. Legislatures have little time left for other crucial state issues after they have repeatedly, if not continually, struggled through with reapportionment. The continued shifting of representative district boundaries has led to a greater number of candidates seeking office. A closer tie between the single legislator and his constituency should result. Crass examples of gerrymandering to favor one party may also diminish, although the politics of reapportionment still centers on the perceived benefits each party will receive. However, the districts must now be nearly equal in population, allowing less of an opportunity for bizarre forms of gerrymandering. Blacks have benefited, with more of them achieving election to state offices. The suburbs, rather than the central cities, have increased their political power to a greater degree. Finally, a shift in policies

[54] H. Frank Way, Jr., "Survey Research on Judicial Decisions: The Prayer and Bible Reading Cases," *Western Political Quarterly*, XXI (June, 1968), 189.

emanating from the state legislatures has not happened to the degree that advocates of reapportionment had hoped. But, policy studies thus far are inconclusive: "While one certainly can find states where reapportionment has brought new faces in the legislature, new leadership, and a better 'break' for the cities in terms of policies, one cannot as yet predict what the general pattern of impact with respect to policy will be, because of our lack of before-and-after studies, forcing us to make inferences from other data. . . ." [55]

The consequences of the *Baker* and *Sims* decisions were expected to be revolutionary. The forecasts of the impact on political parties prophesied substantial changes. An urban-nationally based political party system would, according to Martin Landau, ultimately replace the now rural-locally dominated party system; federalism might become a thing of the past to be replaced by a system more attuned to the demands of a modern era.[56] We have some indications of change but more studies are needed. Robert Dixon describes the changing "political map," but no revolutionary alterations in the political system have yet transpired.

> In the South the sharp increase in urban-suburban seats has brought a better educated, more vigorous breed of politician onto the scene, and in some states has planted the seeds of a two-party system. In the North sharp Republican losses in rural areas have been at least partially compensated by gains in the suburbs. The reapportionment upheaval, by throwing many incumbents together in revised districts has allowed both parties in some states to clean out some deadwood. In most populous states the primary beneficiaries . . . have been suburbs not central cities. In many states . . . a new brand of coalition politics among three groups, no one of which can dominate the legislature—central city, suburbs, rural-small town [has resulted].[57]

Certainly, the increased activity in legislative reapportionment stimulated by the 1970 census presents an opportunity for impact scholars to test the development of past trends and to detect the possible revolutionary consequences.

[55] Wasby (n. 1 above), p. 126.
[56] Martin Landau, "*Baker* v. *Carr* and the Ghost of Federalism," in Glendon A. Schubert, *Reapportionment* (New York: Charles Scribner's Sons, 1965).
[57] Dixon (n. 25 above), p. 585.

The final political area to be reviewed in our investigation of impact studies deals with local police officials. The rights of the accused have been vastly expanded in recent times. *Mapp* v. *Ohio*, 367 U.S. 643 (1961); *Gideon* v. *Wainwright*, 372 U.S. 335 (1963); *Escobedo* v. *Illinois*, 378 U.S. 478 (1964); *Miranda* v. *Arizona*, 384 U.S. 436 (1966); and *In re Gault*, 387 U.S. 1 (1967), are a few of the major cases which have necessitated changes in police procedures. Most of the studies dealing with police practices as they relate to the Court decisions have dealt with the degree of compliance rather than with the reasons for the variance in observance of high-court mandates. Nonetheless, some reasons have been suggested, even though they explain the variance in one specific police jurisdiction and may be inapplicable to other locales. Time is clearly one explanation for variance. Few police officers adhered to the standards of *Escobedo* and *Miranda* shortly after the decisions were handed down, but compliance increased over time. In New Haven, two weeks after the *Miranda* ruling, only about one-half of those arrested were informed of some of their rights. Within three months, approximately two-thirds were so informed.[58] In Washington, D.C., a similar change was evident. The efforts to educate the police officers and the degree of professionalization of those officers had a favorable impact on their responses to the Court's mandates.[59] And the more serious the crime, the more likely the arresting officers would inform the accused of his rights. The police were more diligent in their informing the suspect when they had sufficient evidence to go to trial, but not enough for conviction. The requirements of *Escobedo* and *Miranda* were also ignored in part when the police needed the name of an accomplice or when they felt the suspect had information on other crimes.

Another dimension of impact deals with the behavior of the suspects. Critics of the Court's decisions warned of the "handcuffing of the police" if the standards of the cases were adhered to. The New Haven study concluded that even after the suspect was informed of his rights, the police were fairly successful in obtaining either a

[58] Michael Wald *et al.*, "Interrogations in New Haven: The Impact of *Miranda*," *Yale Law Journal*, LXXVI (July, 1967), 1600.

[59] Neal Milner, "Comparative Analysis of Patterns of Compliance with Supreme Court Decisions: *Miranda* and the Police in Four Communities," *Law and Society Review*, V (August, 1970), 119.

confession or some incriminating information. In Washington, D.C., there was an increase in the request for counsel and in the refusal to give statements when the suspects had been informed of their rights. But, even after police warnings, one-third of the accused requested no counsel and 40 percent continued to supply information. The suspects' refusal to take advantage of their rights was attributed to their inability to understand fully those rights.[60] But the ordinary suspect was not the only individual to fail to understand the implications of the Court's *Miranda* and *Escobedo* rulings. College faculty, staff, and graduate students also did not comprehend the full meaning of the cases. When fully instructed about their rights, they utilized them, but previously they had cooperated with the FBI in its investigation of antidraft activities.[61]

Prior to the *Escobedo* ruling, the Detroit police obtained confessions in 60.8 percent of their cases and the confessions were necessary in only 13.1 percent. But by 1965 the confession rate had dropped to only 58 percent and admission of guilt was essential in only 11.3 percent of these cases. Thus, Theodore Souris concluded that the loss in the number of confessions was compensated for by the greater efficiency of the police.[62]

In sum, the impact of the several cases dealing with the rights of the accused has been, thus far, minimal. James Ridella states: "The total effect of the Supreme Court ruling in *Miranda* and other cases does not hinder police activities. Rather the innovations made following *Miranda* should enable the police to function within . . . Court guidelines and perform their work more effectively." [63] Police effectiveness has remained about the same and only procedures have changed.

[60] Richard J. Medalie, Leonard Zeitz, and Paul Alexander, "Custodial Police Interrogation in Our Nation's Capital: The Attempt to Implement *Miranda*," *Michigan Law Review*, LXVI (May, 1968), 1347.

[61] Note, "A Postscript to the *Miranda* Project: Interrogations of Draft Protesters," *Yale Law Journal*, LXXVII (December, 1967), 300.

[62] Theodore Souris, "Stop and Frisk or Arrest and Search—The Use and Misuse of Euphemisms," *The Journal of Criminal Law, Criminology and Police Science*, LVII (September, 1966), 254.

[63] James Ridella, "Miranda: One Year Later—The Effects," *Public Management*, XLIX (July, 1967), 190. See also A.J. Reiss, Jr., and D.J. Black, "Interrogation and the Criminal Process," *Annals*, CCCLXXIV (November, 1967), 56.

SOCIAL IMPACT

The study of social consequences of court cases is long on theory and short on data. The research regarding social impact falls into two general classes. First, most studies are directed toward an understanding of the role of law in society generally. Second, and of greater concern to impact scholars, some research centers on the reasons for the varying influences of law (especially as enunciated by courts) on society. For example, the relationship between the Supreme Court's rulings liberalizing the law of obscenity and the moral behavior of the public would need to be thoroughly investigated. Obviously, a variety of other factors would account for a change in the public's view of what constitutes acceptable moral behavior, but the rulings of the Court may well be one of the leading variables. Although we know little about change in individual attitudes regarding obscenity which stem from Court rulings, apparently the high court has contributed to a "new freedom and maturity" in film making.[64]

Anthropologists, political scientists, sociologists, and legal scholars have all contributed to theories dealing with the relationship of law to society. Harold J. Berman views law as perpetuating history, settling disputes, teaching right behavior, and controlling deviant behavior.[65] E. Adamson Hoebel, an anthropologist, credits law with an integrating function which defines the relationships between individuals and groups. Law also channels force into constructive functions, decides disputes as they arise, and redefines social relations as change demands.[66] Law can be defined as a set of rules that codifies custom and morality. Or law can be the dictates of those with power over the powerless. It is quite beyond the purposes of this review to reiterate the numerous theories of law in society. The point is that theories of the role of law in society are much in evidence. What is needed is more data to test these various theories within an impact context. The difficulties with accumulating data

[64] Richard S. Randall, *Censorship of the Movies: The Social and Political Control of a Mass Medium* (Madison: University of Wisconsin Press, 1968).

[65] Harold J. Berman, *The Nature and Function of Law* (Brooklyn: Foundation Press, 1958).

[66] E. Adamson Hoebel, *The Law and Primitive Man* (Cambridge: Harvard University Press, 1954).

are great, but not insurmountable. The impact of any series of court cases on social behavior often involves a time span of generations. If integration in public schools has changed the attitude of races toward one another, we would not know for some time the degree and direction of that change. Also, many other factors may influence a change. Parental, teacher, and peer attitudes may intervene to affect a given student's view of his fellow student, quite apart from what the law is. In the long run, study of the law (courts) and society presents the greatest challenge to impact scholars.

The paucity of impact studies on social consequences is due partly to the difficulty of separating that which is due to court action from that which is due to legislative, executive, or group measures. Further, we often can measure attitudinal changes as a result directly, or indirectly, of a Supreme Court ruling, but the corresponding behavioral changes may not be observed. The assumption, of course, is that specific behavior follows from certain attitudes. In reference to the first difficulty, James Levine suggests three connections between court decisions and social outcomes which must be considered by the student of impact. First, the relations between a court decision and its consequences are "probabilistic rather than deterministic." Outcome A does not always follow decision B. Other factors will intervene. Second, the relations between decision and consequences are "sequential." The Supreme Court decides but the outcome may be far removed in time, again allowing for more intervening variables to influence the results. The Supreme Court, for example, decided *Brown* in 1954; 1955–64 saw civil rights as a political controversy; in 1964, the Congress entered the sequence through legislation; between 1966 and 1970, the Department of Health, Education, and Welfare, and the Justice Department instituted administrative and court actions; and by 1971–72, substantial integration was achieved. All of these incidents and agencies made their contribution, but to what degree was the Court responsible? Third, the decision-consequences relation is "contingent: if the Court acts, certain outcomes will follow, but only if other circumstances prevail." Thus, Levine sees the Supreme Court as a catalyst of social change rather than as the direct cause of that change.[67]

[67] Levine, "Methodological Concerns" (n. 4 above), pp. 589–90.

Joel Grossman has recognized the second difficulty concerning the attitudes-behavior relationship: "While changing behavior is likely to be reinforced by consonant attitudes, or attitude changes, it is not necessary to change attitudes in order to achieve behavior changes." It should be added, that impact studies ultimately are aimed at measuring behavior, not attitudes. We often mistakenly assume that attitudes and behaviors are directly related in cause-and-effect sequence.[68]

William K. Muir, Jr., investigated the changes in attitudes toward prayers in public schools resulting directly or indirectly from the Court's decisions and found that, indeed, an attitudinal change favorable to the banning of the practices resulted. School officials in the community he observed, started out after *Engel* with ambivalent attitudes. The *Schempp* decision and a threatened law suit forced them to resolve their indecision. The interactions of the school officials with other groups according to Muir, eliminated many of their misgivings about the correctness of the decisions; and the diverse community environment protected them from immediate and painful consequences when they abided by the Court's rulings and banned religious practices in their schools. Although overstated, Muir's concluding remarks are worth quoting at length:

Can law change deep-rooted attitudes? Of course it can. It has done so—in reshaping in less than a generation this nation's views about racism; in altering in even a shorter time police attitudes toward criminal behavior; in ennobling the city dweller as the backbone of American democracy; in imparting an understanding of poverty; in recasting our ideas about leisure; in maintaining certain attitudes of good sportsmanship apparently essential to a competitive market economy; in stemming religious prejudice; in establishing heightened standards of honesty and public service. . . . Judiciously used, law can and does manipulate our deep-rooted attitudes, our personalities.[69]

And the Supreme Court has played a decisive role in that law.

[68] Joel B. Grossman and Mary H. Grossman, eds., *Law and Change in Modern America* (Pacific Palisades, Cal.: Goodyear Publishing Company, 1971). This collection contains some fine readings on the social impact of law generally.
[69] William K. Muir, Jr., *Prayer in the Public Schools: Law and Attitude Change* (Chicago: University of Chicago Press, 1967), p. 138.

Little doubt remains that courts can legislate morals. But it is far from being clear yet under what conditions, to what degree, and through which methods optimum attitudinal changes can be rendered. Also, research on the long-range social consequences of court decisions begs the ultimate question—whose morals ought we to legislate?

CHAPTER SIX

Systems Models

DESCRIPTION AND ANALYSIS OF SYSTEMS MODELS

Academic disciplines are often wrought by periodical reappraisals by their practitioners of the content, form, and direction of their area of scholarly concern. Political science was, and is, not free from self-criticism. A major question for many in recent years has been the validity of the scientific method for political science and the relation of this method to moral philosophy. David Easton, a leading participant in the dialogue within the profession in the fifties, has summarized this concern: "At the very time that an attempt is being made to introduce a more exact conception of science into the study of politics, many social scientists and philosophers have begun to grow extremely cold and skeptical about its effectiveness in social research as a whole. In all social research a forceful challenge has gone out about the use of this method and its goal." [1] To Easton the malaise in political science "flows directly from an immoderate neglect of general theory." [2] He urged political scientists to reassess their concerns, revitalizing the study of politics through an acceptance and refinement of a general systematic theory fashioned around the idea that political science is the study of "the authoritative allocation of values." [3]

From this beginning, Easton himself in subsequent writings urged adoption of a conceptually-oriented systems approach.[4] Although not

---

[1] David Easton, *The Political System: An Inquiry into the State of Political Science* (New York: Alfred A. Knopf, 1964), p. 23.

[2] *Ibid.*, p. 47.

[3] *Ibid.*, p. 129.

[4] David Easton, "An Approach to the Analysis of Political Systems," *World Politics*, IX (April, 1957), 383; *A Framework for Political Analysis* (Englewood Cliffs, N.J.: Prentice-Hall, 1965); *A Systems Analysis of Political Life* (New York: John Wiley, 1965); and *Varieties of Political Theory* (Englewood Cliffs, N.J.: Prentice-Hall, 1966).

regarded as a model, *per se,* the systems approach fulfills what is required of a model. The framework assists in the selection, organization, and analysis of data. Systems are not unique with political science. Biology, economics, sociology, and cybernetics have all assisted in the development of systems analysis; and most of the systems efforts in these disciplines predated Easton's study.

Easton's purpose was to provide a scheme by which all data relevant to the authoritative allocation of values could be investigated. This comprehensiveness is both the utility of and the difficulty with systems. As already seen, the judicial process is clearly one aspect of the allocation of values within a political system. It can constitute a system by itself.[5] Even though it allocates values as does the legislature or an administrative agency, its procedure and authority are unique.

Characteristics of systems models are comprehensiveness, boundaries, and interdependence.[6] The *comprehensiveness* characteristic answers the criticisms Easton and others have had regarding the limits of past approaches.[7] Political scientists had been too myopic. Under the systems approach, all factors relating to the major function of the system are to be a source of study for the political scientists. However, some things are not related to the system. It is the *boundaries* that determine what will be considered within the

[5] S. Sidney Ulmer, "Homeostatic Tendencies in the United States Supreme Court," in S. Sidney Ulmer, ed., *Introductory Readings in Political Behavior* (Chicago: Rand McNally, 1961), p. 167; James Herndon, "The Role of the Judiciary in State Political Systems: Some Explorations," in Glendon A. Schubert, ed., *Judicial Behavior: A Reader in Theory and Research* (Chicago: Rand McNally, 1964), p. 153; Walter F. Murphy, *Elements of Judicial Strategy* (Chicago: University of Chicago Press, 1964), p. 31; Glendon A. Schubert, *Judicial Policy-Making* (Chicago: Scott, Foresman, 1965); Jay Sigler, *An Introduction to the Legal System* (Homewood, Ill.: Dorsey Press, 1968); Joel B. Grossman, "A Model for Judicial Policy Analysis: The Supreme Court and the Sit-In Cases," in Grossman and Joseph Tanenhaus, eds., *Frontiers of Judicial Research* (New York: John Wiley, 1969), p. 405; Thomas P. Jahnige and Sheldon Goldman, eds., *The Federal Judicial System: Readings in Process and Behavior* (New York: Holt, Rinehart and Winston, 1968); Goldman and Jahnige, "Systems Analysis and Judicial Systems: Potential and Limitations," *Polity,* III (Spring, 1971), 334; and Goldman and Jahnige, *The Federal Courts as a Political System* (New York: Harper & Row, 1971).

[6] Gabriel Almond and James Coleman, *The Politics of Developing Areas* (Princeton: Princeton University Press, 1962), Chapter 1.

[7] E.g., Roy C. Macridis, *The Study of Comparative Politics* (New York: Doubleday, 1957).

system and what will remain outside as part of the environment. Anything relating to the authoritative allocation of values is part of the political system. Thus the nature of authority defines the boundaries. When demands are made on those able authoritatively to allocate (and the demands are heard), then those demands have crossed over the boundaries and are within the jurisdiction of the system. Once into the system, a demand has an impact on all other factors within that system. The *interdependence* of all parts of the system is illustrated by inputs, conversion, outputs, and feedback. Inputs are converted into outputs, resulting in feedback. A change in an input leads to a corresponding change in an output and feedback. Interdependence is thereby manifested.

A system is analogous to an organism which must deal with the stresses and strains of the environment in which it lives. The development of an understanding, description, analysis, and prediction of the exchanges between the system and its environment on the one hand, and the relationships among the system's components on the other, is the purpose of the systems model. Consequently, statements about boundaries—where the system begins and environment ends—are crucial. Further, in developing a systems model, the researcher must be concerned with the logic of the system. The logic of a system, that which holds it together separate from other systems in the environment, is determined by the interdependency of the components. A change in one part brings about some related change in another and both changes are necessitated by environmental pressures. A condition of equilibrium results as a system meets the stresses and strains of the environment through the adjustment of one component with another. Persistence through equilibrium or homeostasis obtains if the system is doing what it should. This drive toward internal balance or equilibrium is one dimension of a system to be understood, and the reactions to and impact on or exchanges with the environment is another. However, the equilibrium is dynamic. That is, the system attempts to meet the demands of the environment. If successful, the system persists; it remains in a dynamic state of equilibrium, in that the outputs balance out the inputs. Failing this, the system is modified or perishes.

In order to meet the demands of the environment, or in other words, in order to perform the necessary functions assigned to it, the system must accept forms of these demands and convert them into actions acceptable to that environment. Thus, a system has inputs, conversion processes, outputs, and feedbacks.

When viewing the judicial process as a system, a legal dispute is seen as a demand input. Oral arguments and written briefs presented by lawyers, the evidence as it develops at the trial level (facts), and *amicus curiae* efforts are among the forms a demand input assumes. Statutes, constitutions, and rules, as they blend with the legal dispute, are also demand inputs. The degree of confidence people have in law and the courts constitutes a support input. Those who applaud a court decision as the right decision are providing specific support, as are those who win their cases, both as litigants and as lawyers or pressure groups. General support flows from the degree of awe, deference, and respect granted to and held for the law, the judges, and the justice they administer. Sources for inputs are the environment and also reactions to previous judicial decisions (i.e., feedback).

The judges and juries constitute major units of the conversion stage. As the demands and supports enter the system, they are converted into decisions. At the appellate level, the conversion stage (involving several judges) begins with the initial review of a petition by the judges and extends through the consideration of written and oral argument by the lawyers, conference discussions and voting, opinion writing and circulation, concluding with the decision announcement. A decision not to review a case constitutes a form of conversion; the judges have decided to let the present situation continue. At the trial level, a judge, meeting in his chambers with contending lawyers, may sanction a plea, or prior to trial, may suggest a solution to the legal issue. Conversion is still involved simply because those responsible for the authoritative allocation of the values embodied in the dispute have decided, even though outside the formal courtroom situation.

The court decision itself is an output from the judicial system. The accompanying opinion that an appellate judge attaches to his decision is designated as an associational output, while the decision itself is an authoritative output. A trial judge, in addition to his or the jury's award, may speak from the bench and, thus, manifest both associational and authoritative outputs. The impact of the decision on the environment is an output. The output may be intended or not.

The impact of the authoritative and associational outputs on the environment results in feedback, in the form of communications which ultimately lead to reactions or counteractions by the judges.

Within a judicial system, feedback can be conceptualized as the communication through formal and informal channels to the judicial authorities of compliance or non-compliance to authoritative output, changes in the level and kind of support, and attempts to limit the authorities and redefine the boundaries of the system. Litigation fed into the system in response to past court decisions is a major form of feedback for a judicial system.[8]

The judicial system is dynamic, ongoing, and self-regulating. An output leads to another input, etc. As long as demands are met, support should increase or at least remain at a tolerable level. The

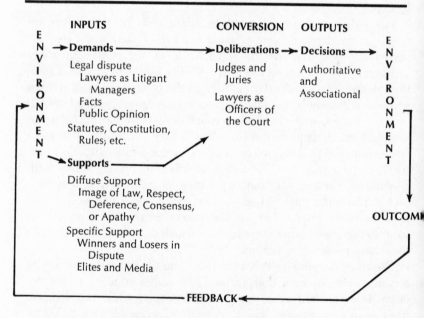

FIGURE 10.   The Judicial System

[8] Goldman and Jahnige, "Systems Analysis," p. 353.

system will persist and thereby display dynamic equilibrium. Should the judicial system fail to satisfy societal demands, those making the demands may well turn to other authoritative allocators of values. The existence of the judicial system, then, is in jeopardy.

Figure 10 illustrates a systems analysis of the judicial process.

CRITIQUE

The values of the systems model flow from its generality. Because inputs, conversion, outputs, and feedback are characteristic of all systems—only the content varies—comparative analysis is encouraged. Even though the judicial system of Louisiana relies upon French antecedents rather than British, it still has inputs, outputs, etc. Within this frame of reference, Louisiana can be meaningfully compared with Maine. Also, the systems model forces the student to be concerned with the influence of the general socio-economic-political environment, which can help explain shifts and changes of court decisions. The courts are institutions which are part of a general political system. No amount of institutional engineering to bring about more objectivity, impartiality, and judicial isolation can nor possibly should change this fact. The systems model allows us not to forget the interdependency of variables involved in legal and political phenomena. What happens at Harvard Law School regarding curricular changes may ultimately have an impact on a judge's perception of his role. Also, the systems model

> . . . is deliberately formulated at such a level of abstraction that it avoids the dangers of becoming tied to any particular type of political system or to any specific variety of sociocultural context. This procedure, of course, sometimes carries with it the danger of loss of content due to high levels of abstraction, but the importance of avoiding biases toward certain types of systems is crucial to comparative analysis.[9]

Finally, because of its emphasis upon equilibrium, some would argue that the systems model helps us to understand change. This is so simply because under certain circumstances, when the demands are greater than the supports and the conversion process is unable

---

[9] Oran R. Young, *Systems of Political Science* (Englewood Cliffs, N.J.: Prentice-Hall, 1968), p. 46.

to convert these inputs into acceptable policies, the system is in disequilibrium and in danger of loss of life. The disparity between balance and imbalance, when understood, constitutes change. Not all would agree with this attribution, however.

Although providing one of the most comprehensive and fruitful models (in a didactic and heuristic sense), the systems approach displays some drawbacks. First, the judicial process involves a variety of delays, appeals, pleadings, counterpleadings, continuances, dismissals, reversals, and remands which are forms of feedback within the system itself. The simple systems model concentrates on that feedback which occurs following decision, thus ignoring the many internal feedbacks. "Withinputs" has been conceptualized to account for these internal communications leading to reactions on the part of judicial decision makers.[10] In order to simplify the model (and that is what models are about), the student may be tempted to limit his system to only the appellate level and to view the trial level or other aspects of the total judicial process as separate systems rather than as withinputs or as feedback. However, such a piecemeal approach may prevent an adequate understanding of the relation of the total judicial system to the larger political or social system of which it is a part.

For example, Jahnige and Goldman exclude state courts from their systems analysis with the observation that "state judicial processes are sufficiently distinct from the federal judicial system to warrant separate systems analysis. . . . The federal courts on the other hand, constitute integrated sets of relationships." But then the rich interchange—having much to do with dynamic equilibrium—between state and federal courts is lost to the analyst.[11]

The systems model, because of its generality, tends to neglect the conversion stage. Emphasis is given to inputs and outputs but what goes on in the "black box" between these two stages remains somewhat obscure. And yet, that black-box stage may be most crucial. To adjust to this gap, some political scientists have shifted their systems emphasis to the conversion stage. Generally, the functional models of the structural-functional approach are merely systems models with a different emphasis. To quote Gabriel Almond, one of the leading authorities on this shift of concern: ". . . Easton's propositions about

[10] Goldman and Jahnige, "Systems Analysis," p. 351.
[11] Goldman and Jahnige, *The Federal Judicial System*, p. 3.

what goes on in the black box of the political system have been kept generically simple. He speaks of inputs of demands, and support and outputs, while I have been stuffing into the black box functional and structural categories which had developed in the creative decades of the empirical political research of the first half of the present century." [12] Recently, Theodore Becker has addressed himself to an application of the systems, or structural-functional, approach to the judicial system. Much of what heretofore has been designated as function in the judicial system is, to Becker, actually structure; and the concern, he believes, should be with the consequences or functions of these structures collectively known as courts.[13]

The judicial system cannot be viewed as a self-contained unit or as a closed system. The systems model presumably achieves internal homeostasis through its own efforts, without regard to the many crucial factors in the larger political world. The judicial system in fact may be in imbalance, and such a state may be desirable.[14] Taking this larger view, equilibrium or homeostasis can be achieved outside the judicial sphere. Courts rule in certain areas and the legislature, outside the judicial process, adjusts the total system by correcting, or building on, the courts' decisions through legislation. An activist Supreme Court may upset the total system through its revolutionary decisions; Congress and the President, through legislative and executive action or inaction, may "correct" these revolutionary aspects of the Court's decisions. Conversely, disequilibrium in the total system may be corrected by the Court. Reapportionment rulings are an example. If the judicial system is viewed as a self-contained and self-balancing system, however, the importance of the larger political world may be ignored. Also, if the systems model

[12] Gabriel Almond, "Political Development," *Comparative Political Studies,* IV (January, 1969), 449.

[13] Theodore Becker, *Comparative Judicial Politics* (Chicago: Rand McNally, 1970), p. 20.

[14] One theory holds that during the fifties the role of the Supreme Court was to take extremely unpopular stands regarding First Amendment freedoms in order to remind the people of their meaning, although Congress continually criticized and "corrected" the Court's interpretations and the public generally thought the Court was "soft on Communism." The point is, however, that the demands and supports (inputs) were different from the decisions (outputs), and thus the judicial system was not in equilibrium. Balance was achieved, though, through congressional or public reaction. See Walter F. Murphy, *Congress and the Court* (Chicago: University of Chicago Press, 1962).

postulates homeostasis as a necessary and inevitable by-product, it is difficult to account for change. Whereas homeostasis is by definition static, change is a process of disequilibrium. Certainly, the judicial system changes and, in fact, change may be the most important phenomenon that the scholar must explain. The systems model may not be an adequate tool for understanding change.[15]

In a problem that is less acute, but still present in a judicial system, systems models generally fail to enlighten us as to when and why certain demands and certain supports become significant and are projected into the conversion process. Many demands are made on a political system. Few are processed. Why? Of course, with the judicial system, the formal filing of a complaint or of arrest, etc., signals the beginning of the input stage (granted that a decision not to prosecute, plea bargaining, a guilty plea, or a decision to settle out of court short-circuits the flow of processes). Nonetheless, with a judicial system it is fairly clear when one type of demand—instituting a formal case—becomes an input. Demands other than instituting a formal case are not so easily identified as inputs, however. When the late Senator Dirksen introduced a constitutional amendment in the Senate which would undo *Baker* v. *Carr,* 369 U.S. 186 (1962), and *Reynolds* v. *Sims,* 377 U.S. 533 (1964), he was making a demand and influencing support. Clearly, the Dirksen Amendment would have had a decisive impact on subsequent outputs of the Supreme Court if adopted. Quite apart from formal attempts to change decisions, do the justices keep a wary eye on what Congress and other political agencies are doing and readjust their decisions? If so, there has been an input into the judicial system. But how do we know when such demands cross the threshold into the conversion process? To anticipate judicial output, we must be able to recognize input initially.

The term "gatekeeping" has been utilized by systems analysts to describe the function of those individuals who, because of rules or choice, are able to prevent certain disputes from becoming legal inputs. A district attorney who fails to prosecute, a private lawyer who arranges an out-of-court settlement, a court which refuses jurisdiction, or a potential litigant without standing are all illustrations of the practice of gatekeeping. These disputes never rise to the input

[15] Young, p. 48.

category. Nonetheless, they can have an impact on the judicial system. Dockets as a result of gatekeeping are not as crowded. Legislatures are pressured by groups or individuals failing to receive a judicial hearing. Different test cases are sought by groups who initially failed to have standing. Even though the gatekeepers have kept such disputes out of the court, subsequent actions may well be a direct result of what transpired at the gate. Should not these actions, then, be analyzed by the student of the judicial process? The answer, of course, is that a model cannot be too comprehensive or the student will be overwhelmed with data. Systems models which are open can at least account for environmental factors when they become sufficiently important to constitute an input. The problem is to determine the degree of importance.

The examples of gatekeeping indicate that although many inputs are easily identified, oftentimes we cannot be sure some inputs will result in any output. A characteristic of a system, as we have mentioned, is the interdependency of its parts. Can we relate an input of an arrest that subsequently is thrown out of the system through a decision not to prosecute, to some system's output? Of course, such a decision is an output but it is a pre-judicial output.

The position of lawyers in the systems model, because of a functional bias of the model, represents a problem. If the scholar utilizes functions as the frame of reference for inputs, conversion, and outputs, the lawyer participates in both inputs and conversion. As litigant manager, the lawyer makes the formal demands on the authoritative decision makers—the judges and juries. But as a partner in the courtroom, the lawyer also suggests decisional alternatives to the judge and thereby participates in the conversion of the demands. But research thus far has failed to enlighten us on the role of the lawyer at the conversion stage. In theory, he is involved in conversion, but in practice, he has been excluded by scholars.

The systems model also suffers, as do many of the approaches to the study of the judicial process, from an imprecision of terms. Agreement is lacking as to what exactly should be classified as an input, conversion, or output variable. The two leading exponents of systems, Goldman and Jahnige, ably illustrate the problems of definitional diversities among the few systems studies of the courts.[16]

---

[16] Goldman and Jahnige, "Systems Analysis" (n. 5 above), p. 334.

Finally, the systems model stresses *what is*. Status quo, equilibrium, or homeostasis are concepts of conservatism as well as of systems. The model can suggest what happened when the system did not persist or suffered from disequilibrium, but it cannot suggest what ought to have happened. Normative considerations are eschewed by the student applying systems models to an understanding of the judicial process. Some would argue that what is needed, especially now, is a model that will tell us how to improve the judicial process, how to improve the administration of justice. Perhaps a return to Plato, Aquinas, or Rousseau is called for.

In sum, the values and drawbacks of the systems approach can be attributed to its generality. Criticism can be leveled at the model's inability to be operationalized adequately to the details of reality. Systems models are too general to allow for measuring, quantification, and data collection which are so sorely needed in studies of the judicial process.[17] But at the same time, they are of value because such models allow comparative analysis, develop a concern for environment, and emphasize the interdependency of variables involved in the judicial process.

SYSTEMS STUDIES

The scope of the systems model has the distinct value of being broad enough to incorporate most of the other approaches and models reviewed in this book. However, the emphasis in the systems model is upon the interdependence of its several components (e.g., inputs as they relate to outputs). A review of systems studies could include applications of such models as decision making (conversion), macro- and micro-group (inputs), and impact (outcome). The author has avoided their inclusion simply because of his stress on the interrelatedness of systems parts, a stress which is often slighted in other models.

Environment

The environment within which the particular judicial system finds itself must make a difference even though we are not altogether sure

---

[17] One exception is Murphy, *Elements of Judicial Strategy*.

of the strengths and causes of the difference. Stuart Nagel has isolated several key environmental characteristics of highly diversified societies, finding that professional judges, jurors, trained lawyers, promulgated laws, and appeals opportunities are common to manufacturing societies and often missing in agricultural societies. Democratic systems are more defense oriented and judges possess less discretion than in dictatorial countries. Collectivist systems emphasize rehabilitation more than individualistic systems do, and bribery and discrimination in decisions are less evident than in the former type of environment. Thus, culture or environment does appear to have a substantial impact on the nature of the judicial system, although Nagel fails to tell us exactly how or why.[18]

After some pioneer studies in the fifties, a rich source of materials has developed in legal anthropology, which isolates important cultural variables accounting for diversities in judicial styles, goals, and procedures. A survey of such studies is beyond the purposes of this review, but it must be noted that the impact of environment has traditionally interested anthropologists; unfortunately this interest has not, until recently, spilled over into the legal and political science disciplines.[19] Too often the anthropologists dwell on the similarities among primitive and modern societies and fail to emphasize the dissimilarities which can be attributed to the environment of the particular societies. But the contributions to an understanding of a judicial system made by cultural anthropologists is clearly recognized:

> [I]f we want to understand the extent to which the judicial structures and functions that we observe in the United States are by-products of specific cultural parameters, then we must undertake

[18] Stuart Nagel, *The Legal Process From a Behavioral Perspective* (Homewood, Ill.: Dorsey Press, 1969), pp. 69–79.

[19] The "classics" in legal anthropology are P. Bohannan, *Justice and Judgment Among the Tiv* (London: Oxford University Press, 1957); M. Gluckman, *The Judicial Process Among the Barotse* (Manchester: Manchester University Press, 1967); E.A. Hoebel, *The Law of Primitive Man* (Cambridge: Harvard University Press, 1954); and Karl N. Llewellyn and E.A. Hoebel, *The Cheyenne Way: Conflict and Case Law in Primitive Jurisprudence* (Norman: University of Oklahoma Press, 1941). A fine review of legal anthropology is given by Klaus-Friedrich Koch, "Law and Anthropology: Notes on Interdisciplinary Research," *Law and Society Review*, IV (August, 1969), 11.

comparative studies. . . . When we study the relatively simple social systems of primitive societies, we may be able to isolate the relevant cultural parameters with greater precision and confidence than we can when we study the complex social system of the contemporary United States.[20]

One of the stated purposes of *Comparative Judicial Behavior*, a collection of works edited by Schubert and Danelski, was, like that of the legal anthropologists, to compare judicial systems in order to isolate the influence of environmental factors. Unfortunately, with few exceptions, the various authors in the collection emphasized environmental similarities and common methods of research rather than cultural differences. Some differentiating environmental observations were noted in the collection, however. The Korean judicial system, for example, has resisted Westernization because of traditional attitudes toward authority and law. Also, in Japan the gradual rather than rapid individualization of decision making can be attributed to a tradition of unanimity on the high bench.[21]

Many of the meaningful studies of the exchanges between environment and the judicial system have come out of comparative state studies of the American federal system. Information on judicial salaries and tenure, selection methods, court organization, and judicial administrative practices tell us much about the level of legal professionalism in any given state political system. High salaries, long judicial tenure, objective judicial election methods, simplified court structure, and efficient court administration lead to a system with high legal professionalism. The higher the professionalism, the more likely that the system is urban, industrialized, and socially and economically heterogeneous. The per capita income will be greater, policy innovations more pronounced, interparty competition higher, and the legislature more professional in a state that displays a high level of legal professionalism. Also, the higher the legal professionalism of a state, the more likely that the dissent rate will be higher

[20] Schubert, *Judicial Behavior* (n. 5 above), p. 85.
[21] Pyong-Choon Hahm, "The Decision Process in Korea," in Glendon A. Schubert and David Danelski, eds., *Comparative Judicial Behavior* (New York: Oxford University Press, 1969); and David Danelski, "The Supreme Court of Japan: An Exploratory Study," in *ibid.*, p. 17.

among the members of that state's court of last resort.[22] From the viewpoint of the systems model, legal professionalism is an input into the legal system. Environment, if not causing professionalism, is at least related to its level.

Jaros and Canon have investigated the impact of environment on the level of dissent in state supreme courts. The degree of urbanization and political competitiveness in a state correlated positively with the dissent rates, especially in those states that have an intermediate appellate level. Dissent is greater in the more urbanized and politically competitive states. The environmental influence was both direct and indirect. First, the nature of the cases and, second, the characteristics of the judges were functions of the particular environment of the state. Jaros and Canon comment: "Variance in dissent in state supreme courts which hear cases filtered through intermediate appellate tribunals . . . is unquestionably related to the socio-economic and political features of the states. . . . This relationship to a considerable extent depends upon the fact that these features affect the environmental characteristics of the judges, which in turn are associated with dissensual behavior." [23] If we view professionalism as an input from the environment and dissent rate as an output, the dynamism of the system becomes evident.

Studies of the judicial selection systems have recently shed more light on the importance of environment to the nature of the judicial system. Throughout the United States a variety of selection systems are employed, allowing for meaningful comparative studies. Gubernatorial appointment, legislative selection, partisan elections, Missouri plans, and nonpartisan elections constitute the basic selection forms. Certain judicial selection methods encourage fairly distinctive environmental exchanges. Partisan elections enhance the influence of political parties and electoral politics. Election by the legislature grants great influence to the majority party in the legislature and makes the choice of judges susceptible to the same influences that any legislative political struggle experiences. Gubernatorial appoint-

[22] Herbert Jacob and Kenneth Vines, eds., *Politics in American States* (Boston: Little, Brown, 1971), pp. 292, 303.
[23] Dean Jaros and Bradley C. Canon, "Dissent on State Supreme Courts: The Differential Significance of Characteristics of Judges," *Midwest Journal of Political Science*, XV (May, 1971), 344.

ment allows for intensive political party as well as pressure-group influence. Law groups dominate the Missouri plan states and non-partisan elections have not eliminated the inputs from political and legal groups.[24] But we must be careful in attributing the different environmental influences to the method of judicial selection alone. For example, in states with strong political parties, party politics will have an impact on judicial recruitment, whether partisan, nonpartisan, or gubernatorial selection systems exist.

Different sorts of lawyers are selected to the bench. To what degree can we attribute the judges' characteristics to (1) the type of selection system in any given state or to (2) the particular environment in those states? The degree of legal professionalism seems not to be a function of selection. The five top-ranked states of Jacob and Vines' legal professionalism scale have selection methods varying from the Missouri plan and gubernatorial appointment, to partisan and nonpartisan elections. It appears that environment is stronger than selection systems. Bradley Canon has shown that regionalism accounts for more of the diversity among judicial characteristics than does selection. For example, party affiliation, religion, career patterns, education, and local origins of the judges can be explained more by the region in which the courts are located than by the type of selection. Canon, however, has found that some characteristics—such as prior judicial experience, prosecuting backgrounds, and education—are also concomitants of selection methods. (See Table 5.)

At the federal level, as at the individual state level, the appointment process allows for the influx of environment. Political party, ideology, patronage, geography, and religion have been environmental criteria referred to by the appointing or nominating officials.

The environment from which the judges come, their jurisdictions, and the types and numbers of cases heard by a particular judge can be designated as elements of a judge's constituency. Richardson and Vines have shown that constituency can explain some important decisional variations among the federal district, circuit, and supreme courts. They have observed:

> Constituencies of political officials often mold their behavior in significant ways. Although one usually thinks of constituencies simply in

[24] Herbert Jacob and Kenneth N. Vines, eds., *Politics in the American States* (Boston: Little, Brown, 1971), p. 279.

TABLE 5. Judicial Characteristics Associated with Region or with Selection System

Characteristics	Region	Selection Systems				
		Partisan Election	Nonpartisan Election	Missouri Plan	Gubernatorial Appointment	Legislative Appointment
Party Affiliation	X					
Religion	X					High-Protestant
Career Patterns	X	Pro-Prosecution Prior Judicial Experience	Prior Judicial Experience	Pro-Prosecution	Anti-Prosecution	Anti-Prosecution Legislative Experience Prior Judicial Experience
Education	X				More Education	More Education
Localism	X					

SOURCE: Adapted from Bradley C. Canon, "The Impact of Formal Selection Processes on the Characteristics of Judges—Reconsidered," *Law and Society Review*, VI (May, 1972), 579.

terms of their location and organization, or as a group of people, their political effects are actually far-ranging. They structure the flow of power; they help to define the character of political clienteles; they determine the boundaries of political activities of institutions; and, finally, constituencies influence the patterns of decision making within political institutions.[25]

District courts within the federal system follow state lines. Appeals courts encompass several states. These differences in constituencies have an impact on the availability of judicial services. In 1966, the district judges in Connecticut had a case load of 187 per judge, while judges in the southern district of Georgia had 409 cases per judge. The Tenth Circuit had 2.8 district judges per appeals judge, while the Sixth Circuit had 5.0.[26] Overloaded dockets and delays obviously vary according to the constituency.

District court decisions tend to reflect the socioeconomic and political nature of the states within which they are located. The courts of appeals display a less parochial view and, of course, the Supreme Court takes a national view. Richardson and Vines isolated a transformation phenomenon as cases move from parochial district courts through the broader appeals courts to the Supreme Court. What initially is a rather common criminal case at the trial level is transformed into a civil liberties issue by the appeals judges. The Supreme Court performs a further transforming function by bringing to bear a broad national viewpoint, which often leads to a reversal of a case in which a district and circuit court have agreed.[27] Courts therefore are products of their respective constituencies or environment.[28]

INPUTS: DEMANDS

Demands and supports constitute the content of inputs to the judicial system. The demands take the form of legal disputes which

[25] Richard J. Richardson and Kenneth N. Vines, *The Politics of Federal Courts* (Boston: Little, Brown, 1970), p. 36.

[26] *Ibid.*, pp. 41–42.

[27] *Ibid.*, p. 154.

[28] See also Kenneth M. Dolbeare, "The Federal District Courts and Urban Public Policy: An Exploratory Study (1960–67)," in Grossman and Tanenhaus, eds., *Frontiers of Judicial Research* (n. 5 above), p. 373.

are regulated by rules (statutory, constitutional, and precedential) regarding jurisdiction, standing, and justiciability. It is the lawyers who manage the disputes submitted to judicial decision makers.

In the most direct and literal sense, demands emanate from litigants, although such demands usually are translated into the legal idiom before being presented to the Court by counsel who are experts in translating lay interests . . . into legal language. . . . We may properly speak of "litigant management" as constituting one method of accommodationships with the government, other organizations, its clientele, etc.[29]

The litigant managers—lawyers—fashion the dispute so as to overcome the rules which limit the types of conflicts courts hear. The characteristics and attributes of the lawyers are important input variables that have an impact on conversion and output. A survey of 130 state judges indicates that the input of the litigant managers constitutes one of the major criteria upon which they rely for their decisions. Eighteen percent of the judges designated the oral arguments of the lawyers as "most important" to their decisions and 23.8 percent felt that written briefs were "most important." The efforts of the lawyers in the adversary process are clearly important and for a significant number of judges, most important.[30] Although these data suggest the importance of lawyers at the conversion stage, they indicate also the input function of lawyers.

But the influence of lawyers goes beyond the presentation of cases. A great number of the legislators who draft and pass laws which judges must apply are lawyers. It is from the ranks of lawyers that judges come. Lawyers are the reference group for judges and are the most crucial source of criticism and support. The input, direct and indirect, by lawyers would appear to be significant therefore. The question becomes: "Do characteristics of lawyers influence the output of the courts?" Stuart Nagel has tested the importance of several

[29] Glendon A. Schubert, *Judicial Policy-Making* (New York: Scott, Foresman, 1965), p. 108. For a review of research on lawyers, consult Olavi Maru, *Research on the Legal Profession* (Chicago: American Bar Foundation, 1972).

[30] Charles H. Sheldon, "Decisional Characteristics of State Judges" (unpublished research report, Washington State University, 1972). The importance of lawyers practicing before the Supreme Court is discussed in Jonathan D. Casper, *Lawyers Before the Warren Court* (Urbana: University of Illinois, 1972).

lawyer characteristics. He has found that age, experience, education, and office organization are related to won-loss records of advocates. The middle-aged lawyers won more than the young or old, and the old lawyers won more than the young. Lawyers with more experience tended to win more than less experienced ones, and those lawyers with two or more college degrees won more cases than those with fewer or no college degrees. The quality of the law school attended and ABA membership seemed to have no impact on whether lawyers won or lost. Members of firms and government lawyers fared better in court than the solo practitioner. Nagel also discovered that the rating system used in the *Martindale-Hubble Law Directory* was a valid indicator of courtroom success. A and B-rated lawyers had better won-loss records than C and unrated advocates. Nationality and religion had no impact on the outcome of cases. In sum, Nagel stated: "There are definite and meaningful relationships between attorney characteristics and courtroom results." [31]

Many years ago, Karl Llewellyn recognized the intimate relationship between lawyers and judges when he wrote: "Courts are made and shaped more by the character of the bar before them than by any other single factor. Courts over the long haul tend in their standards and in their performance to fit the character of the bar with whom they deal." [32] Jerome Carlin's surveys of individual practitioners in Chicago and New York City support Llewellyn's observation. The solo lawyer's practice and lower court environment tended to form a mutually reinforcing system in which the canons of legal ethics for both lawyers and judges were often ignored, official rather than legal doctrines were manipulated, and rarely were judges or lawyers called upon to exercise a high degree of legal skill. [33]

The best legal talent was (and still is) recruited into the large firms. The solo practitioner remains at the bottom of the status, income, and talent ladders. Consequently, "there has been extensive elaboration of legal procedures to handle problems of corporate enterprise . . . [and] developments in public and private welfare,

[31] Nagel, *The Legal Process* (n. 18 above), p. 124.

[32] Karl N. Llewellyn, "The Bar Specializes—With What Results," *The Annals*, CLXVII (May, 1933), 179.

[33] Jerome Carlin, *Lawyers' Ethics* (New York: Russell Sage Foundation, 1966), Chapter 5; and Carlin, *Lawyers on Their Own* (New Brunswick, N.J.: Rutgers University Press, 1962), p. 210.

personal injury, divorce, home finance, etc., have been less dramatic." [34] The disparities in legal development can be attributed to the interaction among types of clients, lawyers, and judges. The recent influx of talented and committed young lawyers into the welfare and consumer spheres has now brought about some meaningful changes in these heretofore neglected legal areas.

The litigant managers fashion disputes into a language and a form appropriate for the judicial process. Cases are the net result. They are the direct and most tangible inputs into the judicial system. Although lawyers are the litigant managers, other participants in the judicial process are also responsible for bringing disputes to the attention of lawyers and judges. The police exercise varying degrees of discretion in apprehending potential litigants. Prosecuting attorneys, often with the assistance of grand juries, decide whether to go to trial or not. Pressure groups active before the courts often have alternatives available which permit them to exercise much discretion regarding choice and timing of litigation. Because of discretionary opportunities, attorneys, police, prosecutors, and leaders of pressure groups, as well as judges, are all regarded as gatekeepers, who are responsible for preventing demand overload.

In 1968, over 70,000 civil suits were filed in federal district courts, constituting over two-thirds of the courts' business. Nearly 31,000 criminal cases were instituted in federal district courts in the same year. Eighty-nine percent of the civil cases were settled out of court, while 83.2 percent of the criminal cases resulted in a conviction either through a trial, guilty, or *nolo contendere* pleas. The courts of appeals heard approximately 9,000 cases, of which 57 percent were civil cases and 24 percent criminal. Administrative rulings and original hearings constituted the remainder of the courts' work.[35] The United States Supreme Court, in 1971, had 1,903 cases on its appellate docket, 2,289 *in forma pauperis* cases, and 20 cases falling under the Court's original jurisdiction. Of the 4,212 cases on various dockets, the high court disposed of 151 after oral arguments through either a written opinion or by scheduling a reargument. The remain-

[34] Jack Ladinsky, "Careers of Lawyers, Law Practice, and Legal Institutions," *American Sociological Review*, XXVIII (February, 1963), 54.

[35] For a fine statistical summary of the case input of federal courts, consult Goldman and Jahnige, *The Federal Courts* (n. 5 above), Chapter 4.

ing cases were either denied review, summarily decided, or carried over for the next term.[36]

Statistics on types of case inputs are most suggestive. First, the issues in the thousands of cases presented to federal courts (e.g., antitrust, bankruptcy, civil rights, or narcotics) supply clues about problems within the environment. Goldman and Jahnige present statistics to show a tremendous increase in robbery, narcotics, and selective service cases between 1964 and 1968, and a decrease in fraud and liquor tax cases during the same time span. The problems in society generally are reflected in the increases and decreases of these cases. Second, case statistics from the various jurisdictions can isolate the regions in which the problems are most prevalent. Third, the great number of cases—386 per district judge in 1960—indicates the necessity of such practices as plea bargaining, pretrial discovery, conferences, and out-of-court settlement procedures. No legal system could long survive if each case initially filed was given a complete and full hearing. Gatekeeping functions are absolutely necessary for a viable court system. Fourth, a review of case statistics indicates the areas in which the judicial process has had an important impact on the total political system. For example, after 1937, the Supreme Court largely withdrew from economic issues and turned its attention to civil liberties so that under Earl Warren, as Tanenhaus and others have shown, the Court would likely grant review of civil liberties cases and ignore requests for review of economic cases.[37] Finally, the nature of particular cases presented to courts provides materials for predicting a judge's decision. Facts, precedent, and rules of law still possess great predictive power as to the outcome of a case. This is not to say that judicial attitudes, ideology, and socioeconomic and political backgrounds are irrelevant. It is only to recognize that judge-made law is relatively stable, with the "facts" of any given case providing the judges with reference points for their decisions. Most likely when the facts are unclear, the precedents conflicting, or the law ambiguous, the judge is given the opportunity for creativity and discretion.

The predictive power of facts, long the source for traditional

---

[36] G.K. Reiblich, "Summary of October 1970 Term" in 91 S. Ct. 169 (1971).

[37] Joseph Tanenhaus et al., "The Supreme Court's Certiorari Jurisdiction: Cue Theory," in Glendon A. Schubert, ed., Judicial Decision-Making (New York: The Free Press of Glencoe, 1963), p. 111.

scholarship, has not been ignored by contemporary students. Courts must apply rules of law which depend upon an appraisal of certain circumstances surrounding the case. Prior to *Gideon* v. *Wainwright*, 372 U.S. 335 (1963), right-to-counsel provisions of the Bill of Rights were made applicable to state action only under special circumstances. The rule of law was "fairness" and as Justice Owen J. Roberts wrote in *Betts* v. *Brady*, 316 U.S. 455 (1942): "That which may, in one setting, constitute a denial of fundamental fairness, shocking to the universal sense of justice, may, in other circumstances, and in light of other considerations, fall short of such denial." Any judge, then, must give considerable weight to the facts of cases involving right to counsel. Fred Kort was able to predict the outcome of right-to-counsel cases on the basis of the absence or presence of special circumstances found in the facts of these cases. Involuntary confession and workmen's compensation cases were also susceptible to prediction when the facts of any given case are measured against a weighted list of circumstances culled from prior decisions.[38] The output of a court is most often dependent upon the facts of a case presented to the judges.

Stuart Nagel has also studied the predictive power of case inputs: "Legal scholars, practicing lawyers, and social scientists interested in decisional outcomes can get much better predictability by analyzing the factual elements within the cases, the characteristics of the judges and jurors, and the characteristics of the litigants" than from analyzing only the characteristics of the lawyers presenting the cases.[39] In reapportionment cases, for example, success can be predicted if the facts of a case indicate that a challenger at the Supreme Court level has (1) utilized either the equal protection clause or the Fifteenth Amendment (or state equivalent); (2) exhausted all remedies, judicial and political; (3) requested declaratory judgments or temporary remedies; and (4) proved that the legislature had affirmatively made representative districts more unequal.[40] The outcome of civil liberties and international law cases can also be

[38] Fred Kort, "Content Analysis of Judicial Opinions and Rules of Law," in Glendon A. Schubert, ed., *Judicial Decision-Making*, p. 133. See also his explanation of the mathematical model used to predict decisions from facts of cases: "Simultaneous Equations and Boolean Algebra in the Analysis of Judicial Decisions," *Law and Contemporary Problems*, XXVIII (Winter, 1963), 143.
[39] Nagel, *The Legal Process* (n. 18 above), p. 124.
[40] *Ibid.*, p. 134.

predicted with some success from an appraisal of factual inputs.[41]

S. Sidney Ulmer also has compiled a list of factual categories or "signs" from lower-court records of civil liberties cases reviewed by the Supreme Court rather than relying, as others have, upon the written opinions of the justices. Ulmer's goal was to determine to what degree Justice Felix Frankfurter's votes could be attributed to certain facts presented by the case. Six factual signs were regarded as important: when the record below indicated the case involved (1) confessions or right to counsel; (2) a black or rights of blacks; (3) communists; (4) a state; (5) a southern state; and (6) an invalidated congressional statute or a sustained state law when questioned in constitutional terms. Frankfurter responded favorably to civil liberties when the facts involved blacks, confession-counsel issues, and when a state was a party. He reacted negatively when communists or invalidated laws were involved. His reaction to the factual sign "southern state" was ambiguous.[42] We are not sure as to why Frankfurter accepted some facts as important and reacted positively or negatively to them, but it is clear from Ulmer's study that facts as demand inputs are related to at least one justice's votes.[43]

Demand inputs often have a more subtle impact on court output than the direct input of cases. Public opinion has both a direct and indirect influence on the courts. Public pressures upon legislators, executives, and groups can influence court appointments, legislation, and enforcement of court decisions.[44] The courts themselves are not entirely isolated from the ebb and flow of public sentiment. During the fifties, the courts were under great public pressure to support legislative attempts to curb the perceived internal communist threat.

[41] *Ibid.*, Chapters 12 and 13.

[42] S. Sidney Ulmer, "The Discriminating Function and a Theoretical Context for Its Use in Estimating the Votes of Judges," in Grossman and Tanenhaus, eds., *Frontiers of Judicial Research* (n. 5 above), p. 365.

[43] Some "whys" are suggested by traditional scholarship. See Wallace Mendelson, *Justices Black and Frankfurter: Conflict in the Court* (Chicago: University of Chicago Press, 1961).

[44] Richard Harris, *Decision* (New York: Dutton, 1971); Walter F. Murphy, *Congress and the Courts* (Chicago: University of Chicago Press, 1962); C. Herman Pritchett, *Congress Versus the Supreme Court, 1957–1960* (Minneapolis: University of Minnesota Press, 1961); and Kenneth M. Dolbeare and Phillip Hammond, *The School Prayer Decisions* (Chicago: University of Chicago Press, 1970).

Such was the pressure that Justice Hugo Black felt compelled to write that "there is hope that in calmer times, when present pressures, passions, and fears subside, this or some later Court will restore the First Amendment liberties to the high preferred place where they belong in free society." [45] His concern for public opinion was echoed in 1961, by Justice William O. Douglas: " 'The most indifferent arguments,' Bismarck said, 'are good when one has the majority of bayonets.' That is also true when one has the votes. What we lose by majority vote today may be reclaimed at a future time when the fear of advocacy, dissent, and non-conformity no longer cast a shadow over us." [46]

But the Court majority failed to accept Justices Black and Douglas' views and followed the public sentiments regarding the degree of freedom to be allotted communists within the American system. "The evidence indicates that in America the rulings of the Supreme Court were consistent with public opinion expressed directly or through groups and Congress. *Douds* and *Dennis* were the products of an aroused public opinion. McCarthyism, the Korean war, and the 'Communists in government' issues exemplified this era." [47]

It is perhaps in the area of the First Amendment freedoms that the Court becomes most susceptible to the pressures of public opinion. Theodore Becker has observed that "the high court is not likely to protect individual liberty—*when it really counts*—against the politically irresponsible mass that becomes aroused so often." [48] But, as Black and Douglas have hoped, in calmer times courts again remind us of the importance of individual freedoms. In 1957, following the demise of the Red scare of the early fifties, the Supreme Court handed down a series of decisions on what was called by the Court's critics "Red Monday," which restored some of the Bill of Rights freedoms that had been restricted earlier.[49]

Although public pressure against the Court reasserted itself fol-

[45] *Dennis* v. *U.S.*, 341 U.S. 494 (1951), at 581.

[46] *Scales* v. *U.S.*, 367 U.S. 203 (1961), at 275.

[47] Charles H. Sheldon, "Public Opinion and High Courts: Communist Party Cases in Four Constitutional Systems," *Western Political Quarterly*, XV (June, 1967), 349.

[48] Theodore Becker, *Comparative Judicial Politics* (n. 13 above), p. 229.

[49] *Watkins* v. *U.S.*, 354 U.S. 178 (1957); *Sweezy* v. *New Hampshire*, 354 U.S. 234 (1957); *Service* v. *Dulles*, 354 U.S. 363 (1957); and *Yates* v. *U.S.*, 354 U.S. 298 (1957).

lowing those decisions, the fact remains that perhaps no other political institution in the American system could perform the all-important function of reminding us of the value of individual freedoms as well as a court of law. Although receptive to public opinion inputs, the courts and jurors can maintain sufficient support to sometimes resist the most crass pressures for restrictions on freedom.[50] And it is in the area of support inputs that we find explanations for the ability of courts to resist immediate public pressures.

INPUTS: SUPPORTS

Most of the studies of public opinion have concentrated on support rather than demand inputs to the judicial system. It is assumed that the greater the public support for courts, the greater the independence of the judges and the compliance with their decisions. In 1965, John Kessel conducted a survey of the public's attitude toward the Supreme Court. Although decisions on reapportionment, school prayers, and rights of the accused had brought the Court into disrepute, he reported that "the largest category of feelings about the Court can best be described as generalized approval." [51] Kessel's study showed that the public was more receptive to the decisions of the Court than to the efforts of the Court's critics. Thus, it appears that the support for courts would increase or decrease more according to what the judges actually do than according to what critics or supporters speak or write about the judges.

Newspaper editorials are indicators of public sentiment. They either lead or follow the perceived opinions of their readers. Nagel also discovered support for the Supreme Court's church-state cases among leading metropolitan newspapers. The politics of the newspapers seemed to explain differences among the editorials more than did the religion of the publishers or the region in which the paper was circulated.[52]

Chester Newland's study of press coverage of Supreme Court de-

[50] Rita Simon's study of the effect of newspaper coverage on potential jurors indicates that when jurors are cautioned by judges to disregard media coverage of the trial (a form of demand input), they, in fact, do just that. "The Effects of Newspapers on the Verdicts of Potential Jurors," in Rita Simon, ed., *The Sociology of Law* (San Francisco: Chandler, 1968), p. 617.

[51] John Kessel, "The Supreme Court and the American People," in Jahnige and Goldman, eds., *The Federal Judicial System* (n. 5 above), p. 79.

[52] Nagel, *The Legal Process* (n. 18 above), Chapter 22.

cisions found, contrary to Nagel, that more newspapers were critical of the Court's prayer cases than supportive, but a favorable response was evident regarding reapportionment.[53] Of course, support for the judicial system has more subtle dimensions than just indications of pro or con attitudes among the public. Murphy and Tanenhaus postulate three conditions which must be met before a court could be determined to have fulfilled its legitimating function (i.e., to have allocated values in the political system acceptably). First, a court must be visible; the public must be aware of its existence although they need not have any detailed knowledge of the court. Second, the public must recognize the function of the court as proper; that is, the judges are accepted as allocators of values. Third, courts must be viewed as carrying out their function impartially and competently. When these three conditions are met, the support inputs will be adequate to the system.

Murphy and Tanenhaus found, in 1966, that 46.2 percent of a national sample could be identified as those to whom the Supreme Court was visible. Nearly 40 percent of the sample was aware of the Supreme Court's constitutional function and, as with visibility, a higher level of education and political knowledge correlated with a higher degree of acceptance of the Court's function. The third condition postulates that there must be a fairly high level of positive support for the Court. Of the 46.2 percent of the public to whom the Court was visible, 31.7 percent indicated a dislike for specific aspects of the Court's work, with only 9.5 percent supporting the Court. When, however, Murphy and Tanenhaus compiled general and diffuse support for the Court, they found that 37 percent liked what the Court was doing and only 21.7 percent viewed the Court unfavorably. Two conclusions follow from their study of support: some members of the public may be critical of some of the specific decisions of the Court, but still support it; and (2) many people who are not knowledgeable about the Court view it favorably. Murphy and Tanenhaus concluded that although far less than a majority of the American public met all three of the support input conditions, the number was more than adequate. In terms of the total sample, and hence presumably the entire adult population of the United States, about one person in eight met all three of the criteria they had estab-

[53] Chester Newland, "Press Coverage of the U.S. Supreme Court," *Western Political Quarterly*, XVII (March, 1946), 16.

lished. But this 12.8 percent, it cannot be too strenuously stressed, constitutes a considerable share of the politically attentive public.[54]

Recent public opinion polls indicate that indeed those who support the Court may be in the minority. Fifty-four percent of a national sample reacted unfavorably to the Court in 1966. This dropped to 46 percent in 1967, and increased to 53 percent in 1968 and 54 percent in 1969.[55] Some caution must be displayed, however, when analyzing poll results. In this case, the questions most often forced the respondent to answer either "yes" or "no," and no attempt was made to measure the degree of satisfaction or dissatisfaction with the Court. Also, to be critical does not necessarily mean that the respondent will do anything about his dissatisfaction. Kenneth Dolbeare's study of public response indicated that few were compelled to act regarding their view of the Court.[56] Finally, respondents may be critical of courts but still support them over time. Many Supreme Court critics continue their support hoping that new appointments to the bench will change its direction.

Where does this leave us concerning public opinion as a support input? Using the support for the United States Supreme Court as our case, the data are not altogether conclusive. And yet, aside from a few halfhearted attempts to impeach some justices, to amend the Constitution, or to withhold certain categories of cases from the Court, no meaningful attempts have been made to change or replace the institution. Adequate support seems to come about from (1) a favorable public impression of the institution and the law it administers, although specific rulings may be criticized; (2) a general public acquiescence allowing the Court to allocate values largely unhampered by public concern; or (3) sufficient support expressed by attentive or relevant segments of the public. We need to know more

[54] Walter F. Murphy and Joseph Tanenhaus, "Public Opinion and the United States Supreme Court: A Preliminary Mapping of Some Prerequisites for Court Legitimation of Regime Rules," in Grossman and Tanenhaus, eds., *Frontiers of Judicial Research* (n. 5 above), p. 295. See also Exercise III in Samuel Krislov, *Judicial Process and Constitutional Law: A Laboratory Manual* (Boston: Little, Brown, 1972), p. 39.

[55] Reported in Stephen Wasby, *The Impact of the United States Supreme Court: Some Perspectives* (Homewood, Ill.: Dorsey Press, 1970), pp. 237–38, and Goldman and Jahnige, *The Federal Courts* (n. 5 above), p. 135.

[56] Kenneth M. Dolbeare, "The Public Views the Supreme Court," in Herbert Jacob, ed., *Law, Politics, and the Federal Courts* (Boston: Little, Brown, 1967), p. 208.

about the ebb and flow of Court sentiment through time among politically relevant segments of the public.[57] We also must begin analyzing demand and support impacts on courts at all levels of the judicial system.

CONVERSION AND OUTPUTS

The conversion phase of the judicial system encompasses those individuals who transform the inputs into policy. Judges, lawyers, and juries—independently and together—convert the inputs into decisions. It is on this particular phase that most of the traditional and contemporary studies of courts have concentrated their efforts. The disagreements over explanations of conversion have consumed a great amount of scholarly energies. Mechanical jurisprudence, legal realism, sociological or historical jurisprudence are but a few of the leading categories into which scholars of conversion have been placed. In political science the behavioral approach seems to have preempted the public law field today. Despite some meaningful differences between the various schools of thought regarding law and judges, all are attempting to understand how and why a judge will decide the way he does.[58] Thus, a large body of materials on conversion is available. Goldman and Jahnige have correctly observed that: "Theories of conversion are considered partial theories and can be included under the umbrella of systems analysis. Certainly the various decision-making models that adorn the judicial behavior literature are not clearly incompatible with the systems framework."[59]

The decision-making, small-group, and role models are often incomplete in that they tend to neglect the input and feedback aspects of the systems approach. The interdependence attribute of the systems approach demands consideration of these phases of the judicial process. Often conversion models therefore require some adaptation to be applicable to systems analysis.

Analyses of conversion models comprise the subject matter of separate chapters in this book. Decision-making, small-group, and

[57] Don W. Brown, "Public Opinion and Judicial Decision-Making" (paper delivered to American Political Science Association Meeting, September, 1972).
[58] Theodore Becker describes the various schools in his *Political Behavioralism and Modern Jurisprudence* (Chicago: Rand McNally, 1964), Chapters 1 and 2.
[59] Goldman and Jahnige, "Systems Analysis" (n. 5 above), p. 351.

role models, when viewed as open models, lend themselves to an understanding of conversion and outputs. Traditional approaches frequently analyze and describe court conversion. Whatever may be the model or approach, to be applicable to systems analysis it must account for the impact of inputs on conversion and on decisional outputs of the court. The former input accounting is seldom difficult to establish and, as critics of decision-making models point out, the latter relationship is seldom satisfactorily established.[60]

A recent survey of 130 state judges shows that decision-making factors are demand-input oriented, although equally important are factors which are internal demands flowing from the intellect and ideology of the judge. Judges were asked to rate various decisional guides on a scale from "most important," "important," "hardly important," to "not important" with the following results as noted in Table 6. Unfortunately, we have no indication of the outputs of various judges who utilize different decisional factors.

Conversion frequently involves two phases which, although in reality they are commingled, can be separated for purposes of study.

> Essentially, there are two analytically separate processes of decision-making on juries and appellate courts. First there is an individual phase in which a judge or juror [or trial judge] turns over in his mind the specific issues and the broader societal context of the case as he perceives them; the legal principles that seem relevant to him; and the implications he believes possible decisions might have. . . . In the group phase the members of the court or jury interact and try at least to justify a particular choice, if not to persuade others that it is the best of all possible alternatives.[61]

The trial judge may also participate in a group phase as he shares decisional tasks with a jury in some cases.

Descriptions of the two phases of the conversion process at the Supreme Court level are ably presented by Walter Murphy in his *Elements of Judicial Strategy*. Each justice, at the individual stage, contemplates inputs in terms of (1) the legitimacy of the demands represented by the case; (2) the desirability of competing demands; (3) the nature and desirability of the demands of other public offi-

---

[60] See especially Becker, Chapter 1.

[61] Walter F. Murphy and Joseph Tanenhaus, *The Study of Public Law* (New York: Random House, 1972), p. 177.

TABLE 6.   Question: "Which of the following do you think are the most important factors influencing your judicial decisions?"

Decisional Guides	Judges' Responses (N = 130) Percentage Designating Factor as "Most Important" *
Direct External Demands	
Law and Precedent	57.6
Lawyers' Written Briefs	23.8
Advocates' Oral Arguments	13.8
Indirect External Demands	
Public Opinion	10.0
Community Values	7.6
Community Needs	3.8
Community Demands	2.3
Political Factors	0.0
Internal Demands	
Common Sense	57.6
Justice	51.5

* Total is greater than 100 because of opportunity to designate several factors as "most important."

SOURCE: Charles H. Sheldon, "State Judicial Roles: Trial vs. Appellate" (unpublished research report, Washington State University, 1972).

cials and public at large; (4) the seriousness of threats and possibilities of sanctions accompanying the respective demands; and (5) the possible changes in supports for each of the policy alternatives available to the judges.[62] At the group stage, the individual input evaluations are presented, and agreement is reached on a decision

[62] Murphy, *Elements* (n. 5 above), p. 34. Unfortunately, Murphy's analysis, although within a systems framework, fails to elaborate on the relationship between inputs and conversion. His study appears to fit more appropriately within the small-group context. See Chapter 2.

and on a justification for that decision. The bulk of Murphy's book concentrates on what strategical alternatives are available to the justices of the high court during the group phase. Hopefully, in the future some scholar will attempt to relate the several strategies to types of inputs and kinds of outputs.

The goal of systems analysis is to predict the outputs and outcomes of various inputs fed into the judicial process. Glendon Schubert's suggestion of pertinent variables ultimately led him to advocate judicial attitudes as the most reliable class of predictive variables. Cultural or environmental factors are important, of course. The environment defines the limits of attributes possessed by judges, jurors, and lawyers; that is, judges with certain kinds of background characteristics come from characteristic environments. The attributes of the decision makers, in turn, are closely related to the attitudes and ideologies held by the judges or jurors. Therefore,

> We expect . . . prediction will be most likely to succeed between adjacent classes of variables: between cultural and attribute variables; between attribute and either cultural or attitudinal variables; between attitudinal and either attribute or decisional variables; and between decisional and attitudinal variables. This implies that the prediction of judicial decision-making behavior will be most successful if it is based upon the observation and measurement of judicial attitudes.[63]

And, as the chapter on decision making observes, Schubert has remained consistent with his concern for attitudes as the most reliable predictor of judicial outputs. At this point we need not again describe the materials relating to decision making, roles, or small groups. These are models of conversion and outputs, and the student is encouraged to review these chapters within the context of the systems approach.

FEEDBACK

Feedback is the communication from the environment back to the allocators of values in the judicial system. Subsequently, feedback becomes new or revised input into the system. The difficulty is to separate feedback from inputs. A feedback demand is a result of

---

[63] Schubert, *Judicial Policy-Making* (n. 5 above), p. 123.

perceptions of what the courts have done or failed to do. At what point does the feedback become a demand? When judges respond to a request or to pressure to act, a feedback is transformed into an input. The important distinction is that the decision makers respond to forces which had previously generated the court action or inaction.

The forms of feedback are numerous, as Chapter Five indicates. The President, Congress, state government, other courts, pressure groups, legal scholars, and the public are all instruments of communications-return to courts. In 1954, the Warren Court handed down the decision in Brown v. Board of Education, 347 U.S. 483 (1954), declaring segregated schools to be in violation of the Fourteenth Amendment. President Eisenhower responded by simply stating that "The Supreme Court has spoken and I am sworn to uphold the constitutional processes in this country; and I will obey." Some have said that the President could not be accused of displaying enthusiasm for the Court's ruling. President Kennedy's response to the Supreme Court's prayer decision (Engel v. Vitale, 370 U.S. 421 [1962]) was somewhat stronger and, because of the President's religion, more sensitive: "The Supreme Court has made its judgment, and a good many people obviously will disagree with it. Others will agree with it. But I think it is important for us if we are going to maintain our constitutional principles that we support the Supreme Court decisions even though we may not agree with them." [64] To what degree was the second Brown, 349 U.S. 294 (1955), decision dealing with the implementation of desegregation and the Schempp, 374 U.S. 203 (1963), case on Bible reading in public schools influenced by earlier presidential enthusiasm or the lack of it?

Congress reacts to court decisions in a variety of ways. The Talmadge Amendment of 1960, although failing to achieve any substantial support, was directed toward undoing the Brown decision. The Dirksen Amendment proposal of 1965 was a reaction to the reapportionment cases, and the Becker Amendment of 1963 was proposed to "correct" the Court's rulings on prayers and Bible reading in public schools. Congress and the states have succeeded in changing a Supreme Court ruling only four times. The Eleventh Amendment of 1795 overrode Chisholm v. Georgia, 2 Dall. 419 (1793); the Thirteenth Amendment corrected Dred Scott v. Sand-

[64] Quoted in Charles H. Sheldon, ed., The Supreme Court: Politicians in Robes (Beverly Hills: Glencoe Press, 1970).

ford, 19 How. 393 (1857); the Sixteenth Amendment was a result of *Pollock* v. *Farmer's Loan and Trust Co.,* 157 U.S. 429 (1895); and the Twenty-Sixth Amendment, granting the vote to eighteen-year-olds in state elections, was a reaction to the Court's *Oregon* v. *Mitchell,* 400 U.S. 112 (1970). Although amending the Constitution as a reaction to court decisions is a long and tedious process leading to limited success, the introduction of amendments is quite common and are expressions of public opinion designed to influence the judges.

Impeachment proceedings of high-court justices have often been threatened by Congress but rarely proposed and only once instituted. These efforts are also largely directed toward influencing rather than replacing judges. For example, the recent threat of impeachment directed toward Justice Douglas could possibly have influenced his decision to disqualify himself in two obscenity cases (*Rosenbloom* v. *Metromedia,* 403 U.S. 29 [1970], and *Byrne* v. *Karalexis,* 401 U.S. 216 [1970]) and in two cases involving publishers of his works (*Decker* v. *Harper and Row,* 400 U.S. 38 [1971], and *Grove Press* v. *Maryland Board of Censors,* 397 U.S. 1060 [1970]).

Congress can also withhold some subjects from courts through legislation. The appellate jurisdiction of the Supreme Court is under the control of the legislators. Part of the 1968 Crime Control Act was designed to allow a trial judge to determine the voluntariness of a confession, although the *Miranda* decision, 384 U.S. 436 (1966), apparently had established sufficient standards. A moratorium on the busing of children for purposes of integration was considered by Congress as a reaction to *Green* v. *New Kent County School Board,* 389 U.S. 1003 (1967), and *Swann* v. *Charlotte-Mecklenburg Board of Education,* 402 U.S. 1 (1971). Congress can change legislation, pass laws to regulate something the court avoids, withhold or grant pay raises and staff assistance to court, increase the size of the Supreme Court, authorize more lower-court judgeships, and exert pressures on the appointment process. State legislatures have some of the same powers over state courts.[65] Not all legislative reactions, of course, are adverse to courts. For example, the 1964 Civil Rights Act helped enforcement of the *Brown* decision. The Criminal Justice

[65] For a review of congressional changes in laws to circumvent Supreme Court rulings, see Jack W. Peltason, *Federal Courts in the Political Process* (New York: Random House, 1955), pp. 59–60.

Act of 1964 was a partial reaction to *Gideon* v. *Wainwright*, in which adequate counsel for the poor in federal courts was assured.

Lower courts, although under the supervision of the Supreme Court or state high courts, can react by vigorously and broadly interpreting high-court decisions or by ignoring or changing the thrust of those decisions.[66] Virgil Hawkins' attempts to get into the University of Florida Law School are well documented. The Supreme Court ruled in 1954, that as a black, he had as much right to attend the law school as a white. They remanded the case to the Florida Supreme Court for reconsideration in light of the *Brown* decision. But the lower court delayed. Hawkins went back to the Supreme Court and the justices said that he must be allowed to enter without delay. The Florida court refused relief again because of fears of violence if Hawkins were allowed to enroll in the law school. Hawkins appealed again to the Supreme Court. The Court refused to review his case but urged him to go to a district court for relief. The Florida District Court denied his request for an injunction and the case went to a U.S. Court of Appeals, which reversed the lower court. The Court of Appeals returned the case to the district court for reconsideration. Finally, in 1958, Hawkins was allowed to enroll in a law school that had refused his application in 1949.[67]

Virgil Hawkins' circumstances may have been unique, but the instances of evasion by lower courts were not. The *Harvard Law Review*, tracing the results of 175 state cases reversed and remanded by the Supreme Court between 1941 and 1951, found that 46 involved further litigation and in almost half of these cases, the party successful before the Supreme Court became the losing party following the remand.[68]

[66] Walter F. Murphy, "Lower Court Checks on Supreme Court Power," *The American Science Review*, LIII (December, 1959), 1017.

[67] See *ibid.*; and Walter F. Murphy and C. Herman Pritchett, eds., *Courts, Judges, and Politics* (New York: Random House, 1961), pp. 606–18.

[68] Note, "Evasions of Supreme Court Mandates in Cases Remanded to State Courts Since 1941," *Harvard Law Review*, LXVII (May, 1954), 1251. See also Note, "Final Disposition of State Court Decisions Reversed and Remanded by the Supreme Court, October Term, 1931 to October Term, 1940," *Harvard Law Review*, LV (January, 1942), 357; Note, "State Court Evasion of United States Supreme Court Mandates," *Yale Law Journal*, LVI (March, 1947), 574; and Note, "Supreme Court Disposition of State Decisions Involving Non-Federal Questions," *Yale Law Journal*, XLIX (June, 1940), 1463.

In the fifties, the Supreme Court ruled that the movie "The Miracle" could not be banned as sacrilegious. But the same movie may well have been kept out of the theaters according to state courts because it was either "immoral," "harmful," or "obscene." [69] The instances of lower-court reactions to and changes in higher courts' rulings are many. As in Virgil Hawkins' case, the higher courts must consider a new demand which had been fed back to them from the actions of other courts.

Opinion leaders often attempt to influence courts through their pronouncements. Billy Graham was shocked by the Supreme Court's ruling on prayers in public schools:

> At a time when moral decadence is evident on every hand, when race tension is mounting, when the threat of Communism is growing, when terrifying new weapons of destruction are being created, we need more religion, not less.
>
> Eighty per cent of the American people want Bible reading and prayer in the schools. Why should the majority be so severely penalized by the protests of a handful? [70]

The Appendix to the *Congressional Record* contains many accounts of reactions of constituencies to the prayer and Bible-reading cases. The hope, of course, is for a new input into the judicial system which will "correct" or reinforce prior court decisions. Although the Supreme Court prayer cases still stand, compliance is not altogether uniform. Perhaps, also, the recent rather ambiguous church-state decisions are a result of feedback symbolized by Billy Graham's warnings to the public (e.g., *Lemon* v. *Kurtzman*, 403 U.S. 602 [1970], and *Walz* v. *Tax Commission*, 397 U.S. 664 [1970]).

Legal scholars and lawyers communicate feedback materials to courts. Conferences of judges, ABA conventions, law reviews, speeches, and *ad hoc* committees of the profession frequently are

---

[69] Peltason (n. 65 above), p. 61; and Alan F. Westin, *The Miracle Case: The Supreme Court and the Movies* (University, Ala.: University of Alabama Press, Inter-University Case Program, 1961).

[70] *New York Times,* June 18, 1963, p. 27.

feedback participants.[71] At the present stage of development of systems analysis of the judicial process, we are unable to trace back an input to the feedback phase with confidence. Speculations like those suggested above are now being, and have been, investigated through impact models. The systems model performs a heuristic function by suggesting hypotheses which can be tested by other models. Impact models, covered in Chapter Five, have been developed to study the environmental ramifications of court decisions. Obviously, feedback is a dimension of impact.

Much remains to be studied. The systems model can be of great assistance in our development of knowledge on the judicial process.

Presently judicial systems analysis offers researchers a comprehensive set of categories for organizing and relating data, an impressive number of important heuristic insights, and the ability to handle microcosm studies displaying predictability. . . . Systems analysis, in spite of some severe shortcomings, provides a major analytical tool for students of public law and judicial behavior. It is likely that systems analysis will be increasingly used and improved and provide solid analytical payoffs.[72]

---

[71] E.g., *Resolutions Adopted at the Tenth Annual Meeting of the Conference of Chief Justices* (Chicago: Council of State Governments, 1958); "Debates of the ABA House of Delegates," *American Bar Association Journal* (October, 1963); selected speeches printed in *Vital Speeches* (Southold, N.Y.: City News Publishing Company); H.A. Long, *The Constitution Betrayed* (Philadelphia: Your Heritage Books, Inc., 1957); and James Voerenberg and James Q. Wilson, "Is the Court Handcuffing the Cops?" *New York Times Magazine*, May 11, 1969.

[72] Goldman and Jahnige, *The Federal Courts* (n. 5 above), p. 284.

CHAPTER SEVEN

The Traditional Approach

CHARACTERISTICS OF THE TRADITIONALISTS

It may seem strange to reserve for the last a review of an approach which antedates all that we have already discussed. The traditional approach has been predominant for years and, until most recently, was responsible for training the vast majority of students of the judicial process. Beyond its predominance through time, the traditional approach has provided, and still provides, the foundation for the political and behavioral models previously reviewed. The author has chosen to discuss the traditional approach last simply because he regards it as the most comprehensive of all the models. The concerns of traditional scholarship are clearly wide. The traditionalist may research the legal, political, and historical variables impinging upon one Supreme Court case or he may cover the entire history of the Court.[1] His sources may be a Supreme Court justice's personal papers, a series of court cases, or numerous historical documents.[2] The traditionalist is limited in his selection of topics only by his own creativity and the documentary sources available. But one could argue that the same unlimited horizons are available to the scholar viewing courts through role, small-group, or decision-making models. Certainly the systems model, as an example, could conceivably be

[1] E.g., Alan F. Westin, *The Anatomy of a Constitutional Law Case* (New York: Macmillan, 1958); Robert G. McCloskey, *The Supreme Court* (Chicago: University of Chicago Press, 1960); and Charles Grove Haines, *The Role of the Supreme Court in American Government and Politics* (Berkeley: University of California Press, 1957).

[2] E.g., Alexander Bickel, *The Unpublished Opinions of Mr. Justice Brandeis* (Cambridge: Harvard University Press, 1957); and L.W. Levy, *Origins of the Fifth Amendment* (New York: Oxford University Press, 1968). S. Sidney Ulmer has reviewed the problems of using personal papers in his "Bricolage and Assorted Thoughts on Working in the Papers of Supreme Court Justices," *Journal of Politics*, XXXV (May, 1973), 286.

used for research into the influence of innumerable and remote social forces. The broad scope of traditional studies, however, encompasses more than the potential for considering a great number of variables.

Glendon Schubert distinguishes a traditionalist from his conventional and behavioral counterparts by the former's reliance upon history, law, and philosophy as explanations for various aspects of the judicial process. The traditionalist tends to possess a philosophical as opposed to a scientific view of the legal system. The traditionalist studies *normative* questions and makes value judgments.[3] This does not mean that the nontraditionalist eschews value judgments. Being human means reaching normative conclusions. But some would argue that the nontraditionalist *wills* to remain as objective as possible, while the traditionalist accepts value judgments as an integral part of his scholarly efforts. Obviously, there is a need for both approaches. To understand what *is*, we must attempt to avoid clouding our observations with subjectivity. But, equally important, we must strive for what is *better*, making moral judgments necessary.

The traditionalist studies *doctrine*. His research is with cases, judicial opinions, and constitutional phrases. He explains for us the meaning of free speech and the First Amendment by beginning, at least, with *Barron v. Baltimore*, 9 Pet. 243 (1833); moving through *Gitlow v. New York*, 268 U.S. 652 (1925), *Dennis v. U.S.*, 341 U.S. 494 (1915); and *Yates v. U.S.*, 354 U.S. 298 (1957); to *U.S. v. Caldwell*, 92 S. Ct. 2646 (1972). The doctrine of the First Amendment as expressed through Supreme Court cases is what concerns the traditionalist. Law is more important than policies, attitudes, voting blocs, roles, or pressure group activities.

History looms large for the traditionalist. The flow of human events provides not only explanation, but also standards for judgment. If the dead hand of the past no longer dictates the direction of the future, at the very least, it provides clues as to the consequences of future alternatives. Benjamin N. Cardozo succinctly expressed the role of history: "I do not mean that the directive force of

[3] Glendon A. Schubert, "Academic Ideology and the Study of Adjudication," *The American Political Science Review*, LXI (March, 1967), 127; and "Ideologies and Attitudes, Academic and Judicial," *Journal of Politics*, XXIX (February, 1967), 3.

history . . . confines the law of the future to uninspired repetition of the law of the present and the past. I mean simply that history, in illuminating the past, illuminates the present, and in illuminating the present, illuminates the future." [4]

The concern for history adds an element to traditional studies which is not ordinarily evident in most behavioral studies.[5] History, for the traditionalist, is not idiographic but nomothetic. What has happened in the past is not unique, but, as suggested by Cardozo, can provide clues about the future. By looking at universal variables rather than at dates, special circumstances, names, or places, the past becomes a vast source of data for testing hypotheses, applying models, and investigating theories.[6] In an important sense *time*, the crucial ingredient of change, is accounted for and explained by the traditional scholar better than by some of his behavioral counterparts.

The traditionalist is not unaware of the force of politics in history.[7] He would recognize that an explanation of *Marbury* v. *Madison* lies in the conflict between the federalist and the Jeffersonians and that the "switch in time that saved nine" in 1937 was not due to a new discovery of precedent on the part of Chief Justice Hughes and Justice Roberts. The best in traditional writing interprets the judicial process in terms of the political forces of the times. But history is also important for the nontraditionalist. An understanding of the interactions among members of a collegial court, for example, has developed from a study of the past.[8] Although behavioral models may be constructed from materials provided by history, they are only rarely applied to the past.

Murphy and Tanenhaus point out that traditionalists have shared three assumptions which have not been accepted uncritically by the

---

[4] Benjamin N. Cardozo, *The Nature of the Judicial Process* (New Haven: Yale University Press, 1960), p. 53.

[5] Donald G. Baker, "Political Socialization: Parameters and Predispositions," *Polity*, III (Summer, 1971), 586.

[6] Adam Prezeworski and Henry Tuene, *The Logic of Comparative Inquiry* (New York: John Wiley, 1970), p. 87.

[7] Since 1925, Robert E. Cushman's case books have always made note of the several political and social forces which are related to the doctrine enunciated by the Supreme Court. Robert E. Cushman, *Leading Constitutional Cases* (New York: F.S. Crofts & Co., 1925).

[8] E.g., Walter F. Murphy, *Elements of Judicial Strategy* (Chicago: University of Chicago Press, 1964).

"new school" of scholars. First, the public law student trained in the traditional approach has assumed that the American Constitution defines the nature and possessors of authority in the American system. Second, according to this view the U.S. Supreme Court is one of the possessors of political power and authority and through its decisions gives content to the definitions of authority. Third, the Court's decisions are seen to encompass law, politics, and policy as well as the philosophical predilections of the justices on the high bench. But the justices are not free to ignore precedent, the wording of the Constitution, political and social forces, nor history.[9]

It is true that the works of some scholars reviewed in this text suggest that they either reject some aspects of the above assumptions or at least form the assumptions into hypotheses to stand the test of empirical research. But by and large, the post-World War II public law experts and their students recognize the truth of the three assumptions. The difference lies only in the kind of emphasis to be given each. The traditionalist generally tends to study institutions rather than processes; he remains parochial in his concerns, emphasizing American institutions; he attempts to describe rather than analyze; he emphasizes the unique as opposed to the commonplace; he seldom constructs models and theories, and rarely tests hypotheses; he is value oriented; he rarely looks to the other social sciences for possible contributions to the understanding of the judiciary; and, for the traditionalist, law is the overriding variable in judicial decisions, not attitudes or policies.[10] Although some may be critical of these emphases, it cannot be denied that a description of the stable and often unique American institutions is essential, that normative judgments must be made, and that law is a standard for judicial decisions.

The traditionalist is not limited to the narrow confines dictated by a formal model or theory. Intuitive impressions or hunches may flow from his perusal of history, constitutions, and cases, so that he may achieve heuristic and predictive results without the "appropriate" model pointing the way. This freedom allows the traditionalist to ask different sorts of questions of the judicial process—questions which

[9] Walter F. Murphy and Joseph Tanenhaus, *The Study of Public Law* (New York: Random House, 1972), pp. 116–17.

[10] M.M. Conway and F.B. Feigert, *Political Analysis: An Introduction* (Boston: Allyn & Bacon, 1972), pp. 9–10.

his behavioral counterparts would avoid. These largely unanswerable questions are pursued by the traditionalist within the framework of some normative view of the law, courts, or society. To discover the relationship of judicial review to democracy, the intent of the framers of the Constitution, the degree of freedom to be allotted political dissidents, or to establish the right balance between the demands of the First Amendment and the needs of national security require little knowledge of statistical inference or model construction. What is required is some belief in or adherence to a philosophy of democracy, free speech, or political obligation. The reason a scholar is called a traditionalist is not that he is trained in law schools or by the case method, and not that he is unfamiliar with or critical of the newer methods, but that he ultimately poses the traditional questions, questions certainly as old as Plato and Aristotle. What is the law? What is justice? What is democracy? What is freedom? Because the traditionalist pursues the ultimate questions, because hundreds of years are available to him for perusal, and because the boundaries of his "model" are ill-defined, his approach is the broadest in scope.

Figure 11 outlines the interaction of the various concerns of the traditionalist.

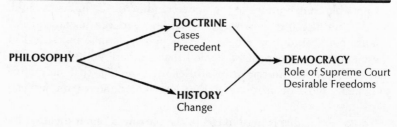

FIGURE 11.   The Traditionalist Model

In the traditionalist model, the change of history is blended with the continuity of cases and precedent as interpreted by the particular normative theory of the scholar in order to arrive at some judgment regarding the role of the Supreme Court in American democracy and the freedoms to be protected by the justices.

CRITIQUE

The traditionalist has generally failed to bring his considerable literary and research talents to bear on courts and judges other than the U.S. Supreme Court. Studies of lower federal and state courts as well as of foreign judicial processes have been missing. Judicial review is not now unique with the American system, and a rich area of comparative study exists which has been only slightly exploited even by the nontraditionalist. Comparative studies of doctrine, judicial activism, executive-legislative and judicial relations, and federalism are possible, for example, for the United States, Canada, Australia, Federal Republic of Germany, and India.[11]

> Traditional political scientists, a few years ago, were not . . . doing research on the judiciary. They were studying constitutional law. They were reading judicial decisions. They were reconstructing judicial philosophies out of the written opinions of members of the Supreme Court. A few were writing judicial biographies. But a concern with the judiciary as a functioning part of the political system, related to other political institutions and processes, had not been developed.[12]

Consequently, these traditionalist scholars became isolated from the general political science profession. They had more in common with their counterparts in the law schools than with their colleagues in the next office. Fewer students concentrated in public law. It was, perhaps, the least popular of all the subfields in political science. The newer methods, statistical techniques, and empirical model construction, which were so instrumental in developing other subfields of political science, came late to public law because of this isolation.

The traditionalist can also be accused of perpetuating several

[11] Exceptions do exist. See Charles Grove Haines, *The American Doctrine of Judicial Supremacy* (Berkeley: University of California Press, 1932); Henry J. Abraham, *The Judicial Process* (New York: Oxford, 1962); Henry J. Abraham, "People's Watchdog Against Abuse of Power," *Public Administration Review*, XX (Summer, 1960), 152; Henry J. Abraham, "Societal and Individual Line-drawing in the British Tradition," *Orbis*, XIII (Fall, 1969), 890; and Charles H. Sheldon, "Public Opinion and High Courts: Communist Party Cases in Four Constitutional Systems," *Western Political Quarterly*, XX (June, 1967), 341.

[12] C. Herman Pritchett, "The Development of Judicial Research," in Joel B. Grossman and Joseph Tanenhaus, eds., *Frontiers of Judicial Research* (New York: John Wiley, 1969), p. 27.

myths about the law, judges, and courts. First, because he uses judicial opinions to explain the law, focuses upon the legal logic embodied in cases rather than upon the judges who heard the cases, and presents criticisms of the Supreme Court which are finely reasoned analyses of how a particular justice or Court misinterpreted or incorrectly applied precedent or violated the rules of logic, he gives a false impression regarding judicial decision making. It appears as if a judge in deciding a case merely took facts from the case; mixed them with constitutional phrases, statutes, and precedent; and thereby discovered the "correct" decision. Although the traditionalist recognizes that the philosophy of a particular judge may well dictate his decision, the traditionalist's concern for rules, precedents, and institutions tends to make the judges appear as mere automatons applying justice through mechanical reasoning by analogy and logic. "Mechanical jurisprudence" or the "slot machine" theory of decision making has now been largely discredited, but the myth was long in dying.[13] Second, when the Supreme Court decides, according to many of the traditionalists, compliance somehow is assured. Impact studies have shown otherwise. Third, the traditionalist has perpetuated the "upper-court myth," diverting the attention of scholars from the equally important position of lower courts—state and federal—in the judicial process. It should be added that the nontraditionalist has also been slow to move into comparative judicial studies of states and lower courts.

The traditionalist has often emphasized the unique nature of the judicial process, preventing the political scientist, with his analytical tools which perform so well in understanding the more political aspects of government, from adequately understanding public law and the judiciary. Schubert comments: "If all institutions are unique . . . then any attempts to develop a systematic body of verified knowledge about human behavior in general, and political behavior in particular, are foredoomed . . . to failure.[14] A political *science* would be impossible on that basis.

The traditionalist assigns great weight to *stare decisis* as a decisional factor in the judicial process. It can be argued that, there-

[13] Associate Justice Owen J. Roberts expressed best the concept of mechanical jurisprudence in his opinion in *U.S.* v. *Butler,* 297 U.S. 1 (1936).
[14] Glendon A. Schubert, *Judicial Policy-Making* (Chicago: Scott, Foresman, 1965), p. 167.

fore, he tends to add a conservative bias to his writing and his criticisms of court decisions. For example, *Baker* v. *Carr*, 369 U.S. 186 (1962), was "bad" law because the justices failed to follow *Colegrove* v. *Green*, 328 U.S. 549 (1946), which had held reapportionment to be a political question and, thus, outside the jurisdiction of a court. Similarly the late Justice Felix Frankfurter was a "good" judge because of his restraintist approach to decision making.

Finally, the traditional critic of newer studies of the judicial process has suggested that the behavioral scholar reaches conclusions that he, the traditionalist, knew all along. But the criticism can be turned around. Even if the nontraditionalist employs "fancy methodologies to prove the commonplace . . . it can hardly be possible that all our truisms and clichés are correct since many tend to contradict one another. Systematic analysis designed to test traditional knowledge cannot, therefore, be wasted even when it tends only to confirm some of our previous impressionistic notions." [15] Impressions, of course, must be validated for they may be wrong.

It has been from the rich traditional literature that newer scholars have drawn many of their insights and hypotheses. Traditional scholars have provided a foundation for empirical studies. No scholar of the judicial process can thus afford to neglect doctrine as explained by the traditionalist. For example, Schubert's decision-making studies in which "C" and "E" scales were designed necessitated considerable knowledge of case doctrine. Further, the traditionalist can make a meaningful contribution by providing general theories of the judicial process for the nontraditionalist to test through models. Quite apart from these contributions, traditional research must not be abandoned simply because, when we no longer ask the ultimate normative questions, we have no hope for the improvement of the human legal condition.

TRADITIONAL STUDIES

In March, 1967, Glendon Schubert published an article in which he reported how political scientists in the public law field rated themselves and others according to behavioral, conventional, and traditional categories. Both self-perception or collegial perceptions placed

[15] Martin Shapiro, "Political Jurisprudence," *Kentucky Law Journal*, LII (1964), quoted in Schubert, *Judicial Policy-Making*, p. 170.

Henry J. Abraham, Paul C. Bartholomew, David Fellman, Robert
G. McCloskey, Walter Berns, Wallace Mendelson, John P. Roche,
Rocco J. Tresolini, and Alan Westin into the traditional classification.[16] As no list of which scholar belongs where could be an adequate substitute for the perceptions of the profession itself, we shall
accept the works of the above scholars as being fairly representative
of traditional studies and shall add only a few political scientists
who have obviously made their impact on public law.[17]

The traditionalist blends doctrine, history, and philosophy into his
writing with the emphases being inextricably combined. He judges
the output of the courts by a study of cases through time. Although
the separation here of these emphases into three categories—doctrinal
studies, historical studies, normative studies—presents the danger of
destroying the life of the total traditional body, it does allow for a
convenient, if not artificial, method for organizing the review of
traditional studies.

DOCTRINAL STUDIES

Perhaps the most common writings found in traditional studies are
analyses of Supreme Court decisions. Apart from these writings,
virtually all historical writing and the philosophical tracts are
founded on a review of case doctrine. To determine what the justices
have said, what they should have said, and whether they were con-

[16] Schubert, "Academic Ideology" (n. 3 above), p. 106. If historians and legal
scholars were included, the list would swell to great proportions. We are basically concerned here with political scientists so that our task is somewhat
simplified.

[17] The amount of important traditional materials is massive. Historians, law
professors, and legal practitioners have all contributed significantly to this
scholarship. What is reviewed here is only a small part of this rich scholarship
and is limited to traditional political scientists rather than historians and
legal scholars (although in the earlier years of our profession the separation
between historians, political scientists, and legal scholars was not always complete). Besides the authors cited in Schubert's study I have chosen to add
Robert K. Carr, Carl Brent Swisher, Edward S. Corwin, Charles Grove Haines,
and Robert E. Cushman.

I recognize that many great names have been excluded from the analysis of
traditional works. Certainly no review would be complete without references
to Charles A. Beard, Alpheus Thomas Mason, Charles Warren, Thomas Reed
Powell, Alexander Bickel, Max Lerner, Roscoe Pound, James B. Thayer, or
Phillip B. Kurland, to name but a few. My purpose has been only to isolate the
leading trends in traditional scholarship and to present examples. A bibliography
of some of the traditional scholarship is in Charles A. Beard, *The Supreme
Court and the Constitution* (Englewood Cliffs, N.J.: Prentice-Hall, 1962),
pp. 147–49.

sistent in what they said is to understand the Constitution and the statutes, which are supposed to be consistent with the basic document. Robert E. Cushman, Paul Bartholomew, and Rocco Tresolini exemplify this level of traditional scholarship. Robert E. Cushman, who began his doctrinal analysis in 1925, wrote in his 1962 edition that "no one can understand fully and clearly how our American national government works, or how it came to be the kind of government it is, unless he is familiar" with the workings of the Supreme Court and, of course, with those decisions which "are milestones in the growth of our American Constitutional system." [18] Tresolini echoes this concern with doctrine:

> During the past few years it has become increasingly apparent that a large number of American students do not understand or fully appreciate the basic principles of democratic government. These students have little awareness of the importance of the Bill of Rights and other constitutional provisions. . . . If our concept of democratic government is to endure and expand, it is essential that students develop an appreciation of concern for our fundamental freedoms.[19]

It is through the case method and the analysis of Supreme Court doctrine that the student will gain an appreciation for the Constitution and an understanding of the democratic system. In particular, analysis of doctrine through the case method was for Tresolini, and is for other traditionalists, by far the best method for achieving this lofty goal. First, case analysis sharpens the intellect—somehow as the study of Latin develops the minds of the young. Second, through cases we can see, in Tresolini's words, "the Bill of Rights for what it is—a living, dynamic, ever-changing protective shield." Third, cases are the original or primary sources for constitutional law. Students become excited by analysis of primary sources not evident in the rehashing characteristic of textbook and lecture materials. By consulting the original sources, the student is engaged in direct research into the most important aspect of the judicial process—the court decisions and their meanings.

Tresolini urged students to utilize the law-school briefing tech-

[18] Robert E. Cushman and Robert F. Cushman, *Leading Constitutional Decisions* (New York: Appleton-Century-Crofts, 1966), p. v. See also his *Civil Liberties in the United States* (Ithaca, N.Y.: Cornell University Press, 1956).
[19] Rocco J. Tresolini, *These Liberties: Case Studies in Civil Rights* (Philadelphia: J.B. Lippincott, 1968), p. vii.

nique to understand Supreme Court doctrine as it develops through cases. Students must understand the facts of a case; cull from the opinions the legal questions that the justices are attempting to answer; give the holding or the Court's answers to the questions; and analyze the opinions of the justices, in which they give the reasons for answering the questions as they did under those factual circumstances. Finally, Tresolini suggested that the student ". . . should personally evaluate the importance of the case, show its relationship, if any, with other cases studied, and indicate its place in the whole stream of American Constitutional law. [The student should also] criticize or praise the opinions or make any other comment that seems significant. . . ." [20]

If the student follows the traditionalist's instructions, he will discover, for example, that *Schenck* v. *U.S.*, 294 U.S. 47 (1919), established the "clear and present danger" test which assists the justices in defining the constitutional doctrine of free speech. An analysis of *Gitlow* v. *N.Y.*, 268 U.S. 652 (1925), shows a change in First Amendment doctrine, with the adoption of the "bad tendency" test to measure what speech and press will be tolerated and what words will be proscribed. *Whitney* v. *California*, 274 U.S. 357 (1927), illustrates a clear application of the clear and present danger test—by the dissenters—but the majority adopted a "reasonableness" test according to which the Court would accept legislative enactments if the justices were convinced that the legislators could have reasonably concluded that certain speech constitutes a danger to the American system. In the fifties, the doctrine of the First Amendment changed in *Dennis* v. *U.S.*, 341 U.S. 494 (1951), to a "gravity of the evil" test; and later the test separated abstract thought and intellectual discussion from illegal actions, protecting the former but proscribing the latter (*Yates* v. *U.S.*, 354 U.S. 298 [1957]).

The commerce clause of the Constitution comes to life as the scholar appraises such cases as *Gibbons* v. *Ogden*, 9 Wheat. 1 (1824); *Brown* v. *Maryland*, 12 Wheat. 419 (1827); *Cooley* v. *Board of Wardens*, 12 How. 299 (1852); *Shreveport Rate Case*, 234 U.S. 342 (1914); *N.L.R.B.* v. *Jones & Laughlin Corp.*, 301 U.S. 1 (1937); *Wickard* v. *Filburn*, 317 U.S. 111 (1942); and *Heart of Atlanta Motel* v. *U.S.*, 379 U.S. (1964). Other cases have indicated different courses for the commerce doctrine, and the efforts of the traditional-

[20] Rocco J. Tresolini and Martin Shapiro, *American Constitutional Law* (New York: Macmillan, 1970), p. 41.

ist document the patterns and isolate the divergences of such constitutional doctrines.[21]

Tresolini, true to the traditionalist pattern, did not avoid value judgments as he traced doctrine. For example, in response to the Supreme Court's doctrine established in *Thompson* v. *Louisville*, 362 U.S. 199 (1960), he wrote that: "The case demonstrates well the fact that 'an active ingredient in the workings of one branch of the most powerful government on earth is compassion. Compassion for the fate of solitary people, of desperate, lonely, untutored and disturbed people. Compassion for human life regardless of its extrinsic worth.' Is it not possible that this concern may well be America's most enduring gift to the world?"[22]

Paul Bartholomew has continued to review each term of the U.S. Supreme Court for the *Western Political Quarterly* in terms of doctrine. David Fellman and others performed the same service for *The American Political Science Review* until the early sixties. The major cases in each term were reported in the form of a brief, with reinforcements or changes in doctrine noted.[23] The obvious purpose of these series of articles has been to keep scholars and interested students up to date on constitutional doctrine. Today, the student often turns to legal periodicals for a current guide to doctrine.[24]

[21] Some of the best in doctrine analysis is illustrated by Edward S. Corwin, *The Constitution of the United States of America: Analysis and Interpretation* (Washington, D.C.: U.S. Government Printing Office, 1963): and, more recently, C. Herman Pritchett, *The American Constitution* (New York: McGraw-Hill, 1968). The analysis of doctrine is still a viable tradition. In such analyses, the commentaries started by Cushman are often expanded, and lower-court decisions may be included to give the student a sense for the dynamism of the decisional process. See, for example, M. Glenn Abernathy, *Civil Liberties under the Constitution* (New York: Dodd, Mead, 1972); Alpheus T. Mason and William M. Beaney, *American Constitutional Law* (Englewood Cliffs, N.J.: Prentice-Hall, 1972); Richard C. Cortner and Clifford M. Lytle, *Modern Constitutional Law* (New York: The Free Press, 1972); Victor G. Rosenblum and A. Didrick Castberg, *Cases on Constitutional Law* (Homewood, Ill.: Dorsey Press, 1973); and Harold W. Chase and Craig R. Ducat, eds., *Corwin's The Constitution and What It Means Today* (Princeton: Princeton University Press, 1973). Lower-court decisions are included in Stanley H. Friedelbaum, *Contemporary Constitutional Law* (Boston: Houghton Mifflin, 1972).

[22] Tresolini, *These Liberties*, p. 87. See also his *Justice and the Supreme Court* (Philadelphia: J.B. Lippincott, 1963).

[23] See December issues of the *Western Political Quarterly* from 1963 through 1969 and 1972. In 1962 and 1970, Bartholomew's reviews were carried in the March issues.

[24] Each year, for example, the *Harvard Law Review* carries a summary of the Supreme Court term and reviews doctrine.

Another example of traditional scholarship which concerned itself with doctrine was Robert G. McCloskey's review of civil rights cases decided in the 1960 term of the Supreme Court. McCloskey not only reviewed, as before, the leading cases; but he also appraised the Court's efforts within an ends-means framework. He analyzed the results of cases and, although the record was somewhat ambivalent, concluded that the Court "did or seemed in the process of doing about as much on behalf of civil rights as we can reasonably expect nine men to do." However, in McCloskey's view, the means by which the justices arrived at these results lacked clarity. The written opinions were confused, badly reasoned, and often contradictory. McCloskey believed that the Court was "not confronting the task of intellectual architecture that is posed by its modern jurisdictional claims in the field of civil rights." The reason for such ambiguity was the "fragmenting and hardening of attitudes" on the bench, making consensus difficult if not impossible.[25] The Court had reached somewhat pro-civil rights ends with means that lacked precision, consistency, and consensus.

Although normative judgments of Court doctrine may have been avoided to some degree by traditionalists, politics and social forces were seldom excluded from the analyses of cases, in which the political and social forces surrounding those cases were explained. Thus, the student of cases gained a sense not only of the law but also of politics. Perhaps this was the major contribution of political scientists to constitutional law, especially as taught at law schools. The realist school of jurisprudence found a friendly reception among the earlier political scientists.[26]

HISTORICAL STUDIES

The use of history by the traditionalist is an extension of his doctrine predilections. It is merely an extension of the study of doctrine through time, often judged by some standard of "right" or "wrong." McCloskey's analysis of Court doctrine from the beginnings of the Republic to the nineteen-sixties led him to divide the span of

[25] Robert G. McCloskey, "Deeds Without Doctrine: Civil Rights in the 1960 Term of the Supreme Court," *The American Political Science Review*, LVI (March, 1962), 87–88.

[26] Walter F. Murphy and Joseph Tanenhaus, *The Study of Public Law*, pp. 14–15.

time into three major periods. From the beginnings of the Court until 1865, Chief Justices Marshall and Taney established and reinforced the image and power of the Court as they faced issues of nation-state relations generated by the young nation.[27] Following the Civil War, capitalism presented to the Court new and trying issues which characterized its life until 1937. The specific question to be answered was that of government-business relations, the Court fairly consistently protecting business from the strictures of governmental regulation. McCloskey comments: "The nation-state relationship, once salient, was now subordinate; the fear that the states would wound or destroy the nation was replaced by the fear that government, state or national, would unduly hinder business in its mission to make America wealthy and wise." [28] After 1937, the Court moved into consideration of government-individual relations, as civil rights issues were generated within the American system.

Each period discussed by McCloskey was a product of historical necessity. The Marshall and Taney Courts were participating in the establishment of a nation finally torn asunder by the Civil War. The post-Civil War Court had to meet the demands of a "new" nation involved in a period of revolutionary economic growth, again, checked by the Great Depression. The post-1937 Court had to face new revolutionary questions of equality and freedom, challenged by a world which from time to time was built upon the negation of those rights. Constitutional doctrine, thus, does not develop in isolation from the ebb and flow of human events. The Court's decisions were, and are, products of history.

But the traditionalist does not merely record history; he draws lessons therefrom. For McCloskey, the contemporary Supreme Court "will be understood and evaluated in light of what has gone before." The question now, as in the past, is: "When should the Court intervene in the political and social forces of the times?" History, according to McCloskey, shows that no single and final answer can be forthcoming. The role of the Court has shifted with national conditions, and should continue to do so. The very nature of the constitutional system dictates an ambivalent answer, for it has fashioned a system of popular sovereignty tempered by the rule of law. The role

[27] Robert G. McCloskey, *The American Supreme Court* (Chicago: University of Chicago Press, 1960), pp. 99–100.
[28] *Ibid.*, p. 105.

of the Court is to balance the ever-changing demands of the majority
with the certainty and security of the law. The Court, as history tells
us, must move into its new tasks slowly and gingerly. In McCloskey's
words, the Court is also obliged to "reckon with America and her
propensities; and America is a nation that moves hesitantly and
changes gradually." But this does not mean that the Court should
exercise restraint to the degree that most tasks are left to other
branches of government. "The Court of history has never assessed
itself so modestly. [Its] "greatest successes have been achieved when
it has operated near the margins rather than in the center of political controversy, when it has nudged and gently tugged the nation
instead of trying to rule it." [29] The historical answer to the role of the
Court can thus be found somewhere between the "activism" of
Justice William O. Douglas and the "restraint" of Chief Justice
Warren E. Burger.

But the contemporary Court under Chief Justices Harlan Stone,
Fred M. Vinson, and especially Earl Warren in the sixties moved
beyond merely nudging and tugging the nation by becoming a
"major initiative-producing agency of modern government." No
longer did a majority of the justices regard their task as negative, as
vetoing unacceptable actions of the political branches. The Supreme
Court initiated change ahead of the other agencies of government.
Although the Court now has become a center of controversy, Mc-
Closkey feels it could sustain this positive action for a time without
damage to its effectiveness.[30]

The various works of Edward S. Corwin and Charles Grove
Haines are excellent examples of descriptive history which blend
comments on the impact of social, political, and economic forces on
Supreme Court doctrine with normative judgments about the proper
role of the Supreme Court. The development of doctrines of substantive due process, liberty of contract, dual federalism, and the
commerce clause received special attention from these scholars. In
the history that surrounded these constitutional doctrines lies meaningful lessons about law and the role of the Court.

Haines's recording of the development of the American practice
of judicial review still stands as an example of the best in constitu-

[29] *Ibid.*, p. 229.
[30] Robert G. McCloskey, *The Modern Supreme Court* (Cambridge: Harvard
University Press, 1972), p. 363.

tional history.[31] His analysis leads him to conclude that there is nothing within the history of Court doctrine that compels the justices to read their own philosophy into such constitutional clauses as due process or commerce and thereby act as superlegislators. Equally strong in Haines is the restraintist tradition that "judicial review of legislative acts . . . be confined to the normal function of defining and applying the express requirements of written constitutions. . . ." [32]

An appraisal of the intent of the framers of the Constitution and of Supreme Court doctrine leads Edward S. Corwin to conclude, like Haines, that the power of judicial review is correctly exercised when the Court impedes the hasty processes of government, instills a respect for the old, and allows for another stage of "discussion, clarification, [and] rationalization of public policies." [33] The histories of Corwin, Haines, and other traditionalists are more than mere descriptive recordings of events. As in the historical analysis of McCloskey, moral judgments are made.[34]

Another form of historical analysis is represented by the works which review the political, economic, social, and legal forces impinging upon one landmark case decided by the Supreme Court. Alan F. Westin exemplifies this form of traditional scholarship in his case study of the *Youngstown Sheet and Tube Company* v. *Sawyer,* 343 U.S. 579 (1952). He traces the case from its beginnings in the political and economic mood of 1952, through the lower courts, to and beyond the Supreme Court decision. His cast of characters includes the President, Congress, labor union and business leaders, the public, lower-court judges, and, of course, the nine justices of the Supreme Court. Westin urges students to utilize these historical

[31] Charles Grove Haines, *The American Doctrine of Judicial Supremacy* (Berkeley: University of California Press, 1932). See also his *The Role of the Supreme Court in American Government and Politics* (Berkeley: University of California Press, 1957), Vols. I and II.

[32] *Ibid.,* p. 540.

[33] Edward S. Corwin, *Court Over Constitution* (Princeton: Princeton University Press, 1938), pp. 208–09. He is especially disturbed by the Court's ruling in *Pollock* v. *Farmers Loan and Trust Company,* 157 U.S. 429 (1895), in which the income tax was struck down.

[34] Two standard works today which carry on the tradition of constitutional history are Alfred H. Kelly and Winfred A. Harbison, *The American Constitution: Its Origins and Development* (New York: W.W. Norton, 1970); and A.T. Mason and William M. Beaney, *The Supreme Court in a Free Society* (New York: W.W. Norton, 1968).

studies as Tresolini suggests they should use cases: "Analysis of constitutional law decisions usually includes inquiries into the wisdom of the law expounded on this particular subject, the standard of judicial review employed by the Court, and the relation of each opinion to the general position of that individual Justice." [35] The recording of events surrounding, and doctrine established by, an individual case performs the same function as that of the more historical works on the Court. Social, political, and economic conditions are re-created to pose, if not answer, basic questions about the position the case occupies in the patterns of decisions and in the role the Court has assumed, and must assume, in the American system.

NORMATIVE STUDIES

For many traditional scholars, an analysis of doctrine and history supplies them with evidence for moral judgments on the importance of freedoms in the American system and on the proper role the Supreme Court should play in protecting those freedoms. Should the Supreme Court or other branches of government lead the way toward protecting and furthering basic freedoms, and what are those basic freedoms? This question brings into focus the issue of judicial activism versus judicial restraint.[36]

For David Fellman, the value of free speech in a democracy surpasses all other political values. "The right to talk politics," however, is not an absolute, but a preferred right. The psychic demands of a system of free speech are great; for "a free society is inescapably a noisy and disorderly one. . . . We believe that life in a noisy society is infinitely preferable to life in a quiet penitentiary." [37] The

[35] Alan F. Westin, *The Anatomy of a Constitutional Law Case* (New York: Macmillan, 1958), p. 179. Similar case studies are Daniel M. Berman, *It Is So Ordered* (New York: W.W. Norton, 1966); Anthony Lewis, *Gideon's Trumpet* (New York: Random House, 1964); Calvin B.T. Lee, *One Man, One Vote* (New York: Charles Scribner's Sons, 1967); Grant McConnell, *The Steel Seizure of 1952* (University, Ala.: University of Alabama Press, 1960); Bernard Taper, *Gomillion versus Lightfoot* (New York: McGraw-Hill, 1962); and Alan F. Westin, *The Miracle Case: The Supreme Court and the Movies* (University, Ala.: University of Alabama Press, 1961).

[36] For a general introduction to activism vs. restraint, see David F. Forte, ed., *The Supreme Court in American Politics* (Lexington, Mass.: D.C. Heath, 1972).

[37] David Fellman, *The Limits of Freedom* (New Brunswick, N.J.: Rutgers University Press, 1959), p. 91.

limits to free speech, the boundaries to a noisy and disorderly society, are far from easily defined and discerned. But violent words must not lead to violent acts, for a democracy "is not obligated to commit suicide." Society has a right to prevent harm to its members. Libel and slander, some forms of picketing, and obscenity are clearly within the right of society to punish. No easy formula is available to determine what is tolerable and what is not; and Fellman—and, it must be added, the justices of the Supreme Court themselves—provide no simple answer. Harm to others in society appears to be the standard; and this is for society to determine. The costs of a free society are great, but it still remains "the greatest bargain in all history." [38]

The right of association is essential to a constitutional democracy, as are the other First Amendment freedoms. Without the right to assemble and to petition government, a democratic system would be ineffective. But again, as with other First Amendment freedoms, some limits exist. Fellman believes that some private and some public rights have priority over the rights of association. Criminal conspiracies and disorderly picketing can be controlled by government. However, beyond this, the government has an obligation to protect free assembly and petition. Thus, Fellman grants to the First Amendment freedoms a preferred, but not an absolute, position in our constitutional system. And typically, he states that protection of these freedoms is the *rule;* and deviations from the rule must remain the exception.[39]

According to Fellman, the right of association (as with other rights), to remain a meaningful constitutional freedom, must allow individuals to associate with "evil" people for "bad" purposes as much as allowing "good" people to join together for "just" causes. Where the right of association is concerned, separating "good" from "evil" and proscribing the latter would make the former meaningless.[40] "We do not have one Bill of Rights for nice people, and another one for bad people." [41]

[38] *Ibid.*, p. 123.
[39] David Fellman, *The Constitutional Right of Association* (Chicago: University of Chicago Press, 1963).
[40] *Ibid.*, p. 86.
[41] David Fellman, *The Defendant's Rights* (New York: Rinehart, 1958), p. 7; and "Association with Bad People," *Journal of Politics*, XXII (November, 1960), 620.

Robert K. Carr, like Fellman, attaches prime importance to the exercise of freedoms espoused in the First Amendment. Government has the obligation not only to shield the individual from state action, but it must also wield the sword of state power to prevent private individuals, mobs, or society from silencing the minority. Carr states: ". . . the Bill of Rights . . . [is] a shield fashioned by a democracy for safeguarding individual freedom against governmental encroachment. Now another instrument has been fashioned, a sword, for which little or no express constitutional sanction exists. But it has been fashioned and its usefulness decisively indicated. . . . The sword is tested. . . . Let us not hesitate to use it." [42] Implied, of course, is that the exercise of freedom will lead to a better society. The exercise of that freedom, however, must be balanced with the demands of society. Since freedom is relative, not absolute, the task is to achieve an adequate balance. According to Carr, federal rather than state or personal responsibility will provide a means for balancing. Also, people must be educated to the belief that freedom should be granted to all. Before liberty can be assured, however, America must build a social order which eliminates economic and social insecurities. [43]

Walter Berns is not willing to assume that freedom somehow carries with it an intrinsic good and that a free society is all that democracy is about. On the one hand, he condemns those writers who rely on American tradition to give content to freedom; on the other, he condemns those who accept no restraints on freedom, simply because it is a natural right flowing somehow from man as a human being, with government presenting the greatest threat to it. First, according to Berns, we must ask what is the right; and then, and only then, can we ask how can the right be done? His criticism is leveled at liberals like Fellman who, he believes, fail to ask the first question and, thus, cannot provide adequate answers to the second. [44]

[42] Robert K. Carr, *Federal Protection of Civil Rights: Quest for a Sword* (Ithaca, N.Y.: Cornell University Press, 1947), p. 210. The book was written before any modern civil rights acts were passed by Congress. The bearer of the sword was the Civil Rights Section of the Justice Department. For a historical analysis of the assumption of positive power by government, see Edward S. Corwin, *Liberty Against Government* (Baton Rouge: Louisiana State University Press, 1948).

[43] *Ibid.*, pp. 191–92.

[44] Walter Berns, *Freedom, Virtue and the First Amendment* (Baton Rouge: Louisiana State University Press, 1957), pp. 26–28.

In his efforts to correct the liberal oversight, Berns points out that the Constitution not only states in the First Amendment that "Congress shall make no law" to regulate freedoms, but also that the government, as stated in the Preamble, was formed to "establish justice." Berns comments: "The problem of the First Amendment is not one merely of protecting freedom of speech, press, religion and political opinion, but is inseparable from the problem of governing, of establishing justice, the central political virtue. A reasonable jurisprudence would be guided by the knowledge that freedom and justice are not always compatible." [45]

Liberals (including Supreme Court justices), according to Berns, mistakenly fail to define good and evil. The "free market of ideas," where virtually all ideas and doctrines compete for public acceptance, will not result in a good society, as libertarians have assumed. Like Carr, Berns believes that government must seize the sword in order to establish justice. But Berns's sword is double-edged. First, government must define what is good and evil, using justice as the standard; second, evil must be eradicated and the good fostered by the instrumentalities of government. Justice or virtue, Berns believes, results from the establishment of "ideal relations among men." Rather than threatening freedom as some liberals assume, government must be used to establish virtue. This means that only those freedoms which are consistent with justice are tolerated by government. In addition, government must assume the responsibility for teaching moral principles. A virtuous society will result.

Berns fails to provide specific guides to the establishment of virtue but regards his task as one of pointing out the dilemma in which contemporary liberals place themselves when they eschew moral philosophy. For without answering the question of what is good and what is evil, we may well miss the opportunity of establishing justice in our society.

Wallace Mendelson accepts, as does Fellman, that "Democracy . . . is the *unfettered exchange of ideas* with public *control* of action in accordance with those thoughts which win acceptance in the market place of reason." [46] The issue for Mendelson is how the Supreme Court fits into a democratic scheme which maintains, how-

---

[45] *Ibid.*, p. 46.
[46] Wallace Mendelson, *Justices Black and Frankfurter: Conflict In the Court* (Chicago: University of Chicago Press, 1961), p. 52.

ever inadequately at times, the unfettered exchange of ideas. Justices Hugo Black and Felix Frankfurter represent two basic approaches to the question of the role of the Supreme Court in the democratic scheme. Justice Black, according to Mendelson, was an idealist who bypassed precedent to achieve justice in the immediate case. Frankfurter, on the other hand, was a pragmatist who followed precedent in order to perpetuate law for all. Black, by doing justice, was an activist; and Frankfurter, by doing justice under the law, was an "humilitarian" or restraintist. Mendelson accepts Frankfurter's approach to the function of the Court. By rejecting the activist role, Mendelson also rejects Berns's approach. The value of separation of powers and diffusion of powers within the American system of government is more important than some arbitrary definition of justice administered by an intellectual and social elite on the high-court bench. Mendelson described Frankfurter's view of the judicial role with obvious approval: "[H]umanitarian ends are served best in that allocation of function through which people seek their own destiny. True to the faith upon which democracy ultimately rests, [Frankfurter] would leave to the political processes the onus of building legal standards in the vacuum of doubt. For in his view only that people is free who chooses for itself when choice must be made." [47]

But, like Berns, Mendelson sees democracy as more than liberty and freedom under the law. Again, Frankfurter epitomized for him what was desirable: "It is not that [Frankfurter] loved liberty less, but rather that he loved democracy—*in all its aspects*—more." [48] Thus, the good judge (meaning Frankfurter)

> . . . must maintain at least formal symmetry while he synthesizes established rules, pragmatic needs, and moral yearnings. He must honor reasonable expectations born of the past, yet accommodate the present and the future. Thus he cannot entirely forsake either rule or discretion. The genius of the great judge is that he finds a happy blend. . . . Above all, he recognizes that the process of legal change—the exer-

---

[47] *Ibid.*, p. 131. Mendelson later believed that Black had the same goals as Frankfurter but used different and inadequate methods to achieve them. See his "Hugo Black and Judicial Discretion," *Political Science Quarterly*, LXXXV (March, 1970), 17.

[48] Wallace Mendelson, *The Supreme Court: Law and Discretion* (Indianapolis: Bobbs-Merrill, 1967), p. 12.

cise of a court's inevitable discretion—must itself be principled and orderly.[49]

Henry J. Abraham appears to accept and also reject aspects of Fellman's, Berns's, and Mendelson's judgments. First, he identifies a double standard in Supreme Court doctrine. The justices have eschewed judicial policy making in the economic sphere since 1937, but have been very careful in their scrutiny of legislative acts dealing with civil liberties. This double standard can be justified. The First Amendment, for example, contains language specifically denying Congress legislative authority in the area of the freedoms therein enumerated. The Amendment begins with—"Congress shall make no law. . . ." Also, the Amendment is a statement of *basic* freedoms upon which all the others rest. No other agency of government is as willing or as capable of protecting the basic freedoms as the courts. Finally, pressure groups organized around an economic or social interest have access to the legislature; but unpopular minorities or individuals, although not entirely alone, cannot gain a hearing in the legislature, necessitating court intervention. Thus, economic issues are resolved elsewhere but the courts take care of questions of liberty.[50] So like Fellman, Abraham assigns to the First Amendment a preferred status; and in his view the role of the Court, contrary to Mendelson's theme, is to foster those basic freedoms.[51]

The Supreme Court, in the long run, has played its role well. Abraham believes that, over time, the Court espouses the trends evident in the more popular branches of government. Thus, for him, the issue of activism versus restraint, so important to Mendelson, is not a burning issue. Even Justices Black and Frankfurter disagree only on when the Court ought to intervene in the popular political processes, not if it should check legislative or executive actions.

Finally, like Berns, Abraham believes that the Court must "play its role as an educator and arbiter—it must remain true to its function

[49] Wallace Mendelson, "The Neo-Behavioral Approach to the Judicial Process: A Critique," *The American Political Science Review*, LVII (September, 1963), 603.

[50] See Justice Stone's opinion in *U.S. v. Caroline Products Company*, 304 U.S. 144 (1938).

[51] Alan Westin sees right to privacy as the *basic* freedom. Without "the opportunities for privacy . . . our whole system of civil liberties may become formalistic ritual. . . ." Alan F. Westin, *Privacy and Freedom* (New York: Atheneum, 1967), p. 399.

as teacher in an eternal national constitutional seminar." [52] The Court teaches moral principles. The question to be asked concerning moral principles, by the Court and by us all, according to Abraham, is "Will the forbidding of freedom of expression further or hamper the realization of liberal democratic ideals?" [53] This stand appears to be not far from Berns's "ideal relations among men."

David Fellman has argued that ". . . . procedural safeguards are absolutely essential for justice. In fact, in large measure justice is fair procedure." [54] But, John Roche believes, more is involved. Due process means procedure, certainly; but due process goes beyond procedure to provide a standard for judging the content of the law. Without the substantive aspects of due process, the procedural protections would be meaningless. According to Roche: "[D]ue process of law is an ideal which governs the subjective content of legal action as well as the objective methods pursued. . . . All the procedural guarantees in existence will not protect liberty unless they are part and parcel of a fundamental atmosphere of freedom. . . ." [55] The substance of the law, however, for Roche, is to be defined by Congress or representatives of the people—not the Supreme Court. Like Mendelson, he feels the Court is unsuited in theory and in practice for such an activist role ". . . it is not the function of judges to determine social and economic policy; their task is to apply those policies decided upon by the responsible organs of government to cases at bar." [56]

Roche's deep belief in the common man and in his ability to govern himself accounts for his support for representative bodies. Of course, the common man is fallible, but certainly his concept of what is good for him and society is no less "wrong" than that of the elite or the privileged few.[57] Roche is further convinced that only by exercising restraint will the Court be able to retain its power and prestige in the American system.[58]

[52] Henry J. Abraham, *The Judiciary: The Supreme Court in the Governmental Process* (Boston: Allyn and Bacon, 1969), p. 117.

[53] Henry J. Abraham, *Freedom and the Court* (New York: Oxford University Press, 1972), p. 205.

[54] Fellman, *The Defendant's Rights* (n. 41 above), p. 4.

[55] John P. Roche, *Courts and Rights: The American Judiciary in Action* (New York: Random House, 1961), p. 91.

[56] *Ibid.*, p. 105.

[57] See especially his *The Quest for the Dream* (New York: Macmillan, 1963).

[58] John P. Roche, "Judicial Self-Restraint," *The American Political Science Review*, XLIX (September, 1955), 772.

One of the major tasks of the traditionalists has been to determine the proper role of the Supreme Court in the American political system. A discussion of the desirability of judicial review provides the basis for this determination; and a rich mixture of doctrine, history, and philosophy are the sources. Ultimately the question can only be answered by an appraisal of the nature of democracy in America. For example, John Roche urges restraint on the Court because of his commitment to representative democracy. But Robert K. Carr, long before David Truman and Jack Peltason, saw American democracy as pluralistic, with groups supplying the demands and government acting as broker. The Court was and is "subject to many of the same forces and influences" as Congress and the President. When the justices are faced with exercising judicial review, the contending groups have merely transferred their struggle from the administrative and legislative arenas to the courtroom.[59] Since politics is pluralistic and the Supreme Court is clearly a political institution, judicial review is an acceptable if not desirable institution.

Edward S. Corwin, one of the giants of traditional scholarship, attributes to the American written Constitution a "higher law" concept which places judicial review in a unique and important position. According to Corwin the Constitution has developed into a "statute emanating from the sovereign people," which then places ordinary legislative enactments into a secondary role. The recourse for individuals to the higher law is the Supreme Court's exercise of judicial review.[60] The bridge to the higher law is provided by the role of the Supreme Court as it weighs and judges the legislative enactments in terms of the sovereign Constitution.

But traveling that bridge, again because of the higher-law attribute of the Constitution, may require payment of an exorbitant toll. Natural-law or higher-law constitutional symbols also allow the judge to exercise his own view of "reason," "justice," or morality in weighing legislative enactments on the scale of constitutionalism. Because of the development of the doctrine of substantive due process as a vehicle of Supreme Court policy making, Corwin comments that

[59] Robert K. Carr, *The Supreme Court and Judicial Review* (New York: Holt, Rinehart and Winston, 1942), pp. 291–92. Prior to the 1937 Court "revolution" Carr was not so sure that judicial review was entirely desirable. See his *Democracy and the Supreme Court* (Norman, Okla.: University of Oklahoma Press, 1936).

[60] Edward S. Corwin, *The "Higher Law" Background of the American Constitutional Law* (Ithaca, N.Y.: Cornell University Press, 1957), p. 89.

"judicial review in the sense of judicial discretion has devoured its progeny, constitutional law." [61]

It appears that some traditionalists are judging judicial review in terms of "whose ox is being gored." The dominance of the constitutional system by the advocates of business, property, and contract—despite the Depression and the efforts of the early years of Roosevelt's New Deal—appears to have brought judicial review into disrepute. But Charles Grove Haines does not condemn the institution simply because in the hands of the "Nine Old Men" it may have been abused: "If it is the customary morality of right-minded men and women which the judges are to enforce, natural law standards as conceived by them and as developed by the scholars and commentators, will serve as an invaluable guide." [62] And Haines is quite clear about this role of the judges. It is not the "right-minded" morality of the judges which is to be enforced, but the morality of the people.

> Not that the voice of the people is the voice of God or that it is always reliable and invariably inures to the public welfare, but that in the long run the voice of the people is more to be relied upon than that of some self-appointed guardians whose chief claim to eminence is an arrogant confidence that they are endowed with a political acumen not vouchsafed to ordinary human beings.[63]

Perhaps following the "switch in time that saved nine" in 1937 Haines might have been more sanguine regarding discretionary judicial review.

[61] Edward S. Corwin, *The Twilight of the Supreme Court* (New Haven: Yale University Press, 1934), p. 101. See also Charles Grove Haines, *The Revival of Natural Law Concepts* (New York: Russell and Russell, 1965); Edward S. Corwin, *Constitutional Revolution, Ltd.* (Claremont, Cal.: Claremont Colleges, 1941); Edward S. Corwin, "The Constitution as Instrument and as Symbol," *The American Political Science Review,* XXX (December, 1936), 1071–85; and Edward S. Corwin, *Liberty Against Government* (Baton Rouge: Louisiana State University Press, 1948). For a complete bibliography of Corwin's works, consult A.T. Mason and G. Garvey, *American Constitutional History: Essays by Edward S. Corwin* (New York: Harper and Row, 1964), pp. 216–29.

[62] Haines, *The Revival of Natural Law,* p. 330.

[63] Charles Grove Haines, *The American Doctrine of Judicial Supremacy,* pp. 538–39. This work is perhaps one of the best on the history of judicial review in America. Experiences in other countries are also considered. See also his *The Role of the Supreme Court in American Government and Politics.*

Now that the 1937 constitutional revolution has returned economics concerns to the legislatures, Corwin feels the justices are exercising judicial review as they should: "The purpose which [judicial review] serves more and more exclusively is the purpose for which it was originally created to serve, the maintenance of National Supremacy." [64] But this doesn't mean that the Constitution as expounded by the Supreme Court no longer functions as a check against government.

> I am far from saying that the concept of Liberty *against* Government is without value any longer, or that Judicial Review, which is its appropriate instrument, should be scrapped. [Its role now is] to protect against hasty and prejudiced legislation the citizen's freedom to express his views—a right of vital importance for the maintenance of free institutions.[65]

As long as "natural rights" means especially the First Amendment rather than the "vested rights" of property in the Fifth and Fourteenth Amendments, then the Court is free to discover the higher law and to apply it to legislative enactments.

The idea of government against liberty does not greatly disturb Carl Brent Swisher. His view of the role of the Court is to return it to the people. In his words, "The Supreme Court succeeds in leading largely to the extent of its skill not merely as leader but as a follower." [66] The Court is to reflect the deep needs and desires of the people and express them so the people will recognize them as similar if not identical to their own.[67] Swisher does not leave the issue of the Court's role with a mere enunciation of high-sounding words with which few would disagree. Two practical methods are suggested by which this marriage of the people and the Court will be consummated. First, the justices must more convincingly present a unified front to the public. Permanent and antithetical blocs on the Court must be avoided. Dissents of course have their place in the history of the Court and should continue, but the justices must make

---

[64] Corwin, *The Constitution of the United States of America: Analysis and Interpretation* (n. 21 above), p. 23.

[65] Edward S. Corwin, *Constitutional Revolution*, p. 115.

[66] Carl Brent Swisher, *The Supreme Court in Modern Role* (New York: New York University Press, 1958), p. 179.

[67] *Ibid.*, p. 180.

a greater effort toward consensus. Thereby will the public grant more credence and deference to the high bench. Second, through time those justices out of step with the need and desires of society will be replaced. New appointments will renew the Court's commitment to society. Thus, Swisher is rather optimistic about the future course of constitutional law and sees little to be apprehensive about unless society fails to reach a consensus itself on the major issues and thus fails to provide the guide for the Court.[68]

Robert E. Cushman also suggests some practical methods by which the justices can become more attuned to contemporary society. First, he argues that the justices must exercise self-restraint and grant to the legislatures more deference. He urges the justices to adopt Associate Justice Oliver Wendell Holmes's view that "I am not God" and that a legislature had "the right to be a cussed fool." By educating the legal profession and the public in the values of judicial restraint, Cushman feels that the President would soon become more concerned with such a dimension when he appoints lawyers to the high bench. Should this fail, the Constitution should be amended to clarify the meanings of the commerce or due process clauses and thus remove from the justices of the Supreme Court the sources of their discretionary rulings. Through such practical measures, the Court would be "divested of its undemocratic assumption of legislating." [69]

The foregoing descriptions of traditional scholarship illustrate the broad scope of this approach. Considerations of time and change are limited only by history itself and by the documentary evidence available. The questions pursued go beyond those posed by behavioralists. What is freedom? What is the proper role of the Supreme Court? What is democracy? But the questions exceed the mere "What is?" and become concerned with "What ought to be?" For these reasons the traditional model or approach to the judicial process is most comprehensive.

[68] Carl Brent Swisher, *The Growth of Constitutional Power in the United States* (Chicago: University of Chicago Press, 1946), pp. 225–27; and *The Supreme Court . . . in Modern Role*, p. 181.

[69] Robert E. Cushman, *The Role of the Supreme Court in a Democratic Society* (Urbana, Ill.: Edmund J. James Lectures on Government published by the University of Illinois, 1938), pp. 59–60.

CHAPTER EIGHT

A Need for Eclecticism

If political scientists were somehow to agree upon one approach or model as the best tool for organizing, analyzing, predicting, and explaining political phenomena, it would mean the end of the discipline. Eugene J. Meehan is quite correct in insisting upon the need for a variety of approaches.

> It is both desirable and necessary that some political scientists concentrate on methodological questions while others search for new data, classify, construct theories, and carry out the other functions of explanation: and it is essential that some attention be given to reasoned criticism of political values. So long as no one insists that one particular aspect of political study is both a necessary and a sufficient definition of the enterprise, only good can come from the division of labor. No phase of the discipline is logically prior or intrinsically superior to the others. The nature of political science is determined by the nature of politics, and not the converse.[1]

And so it is with models and approaches to the study of the judicial process. A division of labor must exist in which each learns from others, but continues to exercise his or her special talents to probe the workings of the judiciary.

It is evident that some scholars of the courts do not accept a division of labor within the discipline. Debates, criticisms, and condemnations have marked this disagreement; but this is altogether healthy for it sharpens the tools of political inquiry.[2]

[1] Eugene J. Meehan, *The Theory and Method of Political Analysis* (Homewood, Ill.: Dorsey Press, 1965), p. 258.
[2] Typical of the debate over methods and models are Wallace Mendelson, "The Untroubled World of Jurimetrics," *Journal of Politics*, XXVI (November, 1964), 914; Fred Kort, "Comment on the 'Untroubled World of Jurimetrics,'" *Journal of Politics*, XXVI (November, 1964), 923; Wallace Mendelson, "An

The debate has been between the traditionalist and the behavioralist. For our purposes we can identify the behavioralist as a scholar who researches the judicial process from the perspective of decision making, micro-groups, role, macro-groups, impact, and systems models; although Glendon Schubert categorizes most of the macro-group and many of the impact scholars in a conventional group.[3] This debate has been leveled at the question of the use of values in research and at the methodologies common to the behavioralists. The dialogue takes a scientific versus non- or antiscientific perspective, with the behavioralist claiming that the traditionalist fails to be scientific enough, and the traditionalist arguing that the behavioralist confuses science with methodology. Neither approach has won over the discipline, however. Robert McCloskey has observed ". . . that the fraternity in general is now receptive to the methods and insights of behavioralism in so far as it finds them *helpful;* that it shows no disposition on the other hand to redefine the discipline in exclusively behavioral terms; that the moment has come to adjourn the debate; and that the discipline is about ready for a new movement and thus a new *casus belli.*" [4]

The new movement is upon us in the political science profession, generally, and in public law, specifically. According to David Easton: "A new revolution is under way. . . . The initial impulse of this revolution is just being felt. Its battle cries are *relevance* and *action.*" [5] The postbehavioral revolution demands that our research be guided by a concern for the world in which we live and be directed toward improving that world. Possibly a synthesis of the

---

Open Letter to Professor Spaeth and His Jurimetrical Colleagues," *Journal of Politics,* XXVIII (May, 1966), 429; Walter Berns, "Law and Behavioral Science," *Law and Contemporary Problems,* XXVIII (Winter, 1963), 185; and John P. Roche, "Political Science and Science Fiction," *The American Political Science Review,* LII (December, 1958), 1026. Theodore Becker and Glendon A. Schubert are continuing the debate. See, for example, sections of Becker's *Comparative Judicial Politics* (Chicago: Rand McNally, 1970), and Glendon A. Schubert and David J. Danelski, eds., *Comparative Judicial Behavior* (New York: Oxford University Press, 1969).

[3] Glendon A. Schubert, "Academic Ideology and the Study of Adjudication," *The American Political Science Review,* LXI (March, 1967), 106.

[4] Robert G. McCloskey, "Political Science: The State of the Profession," *Political Science Quarterly,* LXXX (June, 1965), 282.

[5] David Easton, "The New Revolution in Political Science," *The American Political Science Review,* LXIII (December, 1969), 1051.

various models and approaches discussed in this book will supply materials for postbehavioral efforts.

The purpose of models and, for that matter, of scientific inquiry, generally, is to organize, analyze, predict, and explain political phenomena. A "new"—or possibly "old"—dimension is now being added to this kind of inquiry: the study of the judicial process should also judge what it organizes, analyzes, predicts, and explains and advocate remedial actions if necessary. The postbehavioral revolution in political science demands that we be concerned for the contemporary world and its problems even if we must sacrifice some of our scientific rigor. In Easton's words, ". . . it is better to be vague than non-relevantly precise." [6] The postbehavioral adherent, echoing some of the traditional condemnations, argues that we must move beyond behavioralism. By the very nature of his endeavor, the behavioralist has been a quiet supporter of the status quo. In describing, explaining, and predicting what *is* and eschewing the *ought,* he tends to support the existing conditions in the world. The realities of the political world tend to be lost in the abstract context of models and data collection. For example, to know that the sentencing behavior of judges varies is to miss the meaning of life in the cell block. An intellectual obligation is not met by the behavioral political scientist. Those with the knowledge of things political have the obligation to utilize that knowledge for good. Time is not on our side. The problems of prison reform, judicial selection and tenure, racism, crime, and disregard for law are not waiting for the quiet, incremental, and detached suggestions of the scholar. So it appears that public law as a field, like its mother discipline, political science, is split between the traditionalist who looks to the past, the behavioralist who looks to the present, and the postbehavioralist who looks to the future. The question is not which approach should prevail, but, rather how can all three work together to help understand and improve our judicial system and the society of which it is an important part? The question suggests a paradigm for the task ahead (Fig. 12):

Three tasks face the behavioralist. First, as has been repeatedly suggested throughout this book, the findings of some models have applicability to other models. Decision-making, role, and micro-group

---

[6] *Ibid.,* p. 1052.

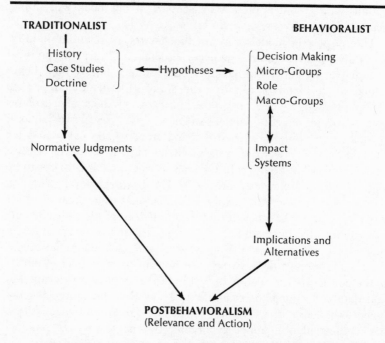

FIGURE 12.   The Study of the Judicial Process: A Synthesis

studies can assist greatly in understanding the conversion stage of the systems model; macro-group studies can contribute to an understanding of the input stage; and impact studies can contribute to an understanding of the output stage. The behavioralist must cooperate more with his colleagues. A science of politics at the very least means that we must build upon what other scholars have done.

Second, the behavioralist must share knowledge with the traditionalist. The cooperation can lead to some exciting scholarship. "Hypotheses sharing" is perhaps the best way of expressing the interchange. For example, traditionalists have suggested that the Supreme Court of the first third of the twentieth century was clearly out of step with the needs and desires of the populace. They have urged upon the Court a greater restraint and a rejection, for example, of substantive due process, in order that the Court might assume its proper role. Impact and systems models are aptly designed to investigate exactly this—the relationship of public opinion to Court decisions. In fact, did the public view the Court as out of step? Applications of role models could tell us how Justices Willis Van Devanter and James C. McReynolds viewed their several roles and whether that view was as closely related to their decisions as the traditionalists suggest. It would be most exciting to discover through small-group or role applications the intracourt relations that prevailed in the Marshall, Taney, Fuller, and White courts. Traditional writings can supply the data. The behavioralist also needs the assistance of the doctrine-oriented traditionalist in order to better understand the decisional output of courts. Many studies are almost completely reliant upon an appraisal of doctrine for their classification of voting behavior. Bloc analysis and scaling, characteristic of micro-group and decision-making models, are cases in point. No student of the judicial process should fail to develop skills in appraising doctrine or doctrinal trends.

What is suggested is that a synthesis of the traditionalist and the behavioralist approaches must involve the traditionalist applying some of the behavioral models to the past and the behavioralist utilizing some of the rich materials of history to test his hypotheses. Should this past- and present-oriented cooperative research indicate that there exist some patterns of behavior, some consistent trends, and some favorable outcomes, then prediction for the future would seem to follow naturally.

The third task for the behavioralist, then, is to suggest the empirical ramifications of the past and present to the future, and to bring forth alternatives with all their implications. At this point the behavioralist "merges" with the traditionalist in a postbehavior synthesis. In carrying out this task the description, analysis, explanation, and prediction of the past and present is judged by normative standards; and advocacy for improvement ensues. The synthesis suggested by the paradigm in Figure 12 might be achieved in the following manner.

The systems model—the most comprehensive of the behavioralists' frameworks—could be developed by utilizing the decision-making, small-group, and role models for an understanding of the conversion stage. Macro-group and role models could develop a greater comprehension of the inputs. Impact and macro-group models could explain the output and feedback stages. The traditionalist could make his contribution by applying one or several of the above models to the past or by assisting the behavioralist in his selecting and interpreting of historical inputs and outputs. The traditionalist's role would be to add the dimension of time and thus change to the study of the judicial process. Finally, the traditionalist can make normative judgments about the output and feedback stages, and suggest to us what is unacceptable and why. Before any scientific study of the judicial process can be sufficiently developed, we must cooperate and build upon each other's efforts. But beyond this, we must attempt to improve not just our knowledge of the judicial process, but also our normative judgment of that process. If judges are to allocate values in society, these allocations must be "correct" and the values ought to be "good." The traditionalist possesses the training and experience for an investigation of values. The behavioralist, on his part, can document the legal, social, and political implications of the several normative alternatives and assist in the choice of courses of action in terms of costs and benefits. The postbehavioral revolution, rather than reintroducing the old or generating a new debate, can therefore provide a meeting ground for all scholars of the judicial process.

CASE INDEX

NAME INDEX

SUBJECT INDEX